Amal + Vaishali. S~

Shrimad Räjchandra's

Ätmasiddhi

Adhyätma Geetä and Ätmopanishad

English Translation with Commentary

By : **Manu Doshi**

Publisher

Shri Satshrut Sevä Sädhnä Kendra
SHRIMAD RÄJCHANDRA ÄDHYÄTMIK SÄDHNÄ KENDRA,
Kobä, Dist.: Gandhinagar, Gujarät, India, 382 007.

Ätmasiddhi - Adhyätma Geetä and Ätmopanishad
English Translation with Commentary
By : Manu Doshi.

Publisher :
Shri Jayantbhai M. Shah, President
Shri Satshrut Sevä Sädhnä Kendra
SHRIMAD RÄJCHANDRA ÄDHYÄTMIK SÄDHNÄ KENDRA,
Kobä, Dist : Gandhinagar, Gujarät, India, 382 007.
Phone : +91 79 327 6219
Fax   : +91 79 327 6486
E-mail : srask@rediffmail.com
Web   : www.shrimad-koba.org

First Edition : June, 2003
Copies   : 5000
Price   : I Rs. 60   US $ 2

Design & Printed by :
Amrut Info Print Pvt. Ltd.
108-First Floor, Indrajeet Complex
13, Manahar Plot Corner
Bhaktinagar Godown Road
Rajkot, Gujarat, India, 360 002.
Phone : +91 281 246 2591
Fax   : +91 281 246 5178
e-mail : amrutinfoprint@yahoo.com
web   : www.amrutindia.com

This book is dedicated

to

Truth Seekers

In all Places, at all Times.

— Manu Doshi

Table of Contents

PUBLISHER'S NOTE

It is our policy to regularly publish noble and life-elevative literature for the benefit of the society in general and of scholars and spiritual aspirants in particular. Majority of our 60 publications have been produced in Gujarati, Hindi, Sanskrut and Prakrut.

With changing times and with more overseas people taking interest in our activity, we started English publications and this book comes to the readers in that category.

Shri Manubhai Doshi is a learned, well-read and dedicated follower of Shrimad Räjchandra's thoughts and literature. He has done considerable work in translating Shrimad's original Gujarati work in English for the benefit of new generation and English-speaking youths abroad and in India. The present book follows that tradition which includes English translation as well as commentary on Ätmasiddhi (Self-Realization). The Publishing Committee at Koba appreciates his scholarly dedication and thanks him for spreading Lord Mahavir's message through Shrimad's writings. Inspite of his age (83 years) Manubhai is hard working and enthusiastic.

In India and abroad, many friends and well wishers have been instrumental in production of the present work. Students of Jain Study Group of Jain Center of Southern California, many members of Khandhar family including Mahendra, Ramesh, Suketu, Hetal, Sumit & Samir Khandhars, Pravin Mehta, Usha Sheth, Dr. Natubhai Shah (London) and Jyotindra Doshi & his son Kumar are mentioned for their help in review and production. The Committee sincerely appreciates all of them, specially Mahendra Khandhar whose incessant efforts, scriptural knowledge and visionary approach made this difficult work possible.

We hope that this book will help the readers in their quest for spiritual knowledge and progress. Corrections and suggestions regarding the contents and format are welcome.

Mahavir Jayanti
15th April, 2003.

Publishing Committee,
Koba.

BOOK AVAILABILITY/ CONTACTS

INDIA:

Shrimad Rajchandra Adhyatmik Sadhna Kendra.
Koba,   Dist. Gandhinagar, GJ, India, 382 007.
Tel: +91 79 327 6219. e-mail: srask@rediffmail.com

Dr. Kumarpal Desai. Institute of Jainology,
501 Mahakant Bldg, Ellisbridge,
Ahmedabad, GJ, India, 380 006.
Tel: +91 79 657 8507. e-mail: kumarpalad1@sancharnet.in

Shrimad Rajchandra Adhyatmik Satsang Sadhna Kendra.
10 B East Wing, Bombay Market, 78 Tardev Rd,
Mumbai, MH, India, 400 034.
Tel: +91 22 2 491 1352. e-mail: srassk@vsnl.net

Shri Nitinbhai I. Parekh
"E" - Mangalam, 155 Jain Society
Sion West, Mumbai, MH, India, 400 022.
Tel : +91 22 2 401 0476. e-mail: nipc@vsnl.net

Shri Pratapbhai G. Mehta.
186 Budhwar Peth, Pune, MH, India, 411 002.
Tel: +91 20 445 4464. e-mail: hitubhai@hotmail.com

Shri Ashokbhai P. Shah.
New # 109 Gengu Reddy Rd, Egmore, Chennai,
TN, India, 600 008.
Tel: +91 44 2 641 1197. e-mail: cok@vsnl.net

Shri Deepakbhai S. Shah.
Sapna Book House, Opp. Tribhuvan Theatre,
Gandhinagar, Bangalore, KT, India, 560 009.
Tel: +91 80 226 6088. e-mail: sapnabooks@vsnl.com

Shri Dolarbhai J. Hemani.
25A Sarat Bose Road, Kolkata, WB, India, 700 020.
Tel: +91 33 2 475 2697. e-mail: rajen_h@hotmail.com

Shri Ashok Kumar Jain.
Bhagwan Mahavir Ahinsa Kendra,
Sarvoday Teerth Ahinsa Sthal, Chhattarpur Rd, Mehrauli,
New Delhi, India, 110 030.
Tel: +91 11 2 328 7045. e-mail:amitvinod@hotmail.com

USA & CANADA:

Shri Pravinbhai K. Shah.
North American Jain Federation (JAINA),
509 Carriage Woods Circle, Raleigh, NC, USA, 27607.
Tel: (919) 859 4994. e-mail: pkshah1@attglobal.net

Shri Manubhai Doshi.
Indira Mansukhlal Doshi Memorial Trust.
931 Goldenrod Lane, Lake Forest, IL, USA, 60045.
Tel: (847) 735 0120. e-mail: mansukhdoshi@yahoo.com

Shri Mahendrabhai K. Khandhar.
6112 Leyte Street, Cypress, CA, USA, 90630.
Tel: (714) 894 2930. e-mail: mkkhandhar@aol.com

Shri Prafulbhai J. Lakhani.
30 Balsam Drive, Dix Hills, NY, USA, 11746.
Tel: (631) 423 9647. e-mail: plakhani@reliablegroup.com

Shri Suketubhai S. Kapadia.
7127 La Granada Drive, Houston, TX, USA, 77083.
Tel: (281) 561 7157. e-mail: getallprint@aol.com

Shri Prakashbhai Mody.
37 Tuscarora Drive, North Park, ON, M2H 2K4, Canada.
Tel: (416) 491 5560. e-mail: mody@sympatico.ca

UK:

Dr. Vinodbhai J. Kapashi.
Mahavir Foundation, 11 Lindsay Drive, Kenton,
Middlesex, HA3 0TA, UK.
Tel: +44 208 204 2871. e-mail: vinod@kapashi.freeserve.co.uk

Dr. Natubhai K. Shah, Jain Samaj Europe,
20 James Close, Woodlands, London, NW11 9QX, UK.
Tel: +44 208 455 5573. e-mail: NatubhaiShah@aol.com

Shri Jayantibhai V. Shah.
Flat 1, Barrads Hall, 2 Beech Avenue, South Croydon,
Surrey, CR2 0NL, UK.
Tel: +44 208 657 0282. e-mail: shaileshmalde@blueyonder.co.uk

Shri Harshadbhai N. Sanghrajka.
9 Conway Close, Stanmore, Middlesex, HA7 3RT, UK.
Tel: +44 208 954 9632. e-mail: harshad@mpcnet.co.uk

WORLD WIDE:

Shri Pradipbhai B. Sanghvi.
47 Jacht Laan, Edegem, Antwerp 2650, Belgium.
Tel: +32 3 448 1350. e-mail: sanghvi48@hotmail.com

Shri Manubhai S. Shah.
P.O. Box: 45778, Nairobi-100, Kenya.
Tel: +254 2 375 1679. e-mail: mcpl@futurenet.co.ke

Shri Rameshbhai B. Vora.
P.O. Box: 13455, Deira, Dubai, U.A.E.
Tel: +971 4 226 4690. e-mail: bj@emirates.net.ae

Dr. Navinbhai H. Khandhar.
P.O. Box: 398, Fairfield, 1860 Sydney, NSW, Australia.
Tel: +612 9620 2001. e-mail: navin_Khandhar@bigpond.com

Shri Naginbhai J. Doshi.
Singapore Jain Religious Society,
783 Mountbatten Road, 1543 Singapore.
Tel: +656 344 3963. e-mail: divyesh@danr.com

Shri Dhirenbhai K. Shah.
Tokyo Jain Sangh, Setagaya-KU, Todoroki 7-6-6,
Tokyo 158-0082, Japan.
Tel: +81 3 3704 6363. e-mail: jayshree56@hotmail.com

FORWARD

In modern times, Shrimad Räjchandra (Räychandbhäi) has taught the path of self-realization to the aspirants, who had strayed from the true path of Lord Mahävir, in a simple language. He had attained the self-realization and his living was saintly without any attachment for a position, wealth, fame, and even his body. He was friendly to all. In 142 stanzas of the "Ätmasiddhi" he has taught the pathway to self-realization, the true meaning of life.

Mahätmä Gändhi was greatly influenced by Shrimad. His teachings had helped Gändhi to develop the non-violent way of life and the non-violent freedom struggle for India. In his autobiography, Gändhiji writes, "No one else has ever made on me the impression that Räychandbhäi did". His pathway of true happiness is a boon to the spiritual aspirants in the 21st century where religion and faith could play major pacifying roles in many of today's conflicts in the world.

I have known shri Manubhai Doshi of Chicago for quite sometime. He is well-read and was a teacher in Jain Pathshala in Chicago for many years. He is active in Jain Society of Metropolitan Chicago. He is the editor of fine publication "Jain Darshan". Shri Manubhai has translated many prose and poems into English for the benefit of young Jains and new generation. Being a teacher and professional, he is meticulous and well organized.

It is indeed gratifying that Manubhai has written this English version with short commentary on Ätmasiddhi by Shrimad Räjchandra. Before embarking on this project, he has carefully researched the related past work and included the essence of it with due credit and references. He has studied Vachanämrutji (the collection of spiritual letters by Shrimad Räjchandra, about 1000 page volume) very well and has provided plenty of references and quotes to elucidate the profound spiritual wisdom behind the simple-looking stanzas of Ätmasiddhi.

Manubhai has organized the book in a way that can be used

by beginners, scholars, Jains and non-Jains alike. For each stanza, he has provided original stanza in Gujarati, followed by English transliteration, English translation and his commentary in terms of explanation & discussion. English translation in verse by Pujya Brahmachāriji is included in Appendix-I for reference and reverence. The Letter of Six Fundamentals in prose, the original basis of this Ātmasiddhi Shāstra, is included in Appendix-II. Shri Manubhai has translated it in English. This way he caters to the needs of most readers. Since Manubhai has studied other Darshans (theological schools), he has been able to bring out the deeper meaning and relate it properly. I am sure, it will go a long way in spreading the teachings of Jainism; by Lord Mahavir and his dedicated disciple Shrimad Rājchandraji.

There are six major theological schools in Indian Aryan culture. Each is right in its own way and has something good to offer. Although there is partial truth in each, none is complete. Jainism has synergistically integrated all of them with due respect. The Six Fundamental tenets deal with these six schools and Ātmasiddhi Shāstra is representative of the same. In pointing out only partial truth in each school, no denigration or disrespect is intended. The purpose is simply to state impartially that Jainism, and Ātmasiddhi in particular, includes and integrates all the six tenets appropriately. Manubhai has treated this issue very well in stanza 44 and elsewhere.

In everyday worldly dealings, repetition is considered unnecessary, improper and often an insult to intelligence. However, in spiritual realm repetition is considered necessary and a virtue. This is due to the fact that worldly souls are used to worldly matters since time immemorial and for them there is no need to repeat anything. For this reason, in schools and colleges subject matter is straightforward without any repetition. But in spiritual matters the worldly souls are strangers and without aptitude for it. Realizing this, Manubhai has adopted the tradition of some repetition in his English translation and commentary without undue elaboration. The thoughtful readers, especially the young new generation, should not feel either bored or insulted by some necessary repetition.

Manubhai earned the Masters degree in Economics & Political Science from the University of Bombay in 1947. He then worked for Government for 28 years and retired as Assistant Commissioner of Industries. He immigrated to USA in 1980. He has been the Founder Editor of "Jain Darshan" since 1990 and a Regional Editor of "Jain Digest" by North American Jain Federation (JAINA) since 1995. He has written and published six books under titles: Dev Vandan, Essence of Jainism, Samayik, Spiritual Code & Restraints, Jain Stories of Ancient Times and Pilgrimage to Shatrunjay (Palitana). Manubhai is an avid reader of Shrimad Räjchandra's writings. As a result, he has translated in English; Shrimad's Chha Padano Patra (Appendix-II), Apoorva Avasar, Bhakti Rahasya (20 Dohara), Amulya Tattva Vichär, some letters and now this Ätmasiddhi. He has also written extensively on Yoga (meditation) and Tattvärtha Sutra. He is very dedicated, healthy, enthusiastic and active even at the age of 83! May he live long healthy life and give us more gems like this. He has three sons and a daughter, all married and settled in USA, with 8 grand children.

I sincerely appreciate this excellent work and congratulate Shri Manubhai for the same. I hope that all readers will benefit from this work; whether they are casual readers, scholars or spiritual aspirants. May Mahavir Swami bless us all.

With best wishes and blessings,

Koba
Mahavir Jayanti
15th April, 2003.

(H. H. Shri Ätmänandji,
formerly Dr. Soneji)

PREFACE

Since I started reciting Ätmasiddhi Shästra during the eighties, I wanted to bring out its English version and prepared its translation. It was, however, noticed that the real significance of the original text could not be brought out within the bare translation. Detailed explanatory notes were necessary. So I started to prepare them. But the more I recited the text, the more I noticed that the notes were far from satisfactory. Therefore, I decided to wait, until I could gain a better comprehension of the text.

The Institute of Jainology (London) wrote me a letter in 1998 suggesting that if I prepare the translation with explanatory notes, it will publish the same on the occasion of the first centenary of Shrimad's passing away. That prompted me to start writing. The work was accordingly completed by the end of 1999. But the Institute later on decided not to publish the same. However, it gets the credit of prompting me to write, since I would not have perhaps embarked upon the project in absence of their suggestion.

Meanwhile I was keeping in touch with Shrimad Räjchandra Ädhyätmik Sädhnä Kendra, Kobä in order to get a `Forward' from the revered Ätmänandji. He responded favorably and agreed to write the Forward, which appears in this book. Encouraged by his response, I tried to figure out whether his Organization would like to publish my work. I am happy that they agreed and the book sees the light of the day.

In writing these notes, I have tried to bring out what is implicit in the great work, particularly taking care that the translation remains true to the original text. To be sure, I presented my translation to Dr. Räkeshbhäi Zaveri of Mumbai (Bombay) and I feel gratified that he has appreciated the same.

Some sanctity is attached to the number 18 in Indian tradition. There are 18 Parva in Mahäbhärat, 18 armies were involved in that war, the war lasted for 18 days, Geetä has 18 Adhyäys (chapters), there are 18 Puräns and 18 Abhisheks are performed on the occasion of Pratishthä. Ätmasiddhi Shästra also can be divided into 18 parts comprising, the background, characteristics of the sectarian, those of the truth seekers, Statement of Six Fundamentals, 6 types of pupil's questions, 6 replies thereto, the pupil's self-realization and the conclusion. In this book I have dealt with these 18 parts in 18 chapters. On the analogy of 18 Adhyäys of Geetä, these 18 chapters of Ätmasiddhi Shästra can be termed as Adhyätma Geetä.

In Vedic tradition, Upanishads are the source of high spiritual wealth. Upanishad literally means the spiritual science that can be learnt by sitting at the feet of a preceptor and that exactly applies to Ätmasiddhi. If one wants to grasp the inner significance of Ätmasiddhi Shästra, it needs to be studied as such. It can therefore be termed as an Upanishad. Since it mainly deals with the soul, it can be called Ätma Upanishad or Ätmopanishad. Many non-Jains have adopted it as such and have been reciting the same regularly.

The presentation in the book has been made in the following order. Every stanza of the original text is first given in Gujarati script followed by English transliteration. Thereafter my translation is given, followed by the explanatory notes and discussion. At the end, there are two appendices. The first contains the versified translation of Ätmasiddhi Shästra prepared by revered Brahmachäriji under the title 'Self-Realization'. The second contains my English version of the Letter of Six Fundamentals by Shrimad and addressed to reverend Laghuräjswämi. It is hoped that this plan will make the book more helpful, effective and acceptable.

I have much respect for revered Brahmachäriji. His writings have helped me in better understanding the writings of Shrimad, and in preparing these notes. Moreover, the sermons of Mahäsati Tarulatäji also have been very helpful. Therefore I express my gratitude to her. I also mention Shri Mahendra Khandhär and Dr. Chandrakänt Shäh, who were kind enough to go through the entire matter. The former has gone through the same very minutely and has made several valuable suggestions for improving the same. Thereafter he continued to take active interest in the matter and made every possible effort to see that this book is published.

April 14, 2003   Manu Doshi
Lake Forest (Chicago), USA

PROLOGUE

Shrimad was the Self-realized entity and is known as a spiritual philosopher of very high caliber. He was born with a high level of Kshayopasham, meaning, he had very few deluding and obscuring Karmas. Consequently, he was able to gain the knowledge of his previous births at the tender age of seven.

His memory was very sharp and he could recollect whatever he read or otherwise came across. He became known for his mnemonic capability during his teens. That capacity increased and at the age of 19 he displayed the extraordinary feat of remaining mindful of 100 activities simultaneously. Thereby he came to be known as Shatävadhäni. Even the British rulers of that time were highly impressed by his performance and offered to make necessary arrangements for him, if he were willing to go to Europe for displaying his capabilities. However, he declined that offer, because he felt that he would not be able to live in Europe according to his religious standards. He also realized that the worldly accomplishments, such as performing the memory feat, were not helpful in spiritual pursuit and therefore he gave them up soon after the above performance.

Shrimad gained right perception at the age of 23 and since then he mainly stayed attuned to spiritual awakening, despite being occupied in the jewelry business. His moral character was very high. His regard for truth, adherence to high moral values in the business and firm determination to do what he saw right inspired those who came in contact with him. Mahätmä Gändhi was highly impressed by his spiritual level and accepted him as his spiritual Guide. When Gändhiji was in South Africa, he came under pressure from his Christian and Muslim friends to adopt their faith. At that time he sought guidance from Shrimad. That guidance showed him that he could reach the highest level of spiritual elevation by continuing in his own faith and need not change his religion. He has reverently written about Shrimad in his autobiography and has paid glorious tributes to him on several occasions.

A high level of enlightenment is evident in the writings of

Shrimad. Its significance may not be clear to a casual reader. However, if one dwells deep into it, he would notice that the writings contain the rare jewels of spiritual wealth. Ätmasiddhi Shästra is the prime jewel of his writings. Revered Ambälälbhäi, revered Saubhägyabhäi and Reverend Laghuräjswämi were instrumental in bringing it out of his heart. All three happened to come in contact with Shrimad in 1890 A.D.. They were lucky enough to notice that Shrimad was the self-realized person and understood that their spiritual well being lay in surrendering to him. By virtue of that, they gained right perception during the lifetime of Shrimad. About half of the letters in Vachanämrut (compilation of Shrimad's writings) have been addressed to them; 245 to Saubhägyabhäi, 126 to Ambälälbhäi and 92 to Laghuräjswämi. Therefore it is pertinent to say a few words about them.

Ambälälbhäi was the first to come in contact with Shrimad. He was a native of Khambhät and was two years younger than Shrimad. Once he had been to Ahmedäbäd to attend a wedding. There, he happened to come in contact with Juthäbhäi, who knew Shrimad as the person with self-realization. Ambälälbhäi was impressed by the letters that Shrimad had written to Juthäbhäi and wished to contact him. That wish materialized in 1890 A.D. when Shrimad came to Khambhät. Ambälälbhäi's esteem for him increased by that contact and from then on, he remained a lifelong devotee of Shrimad. He was very intelligent and easily understood what Shrimad had to convey. Shrimad has written to Laghuräjswämi on several occasions that Ambäläl would understand his letters better. The brief explanatory notes on Ätmasiddhi Shästra, prepared by him and reviewed by Shrimad, are published in Vachanämrut (# 718) below the text of Ätmasiddhi. Unfortunately, he died at an early age of 37.

Saubhägyabhäi was a native of Säylä in Sauräshtra (Gujarät) and was 44 years older than Shrimad. In 1890 A.D. when he came to know about Shrimad's exceptional capabilities, he was inspired to show him a secret Mantra, which was termed as "Seed of Enlightenment". However, when he met Shrimad, he noticed that Shrimad was already enlightened. By

virtue of his clairvoyance, Shrimad could   make out why
Saubhägyabhäi had come. From that time Saubhägyabhäi
accepted Shrimad as his Guru and remained totally faithful to
him until the end of his life in 1897 A.D.. During that period of
seven years, he addressed to Shrimad whichever ideas and
questions occurred to him and elicited the enlightening replies.
Shrimad also was pleased to notice in him a real truth seeker and
wrote him many letters on his own indicating the inner state of
his mind. Saubhägyabhäi's death was a great loss to Shrimad.
While writing eulogy over his death, Shrimad observed
(Vachanämrut # 782) as follows.

"It is no doubt that while leaving the body, Shri Sobhäg
gained unprecedented well being by maintaining the state of self
consciousness with unwavering detachment, which is very hard
even for great ascetics. ... We repeatedly feel that it would be
rare, in this part of the world at this time, to come across a man
like Shri Sobhäg. ... No liberation seeker should ever forget Shri
Sobhäg. ... His straightforwardness, firm determination about
the ultimate objective, benevolence towards truth seekers and
other qualities are worth reflecting again and again."

Laghuräjswämi, also known as Lalluji, was a Sthänakwäsi
Jain monk. He was 14 years older than Shrimad. In 1890 A.D.,
while he was in Khambhät, a doubt arose in his mind about a
precept of Bhagavati Sutra. At that time Ambälälbhäi was
talking with his associates about the letters from Shrimad.
Lalluji called him and mentioned his doubt. Ambälälbhäi said
that Shrimad was very knowledgeable and could give
satisfactory replies to all such questions. He showed the letters
of Shrimad that he had brought from Juthäbhäi. Laghuräjswämi
was impressed by their contents and decided to contact
Shrimad. The personal contact led him to accept Shrimad as his
Guru. He survived Shrimad by 35 years and had the opportunity
to spread the message of Shrimad. He founded the well-known
Shrimad Räjchandra Äshram at Agäs, located about 60 miles
south of Ahmedäbäd in Gujarät State (India).

In 1894 A.D. when Laghuräjswämi was in Surat, he was
suffering from fever for about a year. At that time, one Lallubhäi

Zaveri died after prolonged illness. Thereupon Laghuräjswämi felt that if he also met the same fate, his life would end without gaining right perception. In that case he would have to continue the infinite wandering in the cycle of birth and death. He therefore wrote to Shrimad to send him something that could help gain right perception.

Thereupon, Shrimad wrote to him the well-known Letter of Six Fundamentals, which is included in the Appendix II. That Letter is called the abode of right perception. Laghuräjswämi was very pleased to receive it and went through it repeatedly. The Letter was then sent to Saubhägyabhäi in 1895 A.D.. He also liked it very much and used to ponder over it again and again. He wanted to commit it to memory. But it was in prose and he found it hard to memorize. So he requested Shrimad to bring out something similar in verse.

Shrimad was inherently compassionate. Moreover, he had a special regard for Saubhägyabhäi, who had been instrumental in bringing out, in the form of letters, what lay in his heart. Therefore in late 1896 A.D. when Shrimad was in Nadiäd, one auspicious evening after returning from a walk, he called Ambälälbhäi and asked him to hold a lamp. While Ambälälbhäi held it as directed, Shrimad started writing and within an hour and a half he wrote the 142 stanzas of Ätmasiddhi Shästra. Mere copying of those stanzas would take longer time than that! The fact that Shrimad brought out that great work in that short time, would give some idea of the great spiritual wealth abiding within him.

Initially only four copies of the Ätmasiddhi were made; one for Saubhägyabhäi, one for Ambälälbhäi, one for Laghuräjswämi and one for Mänekläl Gheläbhäi Zaveri. Saubhägyabhäi was much elated to get it. He was highly impressed by its contents and committed it to memory. He wrote, "Ätmasiddhi is the essence of 14 Purva. Gosaliä (Dungarshi Gosaliä, who also had become a follower of Shrimad) and myself regularly read it and enjoy it very much. ... After reading it, one is not inclined to read anything else. ... It would have been hard for this body to survive, if you (Shrimad) had not sent Ätmasiddhi. I get delight in reading it and thereby I am able to survive. After reading Ätmasiddhi, nothing remains to be asked. Everything becomes clear."

Laghuräjswämi also was very pleased to get Ätmasiddhi. Since he was asked to read it alone, he used to go away from the residential area and read it in the wilderness. He wrote, "By reading that and reciting some of its stanzas, my soul was overjoyed. I felt that there is unprecedented significance in every line of it. The regular study of Ätmasiddhi Shästra and its contemplation led to internal peace. It stayed in my mind, while talking with any one or while undertaking any other activity." He noted that its reading was helpful to every spiritual aspirant and after setting up Räjchandra Ashram at Agäs, he laid down its reciting as a regular feature for its resident aspirants.

The subject matter of Ätmasiddhi is the soul and it deals with soul's existence, everlastingness, acquisition of Karmas, bearing the consequences, liberation therefrom and the way of attaining liberation. The subject has been carefully and adequately presented. Nothing worthwhile has been left out. Every stanza is full of significance and some of them are the most precious jewels of the spiritual realm. In composing Ätmasiddhi, Shrimad has virtually contained the sea of spiritual science within the bowl of the book. If one wants to realize the Self, studying that text and putting its precepts into practice would suffice and one need not look for any other source.

The known religious philosophies can be grouped within the six ideologies known as Shaddarshan, which used to form a part of the scholastic curriculum in India. Ätmasiddhi Shästra is the gist of all of them and hence, it is the essence of all spiritual sciences. The religious philosophies generally contain intricate terms and their technicalities are hard to understand. But Ätmasiddhi Shästra is presented in easy to understand language. Even a layman can make out its basic concepts. Moreover, except for a few terms, it contains no terminology that can be considered exclusively Jain. This makes it acceptable to people of all faiths. In that connection, Revered Brahmachäriji observed as under.

This unparalleled composition of Shrimad is versified. It is the duty of the discerning reader to calmly elaborate it. Shrimad himself has stated that 100 stanzas can be written on each of its 142 original stanzas. It is such a great composition. But it is presented in a style whereby every one can gain something that he is worthy of and the deeper one goes into it, the more evident would be its significance.

To present the stupendous aspects of the religious philosophy in such a simple language is the function of highly enlightened. The pattern of Ätmasiddhi differs from other writings of Shrimad. This work, composed in short and simple words, devoid of logical concepts and inferences or of the complicating proofs and disproofs and filled with the beneficial matter of use to every one from child to the aged, has become very popular.

The following verse in praise of Ätmasiddhi by revered Brahmachäriji emphasizes its importance and holiness.

Patit Jan Pävani, Sur Saritä Sami,
    Adham Uddhärini Ätmasiddhi;
Janma Janmäntaro Jänatä Jogie,
    Ätma Anubhav Vade Äj Didhi.
Bhakta Bhagirath Samä, Bhägyashäli Mahä,
    Bhavya Saubhägyani Vinatithi;
Chäruttar Bhuminä, Nagar Nadiädamän,
    Purna Krupä Prabhue Kari Ti.

The first line states that Ätmasiddhi Shästra purifies the down trodden like the heavenly river Gangä and it uplifts even those who have fallen to the lowest level. The second line states that the composition has been brought out of Self-experience of the great ascetic, who knew many of his previous lives. Since it was brought out at the request of Saubhägyabhäi, he has been compared in the third line with king Bhagirath, who brought down the holy Gangä. The remaining part of the third line and the last line state that Shrimad has extended the utmost favor by composing it at Nadiäd in the region of Charotar.

With this background, let us first remember the blissful Navkär Mantra and other Mängliks so as to complete this work without any difficulty.

* Namo Arihantänam
  (Obeisance to the omniscient Lords)
  Namo Siddhänam
  (Obeisance to the liberated souls)
  Namo Äyariyänam
  (Obeisance to the heads of religious order)
  Namo Uvazzäyänam
  (Obeisance to the masters of scriptures)
  Namo Loe Savva Sähoonam
  (Obeisance to all the monks in the universe)
  Eso Panch Namukkäro,
  Savva Pävappanäsano,
  Mangalänam Cha Savvesim,
  Padhamam Havai Mangalam.
  (This fivefold obeisance is eradicator of all sins and is the foremost among all blissful aspects)

* Sahajätma Swarup Paramguru.
  (This means : Abiding at ease in Self is characteristic of the Supreme Guru. Alternately it means: One's own Self, pure and natural, is his supreme Guru or teacher)

* Mahä Divyähä Kukshiratnam Shabdajit Ravätmajam
  Räjachandramaham Vande Tattvalochan Däyakam.
  [I bow to Shrimad Räjchandra, the master of words, the jewel born of the womb of mother Devbai (great divinity), the son of Ravajibhäi and bestower of spiritual eyesight]

* Ajnäna Timirändhänäm Jnänänjana Shaläkayä,
  Chakshurunmilitam Yena Tasmai Shri Gurave Namah.
  (I bow to the graceful Guru, who opened with the anointing stick of enlightenment, my eyes blinded by darkness of ignorance).

Chapter 1 : Background

There are 23 stanzas in this introductory chapter. Here, Shrimad gives the vital factors of the Ätmasiddhi Shästra like Mänglik, its purpose, characteristics of lifeless ritualist and bare knowledgeable person, importance of Guru in spiritual pursuit, characteristics of true Guru and the guidance for an aspirant in the absence of Guru.

જે સ્વરૂપ સમજ્યા વિના, પામ્યો દુ:ખ અનંત;
સમજાવ્યું તે પદ નમું, શ્રી સદ્ગુરુ ભગવંત.

||૧||

Je Swarup Samajyä Vinä, Pämyo Dukh Anant;
Samajävyun Te Pad Namun, Shri Sadguru Bhagavant.

In absence of understanding the true nature of soul, I experienced endless suffering. I bow to the graceful Guru who explained the true nature of soul.

- 1 -

Explanation & Discussion:

In Äryan tradition, a spiritual composition usually begins with presentation of four aspects: (1) **Mänglik:** prayer for blessings, (2) **Sambandh:** the context or the relation in which the composition is presented, (3) **Abhidheya:** the subject matter of the composition, and (4) **Prayojan:** the purpose of the composition. The first two are covered in this stanza. The Mängalik is in paying homage to the graceful Guru and Sambandh is in the form of Guru explaining to pupil. The remaining two aspects are in the next stanza.

From time immemorial, the worldly soul has been going through cycles of birth and death. Its main pursuit has been to gain happiness, but actually it only ends up in suffering. In spite of trying hard to mitigate that suffering, the soul fails in reducing the same because it does not make out the cause of suffering. Delusion, the real cause of suffering, prevents it from understanding its true nature and hence deprives it of its inherent happiness. By virtue of delusion, the soul identifies itself with the body and treats the comforts and discomforts of the body as its own. This is the root cause of its misery, wandering from birth to birth and suffering from old age, disease, death, etc. Thus Shrimad summarizes in this stanza the basic tenets of Jainism, the cause and the remedy for human suffering and misery.

This suffering cannot end, unless the soul realizes its true, blissful nature. That realization can come only with the help of a true Guru who has realized the self (soul). One, who has not realized the soul, can never explain its true nature. Here, explaining does not mean merely clarifying the terms, as is done in school. That type of explanation, the worldly soul might have got on innumerable occasions during its infinite wandering. If it got the right explanation at times, the same remained at the superficial level and never reached the depth within. However scholar one may become by reading books and studying scriptures, he still cannot bring an end to suffering and misery until he realizes and experiences the soul (attains self-realization).

Explanation coming from the heart of a self-realized Guru convinces the pupil thoroughly. The pupil therefore makes efforts with all his heart in the direction the Guru has shown. The genuine efforts enable him to understand the true nature of the self, which leads to calming down the worldly desires. Shrimad observes (Vachanämrut # 651) that understanding means to know and experience the true nature of soul as it is. Such understanding changes one's orientation from external to internal. When the orientation turns to its true nature, the soul stays tuned to that. Thus in spiritual pursuit, the importance of such an enlightened Guru is enormous. It is therefore only appropriate that Shrimad starts with the homage to the graceful Guru who explained the true nature of the soul.

This stanza can also be interpreted as covering all six Fundamentals, which form the basis of Ätmasiddhi Shästra. The soul undergoing suffering points to its **existence**, endlessness of suffering signifies that the soul is **everlasting**, undergoing suffering in absence of understanding indicates that the soul has been acquiring **Karmas** and has been bearing its **consequences**, true nature of the soul indicates the state of **liberation** and explaining of that nature points to the **means** of attaining it.

વર્તમાન આ કાળમાં,   મોક્ષમાર્ગ બહુ લોપ;
વિચારવા આત્માર્થિને, ભાખ્યો અત્ર અગોપ્ય.

॥૨॥

Vartamän Ä Kälamän, Mokshamärga Bahu Lop;
Vichäravä Ätmärthine, Bhäkhyo Atra Agopya.

Currently, the path of liberation has been mostly lost. It is described here for the contemplation of the truth seekers, without any reservation.

- 2 -

Explanation & Discussion:

The remaining two aspects of the composition are covered here. The subject matter of the composition, Abhidheya, is the path of liberation. The purpose of the composition, Prayojan, is contemplation by the truth seekers.

People are deeply engrossed with the material well being in the false hope of achieving peace and happiness. We have been pursuing material comforts almost to the exclusion of spiritual and other objectives. With that end in view, we have embarked upon scientific exploration, which has provided the comforts and amenities that were unimaginable only a few years back. Has that, however, made us happy?

Shrimad wrote this more than a century before in light of the situation then prevailing. Since then, the human race has made tremendous progress in the material field. It has split the atom, probed the psyche, spliced the gene and cloned sheep. It has invented radar, microwave and silicon chip. It has revolutionized the means of transport and communication by introducing automobiles, airplanes, rockets, satellites, telephones, televisions, computers, and internet. It has radically revised the prevalent theories in the areas of logic, learning, physics, chemistry, medicine, mathematics, space, and time.

In the spiritual field, however, the mankind has made no progress. On the contrary, there has been evident regress. The material progress has not brought the lasting happiness to the people. True happiness lies in the state of liberation and the worldly soul needs to look for the path, which has been consistently ignored. As that path has not been traversed since long, it has almost been lost sight of. The situation is thus deplorable.

The everlasting happiness can only come from within and by following the path of liberation. Shrimad, the enlightened Guru, shows the path without any reservation for the truth seekers. This is done out of innate compassion.

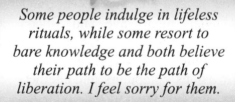

કોઈ ક્રિયાજડ થઈ રહ્યા, શુષ્કજ્ઞાનમાં કોઈ;
માને માર્ગ મોક્ષનો, કરુણા ઉપજે જોઈ.

॥૩॥

Koi Kriyäjad Thai Rahyä, Shushka Jnänamän Koi;
Mäne Märag Mokshano, Karunä Upaje Joi.

Some people indulge in lifeless rituals, while some resort to bare knowledge and both believe their path to be the path of liberation. I feel sorry for them.

- 3 -

Explanation & Discussion:

The path of liberation consists of right perception, right knowledge and right action. Since perception and knowledge go hand in hand, it can also be said that the path consists of knowledge and action. The seers have therefore said: "Jnänakriyäbhyäm Mokshah". It means that liberation can be achieved by the combination of knowledge and action. Knowledge without the follow up action is sterile. It leads nowhere and tends to give rise to vanity. On the other hand, action without knowledge leads to a blind alley. It would be difficult to come out of that.

Most aspirants do not realize the importance of pursuing both those aspects simultaneously and appropriately. Absence of such understanding is the principal cause of drifting within the sea of birth and death. Some aspirants believe that performing auspicious rituals is enough. They expect to earn Punya (good or wholesome Karma), which will lead them to a better life hereafter. They perform the rituals as per tradition without understanding their purpose. Such people are termed as lifeless ritualists.

On the other hand, some happen to read books and scriptures, and conclude that intellectual understanding of the soul and its nature will lead toward the manifestation of its true nature. Such intellectual understanding is not enough for Self-Realization. Mere intellectual understanding actually leads them astray. They are called bare knowledgeable persons. It is the application of the knowledge acquired from religious books into routine activities that translates knowledge into right understanding.

Both these groups are mistaken. Shrimad observes that majority of the religiously oriented people belong to one of the two groups. They insist upon the truthfulness of their own viewpoint only. He feels compassionate that the people are holding such one-sided view. The next two stanzas define in detail the lifeless rituals and sterile knowledge.

બાહ્ય ક્રિયામાં રાચતા, અંતર્ભેદ ન કાંઈ;
જ્ઞાનમાર્ગ નિષેધતા, તેહ ક્રિયાજડ આંઈ.

॥૪॥

Bähya Kriyämän Rächatä, Antarbhed Na Känyi;
Jnän Märga Nishedhatä, Teh Kriyäjad Änyi.

Lifeless ritualists are those who
cherish the external rituals
without inner discrimination, and
they reject the path of knowledge.

- 4 -

Explanation & Discussion:

Here the characteristics of the lifeless ritualists are described. Those, who rely merely upon rituals and cherish in performing them without keeping in view their purpose, are lifeless ritualists. The term ritual connotes some formality. The religious activities undertaken by Jain Shrävaks (householders) as their daily routine, such as, going to the temple, performing Pooja, doing Samayik and Pratikraman, etc. become mechanical and monotonous since they are performed in language that they do not understand. Also, they undertake the rituals without understanding their significance and meaning behind it. The greatest drawback is the false notion behind these activities. The ritualists erroneously think that these activities will reduce their Karmas and take them to the path of liberation.

It should be noted that rituals are not totally rejected here. They are generally meant to benefit average aspirants and beginners. There is therefore no reason to denigrate the importance of the rituals, but some of them have lost their relevance at present. Moreover, every ritual has some purpose. The purpose behind the rituals and their relevance should always be kept in mind while performing them, otherwise they become mechanical or lifeless, and do not yield the real expected benefit. The rituals are primarily meant for cultivating detachment and for augmenting the sense of devotion. Their ultimate objective is to gain equanimity. The lifeless ritualists fail to understand this fact.

Austerities also are mostly observed with such notions. The main purpose of the external austerities is to develop bearing capability so as to maintain equanimity under difficult circumstances. For example, fasting is meant for developing capability to stay without food for some time, and Äyambil for getting used to fatless and tasteless foods. Those purposes are often lost sight of, and people mostly observe austerities with a view to earn Punya.

The lifeless rituals are often carried out with ulterior motives. The desire to be known as a religious person in the community, the desire to have heavenly pleasures in the next life, the desire to follow the family traditions, and the fear of hell's miseries are some examples of ulterior motives. The lifeless ritualists believe that mere observance of austerities and other restraints, reciting prayer, going to temple, etc. would result in eradication of the unwholesome Karma and lead them to the Karmaless state. They overlook the fact that lifeless observance of the rituals would lead to wholesome Karma adding cycles of birth and death, and will never lead to the Karmaless state.

As a matter of fact, no activity without internal bearing and true understanding can lead to liberation. The people, devoid of internal discrimination, thus stay deluded about liberation. They do not realize that during the infinite period of wandering, they must have performed rituals and observed austerities countless number of times. That has not brought the lasting well being, nor has it led them on the path of liberation. They are naive to believe that observance of any ritual without an eye towards its purpose can be helpful.

Not only that, they object to the people who try to follow the path of knowledge. They think that the path of knowledge is slippery and hazardous. There are too many pitfalls, and therefore, it is not meant for them. As such, they turn their back towards knowledge. Therefore, Shrimad warns in this stanza about lifeless rituals without inner discrimanation, as well as about misconceptions pertaining to that.

Lifeless rituality occurs even among the followers of Shrimad. Many of them ritually recite the Ätmasiddhi Shästra and other compositions mechanically in their daily routine. It is a parody that even this stanza is often mechanically recited. Very few people remain vigilant about the true meaning of what they recite.

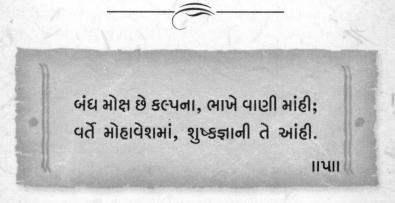

બંધ મોક્ષ છે કલ્પના, ભાખે વાણી માંહી;
વર્તે મોહાવેશમાં, શુષ્કજ્ઞાની તે આંહી. ॥૫॥

*Bandh Moksha Chhe Kalpanä, Bhäkhe Väni Mänhin;
Varte Mohäveshmän, Shushka Jnäni Te Ähin.*

> *Bare knowledgeable people are those*
> *who verbally talk of bondage and*
> *liberation as being imaginary; but who*
> *behave under the influence of delusion.*
>
> *- 5 -*

Explanation & Discussion:

This stanza explains the characteristics of the bare knowledgeable people. A bare knowledgeable person is the one who has acquired information from scriptures but has not applied it in his beliefs and daily life. There are people who come across the spiritual books dealing with the basic and absolute purity of the soul. They conclude that since the soul is intangible, it cannot be defiled; it is incorruptible and stays pure forever. The philosophy of Vedänt states that the soul can never be polluted and its defilement is merely imaginary. It always stays pure and does not incur any bondage. Therefore, nothing is required for liberation, except understanding the soul's inherent pure state.

By virtue of the belief in purity of the soul, such persons may perhaps stay away from gross passions, but they usually remain unconcerned about the subtle ones. Believing that sense organs have nothing to do with the soul, they are also likely to indulge in the sense objects. They fail to realize that the spiritual knowledge does not leave scope for attachment to any worldly object or for indulging in anger, animosity, arrogance, or other defiling instincts. The truly knowledgeable people invariably refrain themselves from indulging in indolence, infatuation, etc.

On account of previous Karma, the sense of attachment or aversion may at times arise even to a truly knowledgeable person, but he understands that such sense is not compatible with the purity of the soul and feels sorry that such a sense arises. Shrimad has stated (Vachanämrut # 819): "When the sense instincts become too powerful, the sensible person feels much grieved to notice the absence of his vigor and continually despises himself. Repeatedly looking at the self with the sense of despise and taking recourse to the words and conduct of the great entities, he generates internal vigor and drives back those instincts even by exerting much force. He does not sit at rest till then nor does he stay complacent merely by being sorry."

Thus a really knowledgeable person identifies any defiling instinct as an alien to his true nature and therefore would not indulge in attachment or aversion. Having developed true detachment for the worldly objects, he does not long for anything. The sense of craving or aversion becomes unbecoming to him. Those, who do not have such understanding at heart, are merely bare knowledgeable people. Despite their scriptural knowledge, they stay deluded about the right path and continue to drift within the sea of birth and death.

વૈરાગ્યાદિ સફળ તો, જો સહ આતમજ્ઞાન;
તેમ જ આતમજ્ઞાનની, પ્રાપ્તિતણાં નિદાન.

||૬||

Vairägyädi Safal To, Jo Sah Ätamjnän;
Temaj Ätamjnänani, Präpti Tanä Nidän.

Detachment, etc. are meaningful, if
accompanied by knowledge of Self;
the knowledge of Self can be
attained if detachment,
etc. are used with the right purpose.
- 6 -

Explanation & Discussion:

The detachment, renouncement, etc. should come out of the true knowledge of soul. Very often people feel detachment due to physical pain, emotional distress, loss of a dear one, or material loss. Such detachment is not derived by understanding the transitory nature of all the worldly objects. Hence it is only temporary and does not last. Those people would again be attracted towards worldly pleasures later on. Under the influence of temporary detachment, they may renounce and may go back to the worldly life later. This happens, because their detachment is not born of true knowledge. Therefore it is stated here that detachment is worthwhile, if it is associated with the knowledge of Self.

The knowledge of Self is thus a prerequisite for lasting detachment. In order to realize that soul is different from the body and is free from craving, aversion and all types of mental defilement, it is necessary to secure appropriate guidance of the realized persons and to contemplate on what they teach. That is the way to gain true knowledge. Thereby one would realize the essentially temporary nature of the worldly life and lose interest therein. Detachment for the worldly aspects would naturally occur to him. Only that type of detachment lasts. Since the lasting detachment thus comes out of true knowledge, it can be termed as indicative of having gained enlightenment. From another viewpoint, the second line of this stanza states that if detachment, etc. are practiced with the purpose of attaining self-realization, they can be instrumental in achieving the knowledge of Self. Thus this stanza shows the importance of detachment and renouncement as the means for attaining the true knowledge of Self.

ત્યાગ વિરાગ ન ચિત્તમાં, થાય ન તેને જ્ઞાન;
અટકે ત્યાગ વિરાગમાં, તો ભૂલે નિજભાન.

॥૭॥

Tyäg Viräg Na Chittamän, Thäy Na Tene Jnän;
Atake Tyäg Virägamän, To Bhoole Nij Bhän.

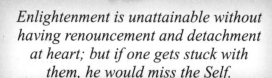

Enlightenment is unattainable without
having renouncement and detachment
at heart; but if one gets stuck with
them, he would miss the Self.

- 7 -

Explanation & Discussion:

The term 'renouncement' is usually understood as giving up worldly life. Such external renouncement is useful, but does not necessarily indicate the internal sense of renouncement. The internal renouncement consists of giving up the internal impurities. This can happen only with the radical change in the belief. If one understands the true nature of self, his inclination for worldly objects will begin to vanish. He realizes that the external objects of any kind cannot give him lasting peace and happiness. In that case the external renouncement and detachment will be in harmony with his true belief. That is the only way to attain enlightenment.

Enlightenment abides within the soul. However, that inherent capability remains obscured, because the worldly soul is under the influence of Karma. It is therefore necessary to eradicate bondage of Karma. Such eradication process is known as Nirjarā. In that connection the Tattvārtha Sutra (IX-3) states: "Tapasā Nirjarā Cha". This means that the eradication of Karma can be achieved by austerities. Many people therefore resort to austerities and restraints in order to shake off bondage of Karma. Most of them, however, forget that so long as there is any inclination for the worldly pleasures, enlightenment cannot arise. Thus Nirjarā takes place only if austerities and restraints are accompanied by overcoming of desires for worldly objects. Hence it is absolutely necessary that the spiritual aspirant develops the true sense of renouncement and detachment.

It should be remembered that the renouncement and detachment are the means, and not the ends, of spiritual pursuit. They are the prerequisites for progress on the spiritual path. After those prerequisites, one needs to go ahead in the pursuit of enlightenment. Some people might feel gratified with the sense of external renouncement, develop detachment, and then they stop at that level. This stanza warns that if they do not move forward, they would not gain enlightenment and miss the real objective of spiritual pursuit.

જ્યાં જ્યાં જે જે યોગ્ય છે, તહાં સમજવું તેહ;
ત્યાં ત્યાં તે તે આચરે, આત્માર્થી જન એહ.

||૮||

Jyän Jyän Je Je Yogya Chhe, Tahän Samajavun Teh;
Tyän Tyän Te Te Ächare, Ätmärthi Jan Eh.

The seeker of truth would everywhere
accept whatever is appropriate, and he
would act accordingly in every situation.

- 8 -

Explanation & Discussion:

In light of what has been stated in stanzas 4 and 5, every spiritual aspirant should examine his particular situation and try to find out what is lacking so as to remedy it. If he has been pursuing the rituals without regard for the purpose thereof, he should keep the attainment of self-knowledge in his view; and if he has been feeling gratified with bare knowledge only, he should try to see that he does not harbor any attachment for the worldly aspects. For controlling the sense of attachment he should integrate restraints, worship, devotion, merits, etc. in his routine life.

Devotion and worship denote some sense of attachment. However, such attachment is wholesome and desirable until one attains high spiritual level, where one can stay tuned to his own soul. Devotion for and worship of the omniscient Lords and Guru are useful to most aspirants, especially in initial development. That approach maintains balanced life and enables one to proceed on the path of liberation.

This stanza can also be interpreted without reference to those two stanzas. In that case, this stanza can be considered as establishing the general criteria for the truth seekers. Such people should be willing to accept the truth in every situation and put it into practice. They should have the discretion to understand what is right and what is wrong, and be willing to adopt the right and discard the wrong. This should be done, irrespective of the tradition in which they might have been brought up. Their objective should be to seek the truth from whatever corner it comes forth. For that purpose they need to have an open mind. Moreover, they should be prepared to notice their own deficiencies as well as drawbacks, and should be willing to adjust their life, if necessary. In other words, they should be guided by the criterion of the right and wrong, and be willing to act accordingly.

સેવે સદ્‌ગુરુચરણને, ત્યાગી દઈ નિજપક્ષ;
પામે તે પરમાર્થને, નિજપદનો લે લક્ષ.

||૯||

Seve Sadguru Charanane, Tyägi Dai Nij Paksha;
Päme Te Paramärthane, Nijpadano Le Laksha.

*Giving up his own view point, if one
serves at the feet of the true Guru,
he would understand the real truth and
proceed towards self-realization.*

- 9 -

Explanation & Discussion:

The primary objective of spiritual pursuit is to get on the path of liberation. The nature of the soul is the ultimate truth and the way it can be realized is Paramärth. The main obstacle in realizing it is that one may either feel satisfied by indulging in the lifeless rituals or may be stuck with bare knowledge. The reason for adhering to such a one-sided approach is that the aspirant has not sought the shelter of a true Guru. While explaining this stanza at length (Vachanämrut # 718), Shrimad has emphasized the vital importance of a true Guru in spiritual pursuit as below.

"The way to overcome lifeless rituality and the bare knowledgeable state is to give up one's own views and to rest at the feet of a true Guru. The lifeless ritualists have taken recourse to the wrong gurus, who do not have self-realization and do not know the right way. They know the path of rituals and physical hardships to which they attract people and get them attached to the family tradition. Thereby such people cease to have the inclination to come in contact with a true Guru. If they happen to come in such contact, they are not receptive to true teaching on account of their rigid sectarian approach.

"The bare knowledgeable persons also have not taken the shelter of a true Guru. They have read the spiritual books according to their own fancy and consider themselves knowledgeable by that, or by listening to the bare knowledgeable people. Being considered as knowledgeable confers a position of honor and they cherish it.

"From a peculiar consideration, the scriptures have laid down the parity of pity, charity, violence, and worship. Without understanding its implications, the bare knowledgeable person makes use of such words merely for being considered knowledgeable. He does not know how such words are to be utilized for gaining the ultimate benefit. As the scriptures have laid down the futility of pity, etc. so have they laid down the futility of learning up to the nine Purva. That signifies the negation of barren knowledge. The bare knowledgeable person, however, does not look at it on account of his ego and the craze for being considered the knowledgeable. That does not give him scope for the right thinking.

"The lifeless ritualists and bare knowledgeable persons, both have been on the wrong track. Their claim to have gained the right path clearly shows their vain persistence. If they had taken refuge at the feet of a true Guru, they would have been induced towards the means for self-realization, whereby they could be treading the right path."

Prior to getting access to a true Guru, the spiritual aspirant might have undertaken different activities as per his understanding. He might have resorted to various gurus and adopted their views. However, all such exercises have not been helpful in realizing the self, because they were undertaken in absence of the guidance form a true Guru.

Here, Shrimad says that whatever the worldly soul has gained so far, has been acquired from the mundane perspective, not from the enlightened one. If he now comes in contact with an enlightened Guru, he must be prepared to leave all other gurus and to give up all his notions and beliefs. He should be ready to adopt the shelter of the true Guru and undertake whatever he commands. Since the true Guru has already walked on the path and knows the obstacles to be faced, he can guide the disciple suitably. He knows the shortcomings of the disciple and can therefore instruct him about right scriptural study and proper means of detachment. Treading that road under the right guidance is the real path for self-realization.

આત્મજ્ઞાન સમદર્શિતા, વિચરે ઉદયપ્રયોગ;
અપૂર્વ વાણી પરમશ્રુત, સદ્ગુરુ લક્ષણ યોગ્ય.

॥૧૦॥

Ätmajnän Samadarshitä, Vichare Udayprayog;
Apurva Väni Paramashrut, Sadguru Lakshan Yogya.

Knowledge of Self, equanimity, activities
as ordained, unparalleled words and
mastery over scriptures are the
characteristics of a true Guru.

- 10 -

Explanation & Discussion:

After stressing the importance of surrendering to a true Guru, this stanza provides five characteristics of such a Guru. Self-realization, equanimity, behavior as ordained, unparalleled speech, and authentic scriptural knowledge are the main characteristics by which one can identify a true Guru. By stating that he should be self-realized, the emphasis is laid on the distinguished knowledge. By saying that he should be imbibed with equanimity, the emphasis is laid on the distinguished perception. By stating that he should behave as ordained, the emphasis is laid on the blissful mode of life. Thus the importance of the right knowledge, right perception, and right behavior is laid down in the first line.

The second line specifies the characteristics of speech and scriptural knowledge. The Guru should have a distinguished way of expression. He should have the capability to use the words, which can uproot the wrong beliefs. Only such words can penetrate the hearts of listeners. Such words do not easily come forth. They are therefore termed here as unparalleled. Only those, who are highly knowledgeable and truly enlightened, can utter such words. It is therefore laid down that the Guru should be well versed and should have mastery over the scriptures.

The explanatory note under this stanza (Vachanämrut # 718) provides another version. It uses the terms Swarupsthit and Ichchhärahit in place of Ätmajnän and Samadarshitä, respectively. Swarupsthit means one who stays tuned to the true nature of the soul. He, who has knowledge of Self, either abides in that state or strives to reach that state. Ichchhärahit denotes the desireless state of mind. This state is implicit in equanimity. Hence, that term makes explicit the principal attribute of equanimity.

Spiritual pursuit rests on surrendering to the true Guru. However, this stanza makes it clear that the aspirant should not surrender to any ordinary person. He should keep the above-mentioned characteristics in mind, while looking for a true Guru, and surrender to the one who fulfills those criteria. Only then the aspirant will get on the right path.

પ્રત્યક્ષ સદ્ગુરુ સમ નહીં, પરોક્ષ જિન ઉપકાર;
એવો લક્ષ થયા વિના, ઊગે ન આત્મવિચાર.

॥૧૧॥

Pratyaksha Sadguru Sam Nahin, Paroksha Jin Upakär;
Evo Laksha Thayä Vinä, Uge Na Ätmavichär.

*Contemplation of Self cannot arise
without realizing that the benefits
flowing from a live Guru are
incomparably superior to those
from the remote omniscient Lords.* - 11 -

Explanation & Discussion:

This stanza states the importance of learning from a live Guru. It says that the instructions of such a Guru are more helpful than the teaching of the remote omniscient Lords, who are no longer available to us. This is not meant to belittle the importance of the Lords' teachings. The omniscient Lords were perfectly enlightened, while the present Guru might be at the stage of self-realization striving for such perfection. As such, there is no scope whatsoever for comparing the two in absolute terms.

What the Lords have said is available to us in the form of scriptures. But those texts have deep underlying meanings, which will not be clear to a person who has not dwelt deep into spiritualism. If one resorts to those texts on his own, he is likely to misinterpret their contents, go astray and become a bare knowledgeable person as outlined in stanza 5. The remote Lords are not going to come down in person and tell that he has incorrectly understood the scriptures. Nor will they be able to guide the disciple about obstacles on the path of liberation. The scriptural books only describe the Path. The essence of the Path is in the heart of a true Guru who has already walked on the Path. The knowledgeable and enlightened Guru would surely point out the aspirant's mistakes and try to bring him back to the right Path. It is therefore said that the secret of the soul lies in the heart of a live Guru. Unless one is convinced of that, he will not conceive of the true nature of the soul.

સદ્ગુરુના ઉપદેશ વણ, સમજાય ન જિનરૂપ;
સમજ્યા વણ ઉપકાર શો ? સમજ્યે જિનસ્વરૂપ.

॥૧૨॥

Sadgurunä Upadesh Van, Samajäy Na Jin Roop;
Samajyä Van Upakär Sho, Samajye Jin Swaroop.

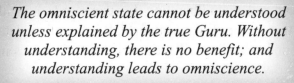

The omniscient state cannot be understood
unless explained by the true Guru. Without
understanding, there is no benefit; and
understanding leads to omniscience.

- 12 -

Explanation & Discussion:

What has been said in the previous stanza is made more explicit in this stanza. It states that the aspirants on their own cannot grasp the true nature of the omniscient state. The worldly soul has always identified itself with the body and its relations. How can he comprehend the bodiless state of the liberated souls or the state of the omniscient Lords? Though being embodied, the omniscient Lords stay beyond the bodily sense. It is very difficult to comprehend the state of those Lords, unless it is explained by an enlightened Guru. The following verse of the saint Kabir is relevant in this respect:

Guru Gobind Dono Khade, Kisako Lägun Päy?
Balihäri Gurudevaki, Jinhe Gobind Diyo Batäy.

It means: Whose feet shall I fall at if God and Guru are both standing before me? The higher beneficence comes from the Guru, because he helped recognize God.

A devotee may pray and worship the omniscient Lords. He may also think that the Lords have rendered obligation by describing the true path, and recite the appropriate verses in token of his devotion. Does he get benefit merely from that? The whole purpose of worship is to get on the path treaded by the Lords. But if one does not know the true state of the Lords, how can he understand the path treaded by Them? What benefit would he then get by merely worshipping the Lords?

If he comprehends the state of the omniscient Lords by explanation from a true Guru, he can also understand the path of liberation laid down by the Lords. Then he will surely go ahead on that path and attain liberation. In other words, he will attain the state that the Lords have attained. It is therefore stated here that right understanding will ultimately lead to omniscience.

આત્માદિ અસ્તિત્વનાં, જેહ નિરૂપક શાસ્ત્ર;
પ્રત્યક્ષ સદ્ગુરુ યોગ નહિ, ત્યાં આધાર સુપાત્ર.

॥૧૩॥

Ätmädi Astitvanä, Jeh Nirupak Shästra;
Pratyaksha Sadguru Yoga Nahin, Tyan Ädhär Supätra.

The scriptures dealing with existence
of soul, etc. can be the recourse for
the deserving aspirants, where direct
contact with the true Guru is not available.

- 13 -

Explanation & Discussion:

The importance of the Guru has been explained in the preceding two stanzas. However, the question is, "How to meet the Guru, who satisfies the criteria laid down in the 10th stanza?" There was shortage of such true Gurus even in good times. It is therefore no wonder that they would be rarely available in the present declining time cycle. If some of them exist, they are likely to stay away from society. It would therefore be improbable to come across a true Guru. Under these circumstances, whom to rely upon would be a problem for spiritual aspirants.

This stanza states the way for the aspirants in absence of a true Guru. It should be noted that this is meant only for the deserving aspirants. It states that the aspirants, who have gained adequate spiritual background, can depend on the right books when a true Guru is not available. The spiritual books, which deal with the existence of soul and related matters would be useful to such deserving aspirants.

It should be noted that these scriptures cannot take the place of an enlightened Guru. However, the spiritual aspirant can continue his progress by resorting to such scriptures in the absence of the true Guru. Then he will remain vigilant and become more qualified to receive the directions from a live Guru, and that will lead to self-realization.

A word of caution is needed here. There are a number of books that purport to deal with the soul and spiritual aspects. Many of them are not written with right perspective and therefore cannot be relied upon. Only those, which have been written by the reliable spiritual authorities, can be depended upon. The persons, who can thus be relied upon, are called Äpta. That term denotes the persons who have no interest other than the well being of the soul. Such persons are self-realized. Only the books written by such authentic persons should be relied upon in the absence of a true Guru.

અથવા સદ્‍ગુરુએ કહ્યાં, જે અવગાહન કાજ;
તે તે નિત્ય વિચારવાં, કરી મતાંતર ત્યાજ.

॥૧૪॥

Athavä Sadgurue Kahyän, Je Avagähan Käj;
Te Te Nitya Vichärvän, Kari Matäntar Tyäj.

> *Otherwise leaving aside different*
> *viewpoints, one should always study and*
> *contemplate the books recommended*
> *by the true Guru for in-depth study.*
>
> *- 14 -*

Explanation & Discussion:

This stanza states the criterion to know about the reliable spiritual books. If the aspirant has come across a true Guru, the latter might have suggested the right books. For instance, reverend Laghuräjswämi has said repeatedly to contemplate over the Letter of Six Fundamentals (Appendix-II), Sadguru Bhakti Rahasya, Yam Niyam and Kshamäpanä. The spiritual aspirant should therefore regularly ponder over their contents. Similarly, if he happens to come in contact with another true Guru, the aspirant should follow his advice and undertake the study of the spiritual books recommended by him. He should go through such literature with his heart and repeatedly ponder over the same with the clear objective of achieving self-realization. It is very important that he first renounce his preconceived and ill-conceived notions and then study the recommended scriptures.

It is very rare to come across a true Guru and get his guidance. Even for those who are lucky to get access to such a Guru, it is not possible to remain in continuous contact with him. Such aspirants therefore need to secure the advice of the Guru about the right literature. It will enable them to pursue spiritual development in the absence of the Guru.

રોકે જીવ સ્વચ્છંદ તો, પામે અવશ્ય મોક્ષ;
પામ્યા એમ અનંત છે, ભાખ્યું જિન નિર્દોષ.

॥૧૫॥

Roke Jiv Swachchhand To, Päme Avashya Moksha;
Pämyä Em Anant Chhe, Bhäkhyun Jin Nirdosh.

One, who restrains self-indulgence,
surely attains liberation. The flawless
omniscient Lords have stated that
innumerable souls have attained it that way.

- 15 -

Explanation & Discussion:

Why has the worldly soul not attained liberation? Of course there are multiple reasons, but the most important one is self-indulgence. It is not that the soul would never have tried to learn about liberation. During the innumerable births that it has taken, it must have been oriented towards its well being on several occasions and might even have tried for the same. But whatever it might have understood and done for the purpose, must have been according to its own viewpoint or self-indulgence. The root cause of self-indulgence is ego or false pride which will not let the person find his own faults. A person cannot eradicate his own self-indulgence. His ego and pride will not allow him to impartially see his own faults.

It has to be born in mind that the soul has been indulging in worldly life since infinity. It never learnt the truth and therefore did not come across the path of liberation. Now, if one tries to seek liberation, how is he going to make out the right path? Without knowing that path, would not his efforts amount to traveling in the dark? Would it not be like a person looking for an unknown place without getting help from someone who knows it?

If a person thus tries to find the place on his own, he would simply wander here and there and not reach the destination. Such effort can be termed as self-indulgence. In the worldly sphere however, one may reach his physical destination by chance without help from any one. But in the spiritual realm, such self-indulgence is of no avail. Since it is impossible to gain right insight without proper guidance, the approach selected by one's own intelligence cannot be right. The intellect, which has never even dreamt of the truth, is not competent to overcome ignorance. A spiritual aspirant therefore needs to give up his self-indulgence and go to a self-realized person. Only such a person can show the right path. That would enable him to proceed in the right direction and reach the destination.

This stanza therefore states that one, who gives up self-indulgence, certainly attains liberation. The omniscient Lords have stated that infinite souls have attained the same accordingly. If one therefore tries to figure out why he still continues to wander, he can conclude that he has not yet given up self-indulgence. Had he given it up, he would have taken recourse to a true Guru, who would have put him on the right track. Giving up self-indulgence is therefore the main precept of the omniscient Lords. Those Lords are perfect and flawless, because they have got rid of all flaws by virtue of eradicating bondage of Karma and have become omniscient. So whatever they have stated cannot be anything but true and flawless.

પ્રત્યક્ષ સદ્‍ગુરુ યોગથી, સ્વચ્છંદ તે રોકાય;
અન્ય ઉપાય કર્યા થકી, પ્રાયે બમણો થાય.

॥૧૬॥

Pratyaksha Sadguru Yogathi, Swachchhand Te Rokäy;
Anya Upäy Karyä Thaki, Präye Bamano Thäy.

Self-indulgence can be overcome
by direct contact with a true Guru;
it would be mostly doubled
by resorting to other means.

- 16 -

Explanation & Discussion:

How can self-indulgence be removed? Of course, it cannot be done by one's own efforts. It is almost impossible to see one's own faults. The right (and easier) way is to get in contact with a true Guru. If he happens to go side way, the Guru is there to bring him back on the right track. Thus he continues to get guidance as necessary. It leaves no scope for self-indulgence. The Guru knows how and when the pupil is likely to fall in the trap of self-indulgence and keeps him in check from falling.

The pupil also knows his weakness and will rely upon the guidance of the Guru. Thus when one tends to rely on someone else, his ego melts and his inclination towards self-indulgence continues to decline. The other way to overcome self-indulgence is to try on one's own. But such effort itself amounts to further self-indulgence! It would be an attempt to overcome self-indulgence with the help of self-indulgence. That can never succeed. On the contrary, it would result in augmenting self-indulgence. It is therefore stated here that self-indulgence is likely to be doubled by resorting to other means.

સ્વચ્છંદ, મત આગ્રહ તજી, વર્તે સદ્ગુરુલક્ષ;
સમકિત તેને ભાખિયું, કારણ ગણી પ્રત્યક્ષ.

॥૧૭॥

Swachchhand, Mat Ägrah Taji, Varte Sadguru Laksha;
Samakit Tene Bhäkhiyun, Käran Gani Pratyaksha.

Renouncing self-indulgence, personal viewpoints, and its insistence, if one acts as directed by a true Guru, that action is termed right perception, being the obvious cause thereof.
- 17 -

Explanation & Discussion:

Self-indulgence, holding one's own views and sticking to the opinions formed thereof, do not allow a person to seek right guidance. If one gives up all of them and seeks the shelter of a true Guru, such a Guru would show him the path that the worldly soul has never come across. One would then proceed on that path and achieve self-realization. Thus going to the right shelter (Guru) without one's own bias is the obvious cause of self-realization. It can therefor be termed as right perception or Samakit.

In this connection, Shrimad has observed (Vachanämrut # 771): "It is not to be taken as a principle that all the monks, nuns, and house holders of the Lord Tirthankars were knowledgeable about the sentient (living) and insentient (nonliving) substances and were endowed with right perception. Many of them were said to have right perception because they had the conviction, willingness, recourse, and firm determination that Lord Tirthankars are the right entities; they have laid down the path of liberation, and the way they have directed, is the right path to liberation."

Every occurrence or event has a cause. Conversely, if there is a cause, its result is bound to come. In other words, the result is inherent in the cause. Therefore the cause itself is sometimes treated as the result. Shrimad here makes use of that logic and states that the molding of life as per instructions of a Guru, being the cause of right perception, is itself right perception.

The causes are of two types. One is the absolute cause known as Upädän, and the other is instrumental cause known as Nimitta. The Upädän is inherent in the subject and indicates its potentiality. For instance, right perception is potentially lying within the soul. The question is to manifest the same. The factor, which is instrumental to such manifestation, is called Nimitta. Thus, going to the shelter of the Guru is the Nimitta that leads to the manifestation of right perception.

માનાદિક શત્રુ મહા, નિજ છંદે ન મરાય;
જાતાં સદ્‍ગુરુ શરણામાં, અલ્પ પ્રયાસે જાય.

॥૧૮॥

Mänädik Shatru Mahä, Nij Chhande Na Maräy;
Jätä Sadguru Sharanamän, Alpa Prayäse Jäy.

Mighty foes like egotism cannot be
destroyed by one's own indulgence;
they can be overcome with little effort
by surrendering to a true Guru.

- 18 -

Explanation & Discussion:

In Jain terminology, the passionate instincts are called Kashäy. Krodh meaning anger, Män meaning ego, Mäyä meaning deception, and Lobh meaning greed are the four main types of Kashäy, which need to be overcome by spiritual aspirants. However, it is the experience of those who have tried to overcome them, that it is very hard to do so. Those passions are therefore termed here as mighty foes. In Vaidic terminology, the passions are actually termed as Ripu, meaning enemies. That tradition lays down sexual instinct, anger, delusion, greed, ego and jealousy as the six enemies of spiritual aspirants. Those enemies are so strong that it would not be possible to overcome them by one's own efforts. It is therefore necessary to seek help. This stanza states that such help can come forth from a true

Guru, and that the passions can be easily overcome by going to the shelter of such a Guru.

Since the four types of Kashäy are usually presented in the order of anger, ego, deception, and greed, one would expect this stanza to begin with Krodhädi (meaning anger, etc.) instead of Mänadi. However, the above order pertains to the time factor in which the Kashäy can be overcome. Krodh, for instance, is very gross and can be easily identified, while other passions are subtle and are not so evident. Therefore, it is comparatively easy to overcome the instinct of anger first; greed or desire is the last to be overcome.

In Vachanämrut (Vyäkhyänsär-1, #199) Shrimad has mentioned the order, in which the Kashäy arises, as ego, greed, deceit, and anger.

Ego or false pride is a predominant Kashäy in humans, being a part of human mentality. If something happens that hurts our ego, we find it hard to bear. We are egoistic and are not willing to let it down. We want to preserve it at all costs. In Sadguru Bhakti Rahasya, Shrimad has therefore written :

Anant Kälathi Äthadyo, Vinä Bhän Bhagawän;
Sevyä Nahin Guru Santane, Mukyun Nahin Abhimän.

It says that the worldly soul has been wandering since the infinity because of the ignorance of its true nature. That happens on account of not surrendering to the true Guru and that in turn happens, because the soul has not given up its ego. Egotism is thus the foremost Kashäy, which is very hard to overcome and which prolongs the worldly life. Shrimad has therefore said (Vachanämrut # 21-83) that had there been no ego (false pride), the world would have been a heaven. Hence this stanza rightly starts with Mänädi.

જે સદ્‌ગુરુ ઉપદેશથી, પામ્યો કેવળજ્ઞાન;
ગુરુ રહ્યા છદ્મસ્થ પણ, વિનય કરે ભગવાન.

॥૧૯॥

Je Sadguru Upadeshthi, Pämyo Kevaljnän;
Guru Rahyä Chhadmastha Pan, Vinay Kare Bhagawän.

One who attains omniscience from
the teachings of a right Guru,
reveres him, even though the Guru
might not have attained omniscience.

- 19 -

Explanation & Discussion:

It would have been clear from the discussion so far that help from a true Guru is of utmost importance in spiritual pursuit. Its importance cannot be overemphasized. This stanza states that the teaching of a Guru can lead the pupil even to omniscience. Therefore, one obviously gives respect to the true Guru. Such respect implies modesty on the part of the pupil. Modesty is a great virtue and helps tremendously in learning what the preceptor indicates. Thereby one can rapidly rise on the path of liberation. It is also possible that one becomes omniscient, even before the Guru attains it.

The term used here for such a Guru is Chhadmastha. Chhadma denotes the cover or the mask that conceals. As such, Chhadmastha indicates the state of concealment. Here, it relates to concealing the omniscient state of the soul. The state, in which the true nature of the soul remains concealed due to bondage of Karma is known as Chhadmastha. This stanza relates to a situation where the disciple has gained omniscience, while the teacher still remains Chhadmastha, i.e., he is self-realized but not omniscient. This has actually happened in several cases. For instance, Gautamswämi could not forgo his attachment for Lord Mahävir and hence did not gain omniscience during the Lord's lifetime. Many of his own pupils, however, gained it and Gautamswämi looked at them with due respect.

There is also the classic example of Chandanbälä and her pupil Mrugävati. On account of the illusion arising out of the Lord's aura, Mrugävati once stayed in the Lord's assembly beyond sunset. As she arrived late at her place, Chandanbälä reprimanded her for violating the code that forbids monks and nuns to stay out after sunset. Mrugävati felt very sorry for that lapse and went into deep remorse. Since the remorse had arisen from her heart, it resulted in destroying all of her Karma and she attained omniscience that very night. By virtue of that omniscience, she could notice, in the dark of the night, a serpent passing by the hand of Chandanbälä, who was fast asleep. Thereupon, Mrugävati lightly moved her hand aside. That caused Chandanbälä to wake up and she came to know of the pupil's omniscience. So she felt very sorry for reprimanding such an elevated soul. She too went into deep remorse and thereby attained omniscience.

Thus, reverence is of fundamental importance in spiritual pursuit. By resorting to that, one can make progress beyond imagination. The pupil, who gains omniscience before the preceptor, does not forsake the importance of modesty and continues to revere the teacher, under whose guidance he pursued the spiritual path and attained the omniscient state.

એવો માર્ગ વિનય તણો, ભાખ્યો શ્રી વીતરાગ;
મૂળ હેતુ એ માર્ગનો, સમજે કોઈ સુભાગ્ય.

||૨૦||

Evo Märga Vinay Tano, Bhäkhyo Shri Viträg;
Mool Hetu E Märgano, Samaje Koi Subhägya.

The holy Lords have stated such a path of
reverence; only a few fortunate can understand
the real significance of that path.

- 20 -

Explanation & Discussion:

Reverence plays a vital role in spiritual pursuit. Its importance has been emphasized by the omniscient Lords in their sermons and is given in the scriptures. Unfortunately, very few people realize that importance. They therefore tend to behave irreverently. That causes worldly life and transmigration to continue.

Here Shrimad states that those few, who understand the importance of reverence, are lucky. The word used for the purpose is Subhägya, which means fortunate. But it also relates to the name of his devotee Saubhägyabhäi by whose request Shrimad had written this Ätmasiddhi Shästra.

અસદ્‌ગુરુ એ વિનયનો, લાભ લહે જો કાંઈ;
મહામોહનીય કર્મથી, બૂડે ભવજળ માંહી.

॥૨૧॥

Asadguru E Vinayano, Läbh Lahe Jo Känyi;
Mahämohaniya Karmathi, Boode Bhavajal Mänhi.

If a wrong guru takes undue advantage
of that reverence, he would be drowned
in the sea of worldly existence by
virtue of intense delusive Karma.

- 21 -

Explanation & Discussion:

After stating the importance of reverence on the part of pupil, Shrimad here indicates what would happen, if a wrong guru takes advantage of the pupil's reverence with a selfish motive. The wrong guru is the one who is not enlightened. The wrong guru takes undue advantage of reverence for the purpose of acquiring name, fame, and recognition. This means extreme disregard for all enlightened (true) Gurus and all others who are on the path of liberation. This is also extreme disregard for his own pure soul. By taking undue advantage, the wrong guru would acquire intense delusive Karma and would stay in worldly existence for very long time.

Everything that one does, attracts appropriate Karma. There are eight main categories of Karma. Of these, the primarily responsible for the worldly existence is the delusive or Mohaniya Karma, which stays for a long time. Its maximum duration is stated as 7000 trillion Sägaropam (uncountable) years. This is known as Mahämohaniya Karma. The wrong guru would be subject to such long lasting Karma. Since the above duration is almost immeasurable, it is said that he would virtually be drowned in the sea of worldly existence.

હોય મુમુક્ષુ જીવ તે, સમજે એહ વિચાર;
હોય મતાર્થી જીવ તે, અવળો લે નિર્ધાર.

॥૨૨॥

Hoy Mumukshu Jiva Te, Samaje Eh Vichär;
Hoy Matärthi Jiva Te, Avalo Le Nirdhär.

One who is a truth seeker
would understand this concept;
one who is sectarian would
arrive at the wrong conclusion.

- 22 -

હોય મતાર્થી તેહને, થાય ન આતમલક્ષ;
તેહ મતાર્થી લક્ષણો, અહીં કહ્યાં નિર્પક્ષ.

॥૨૩॥

Hoy Matärthi Tehane, Thäy Na Ätam Laksha;
Teh Matärthi Laxano, Ahin Kahyän Nirpaksha.

> *One, who is a sectarian, cannot*
> *turn towards the soul; the*
> *characteristics of such a sectarian*
> *are laid down impartially hereunder.*
>
> *- 23 -*

Explanation & Discussion:

The spiritual aspirants are divided into two main categories. One pertains to those who have realized the futility of pursuing the spiritual goal on their own. They would seek the refuge of an enlightened Guru so as to get on the right path of liberation. The term used for them is Mumukshu, which literally means a liberation seeker. They are necessarily truth seekers.

The other category relates to those who are engrossed in self-indulgence and cling to their own viewpoints. They would consider the beliefs and rituals of a particular sect as the only right ones which can lead to liberation. They would also try to understand the Lords' precepts as per their own concepts. Such people are called Matärthi or sectarian. The intellect or mind of the worldly soul has been perverted by indulging in the worldly life since long. Hence, it is not possible to reach the right path by one's own intelligence. A sectarian does not realize his inability to correctly interpret what has been stated by the Lords. Hence he is prone to draw wrong conclusions. The characteristics of such a sectarian are impartially described in the next chapter.

Chapter 2
Characteristics of Sectarians (Matärthis)

There are different viewpoints from which an object or situation can be presented. When it is presented from one particular viewpoint, it is called Nay(नय). Jainism lays down seven categories of Nay, which can be broadly classified into two categories, (1) absolute viewpoint known as Nishchay Nay, and (2) practical or worldly viewpoint known as Vyavahär Nay. When an object is described in its original unadulteraded form, it is Nishchay Nay. The soul, in its true form, is pure, unadulterated, blissful consciousness; it is full of happiness, knowledge, perception, etc. To describe it that way is Nishchay Nay. The worldly soul is, however, found in unhappy and ignorant state. To describe it in that form, to state that the soul is smeared with Karma, is Vyavahär Nay.

Both of these viewpoints are correct in their own context and should therefore be taken into consideration for reaching the right conclusion. If one adopts only the absolute viewpoint, he would come to the conclusion that soul is immutable and incorruptible. As such, he would tend to believe that devotion, detachment, restraints, etc. are of no avail and would therefore give them up. Resorting to the absolute viewpoint to the exclusion of the practical or worldly viewpoint thus leads to an illusive conclusion. The term for this illusive impression is Äbhäs. Exclusively resorting to the absolute viewpoint is therefore not Nishchay Nay; it is Nishchayäbhäs, meaning illusory absolute viewpoint. Similarly, only considering the practical viewpoint to the exclusion of the absolute viewpoint is not Vyavahär Nay, it is Vyavahäräbhäs.

Lifeless ritualists and bare knowledgeable people were described in the last chapter. A lifeless ritualist insists upon ritual practices to the exclusion of knowledge and is therefore Vyavahārābhāsi. A bare knowledgeable person insists upon the absolute view to the exclusion of worldly realities and is therefore Nishchayābhāsi. This sort of one-sided thinking is not helpful in arriving at the truth. The people belonging to either of these categories are Matārthi, because they try to tread on the path of liberation by resorting to their one-sided viewpoint.

In this chapter Shrimad has described the characteristics of such one-sided people. The first five stanzas are devoted to the characteristics of the Vyavahārābhāsi, the subsequent three stanzas to those of the Nishchayābhāsi, and the remaining two stanzas are common to both of them.

બાહ્યત્યાગ પણ જ્ઞાન નહિ, તે માને ગુરુ સત્ય;
અથવા નિજકુળધર્મના, તે ગુરુમાં જ મમત્વ.

॥૨૪॥

Bāhya Tyāg Pan Jnān Nahin, Te Māne Guru Satya;
Athavā Nijakuldharmanā, Te Gurumān Ja Mamatva.

The sectarian believes those as true gurus,
who have outwardly renounced, but do not
have enlightenment; or he has the affinity for
the family gurus, who belong to his sect.

- 24 -

Explanation & Discussion:

Spiritual pursuit consists of treading on the path of liberation. Since the right path for the purpose is unknown, a spiritual aspirant needs to know the same from a true Guru. Those who are truth seekers can recognize a true Guru from the characteristics stated in the 10th stanza. But a sectarian holds wrong beliefs about the gurus. Either he goes in for the outward symbols or attaches importance to the family and sectarian aspects. He is impressed by the external renouncement and would therefore accept such persons as gurus. Those gurus could even be devoid of knowledge and without any sense of internal detachment. Therefore, they might be indulging in passions as well. But a sectarian does not care for that. He goes by the outward signs and regards those as gurus, who wear the monk's cloths, perform different types of rituals, and observes external austerities.

The question may arise, "Is external renouncement of no importance?" The omniscient Lords primarily described the path of renouncement. If that were of no avail, why did Tirthankars and other great persons give up family life and become monks? External renouncement is no doubt useful, but it needs to be associated with internal detachment, resulting from enlightenment. The internal detachment comes from understanding the true nature of the soul. This can take place only when a spiritual aspirant surrenders with great reverence to a true Guru who is enlightened. The absolute and unconditional surrender to a true Guru must take place with the renouncement of wrong beliefs. Only then it will lead to enlightenment. With enlightenment, external renouncement will follow, unless an aspirant has to stay in the worldly life as a consequence of previous Karma. Bare external renouncement, without any implication of an internal one, has little significance in the spiritual realm.

Those so-called gurus have no renouncement at heart nor are they enlightened. They might have renounced the family life in line with their tradition or on account of some other external considerations. They might adopt the dress of a monk, but they have no inclination for the knowledge of the Self. But, a sectarian would consider them as reliable true gurus. He would have more regard for the traditional family guru or for one belonging to his own caste and creed. In most cases, the sectarian, traditional, or family guru is accepted with some ulterior motives such as to support his desire to nurture ego or pride or to earn respect from the community in general. Such a guru gets his followers attached to the family traditions and makes them non-receptive to true teaching.

Such wrong perception about a guru would include a similar perception for the divinity as well. This is Mithyätva (wrong, perverted belief) which is the main cause of transmigration and worldly wandering.

જે જિનદેહ પ્રમાણ ને, સમવસરણાદિ સિદ્ધિ;
વર્ણન સમજે જિનનું, રોકી રહે નિજ બુદ્ધિ.

॥૨૫॥

Je Jindeh Pramänane, Samavasaranädi Siddhi;
Varnan Samaje Jinanun, Roki Rahe Nij Buddhi.

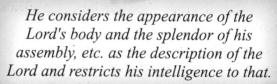

He considers the appearance of the Lord's body and the splendor of his assembly, etc. as the description of the Lord and restricts his intelligence to that.

- 25 -

Explanation & Discussion:

After describing the sectarian approach arising from the wrong perception of a guru, this stanza lays down the one arising from misconception of the Lord. Such a person has faith in the omniscient Lords, but he misunderstands their true image. The Lords have attained perfect purity. The soul has infinite capabilities and the omniscient Lords have fully manifested the same. As such, they are endowed with many accomplishments. Even the heavenly beings take pride in serving them. The Lords also have marvelous bodies. Most people are amazed to know about the magnificent physique, and the pomp & splendor associated with their assemblies & movement. When they read that the Lords' assemblies are organized by celestial beings, splendidly decorated in jewels and diamonds with golden lotuses placed wherever the Lords put their feet, they are awe struck and believe that those aspects constitute the main attributes of the Lords. Thus they overlook the internal attributes, which constitute the true image of the Lords.

Here the questions may arise, "What is the purpose of underestimating the above mentioned antecedents of the Lords? Moreover, their form, their voice, their aura, canopy over their head, Ashok tree, showering of heavenly flowers, etc. are adored even by the celestial beings. Why should such extraordinary aspects be considered of little significance or be treated as subservient to other attributes?"

Those antecedents are, of course, extraordinary. But they are insignificant as compared to the inner majesty of the Lords. When the people remain in awe with only the external aspects, they cannot conceive of the Lords' inner state. They forget that the external aspects, however magnificent they may seem, are ephemeral and do not present the lasting image of the Lords. The external attributes are incidental to their inner achievements. They are by-products of the inner state. Inner majesty consists of absolute purity of the soul, which is blissful, immutable and everlasting. That is the real image of the Lords. But the sectarians do not look at that. They are impressed with only the external accomplishments and consider the same as the true image of the omniscient Lords. The scriptures consider such a concept as misplaced and misleading. It is analogous to describing a capital city as the king.

પ્રત્યક્ષ સદ્ગુરુયોગમાં, વર્તે દૃષ્ટિ વિમુખ;
અસદ્ગુરુને દૃઢ કરે, નિજ માનાર્થે મુખ્ય.

॥૨૬॥

Pratyaksha Sadguruyogamän, Varte Drashti Vimukh;
Asadgurune Dradh Kare, Nij Mänärthe Mukhya.

> *In the case of direct access to a true Guru, he turns about his face and reaffirms his belief in the wrong guru, mostly for the sake of his ego.*
>
> *- 26 -*

Explanation & Discussion:

This stanza deals with the misplaced faith of a sectarian in his wrong guru. He has cultivated firm faith in his guru and feels sure that the path of liberation lies in the way his guru says. As such, he is not receptive to any other way. If he comes across a true Guru, that Guru would obviously exhort him to give up the wrong notions and prejudices that he might have formed. The sectarian is scared to hear that and would turn his face away, thinking that what the true Guru says is wrong and is not in the interest of his well being.

He would then go to his traditional wrong guru and display how much he respects him and how staunchly he follows the traditional aspects. That also helps in preserving his ego, because his guru would feel pleased by his sense of devotion and would praise him for being a true follower. He would thus get esteem for his faith in the traditional approach.

દેવાદિ ગતિ ભંગમાં, જે સમજે શ્રુતજ્ઞાન;
માને નિજ મત વેષનો, આગ્રહ મુક્તિનિદાન.

॥૨૭॥

Devädi Gati Bhangamän, Je Samaje Shrutjnän;
Mäne Nij Mat Veshano, Ägrah Mukti Nidän.

He takes the classification of heavenly and other states of existence as constituting the scriptural knowledge, and believes that insisting on his views and on the sectarian attire will gain him liberation.

- 27 -

Explanation & Discussion:

This stanza deals with the wrong concept of the sectarian regarding scriptural knowledge. Jainism lays down five categories of knowledge. The first two are related to the intellectual and scriptural knowledge, which are termed as Mati Jnän and Shrut Jnän, respectively. Gaining knowledge starts from that level and ends in omniscience, which is known as Kevaljnän.

The scriptures divide worldly life in four categories of heavenly, human, animal, and infernal (hellish) existence. The unhappiness and misery associated with the worldly life of those four categories are explained at length in the scriptures. They have laid down 198 subdivisions of the heavenly beings, 303 of the humans, 48 of the animals, and 14 of the infernal category for a total of 563. A sectarian does not make out that the purpose of such a description is to show the variety of life in which the worldly soul has been wandering. Instead, he would consider those details as constituting the essence of scriptural knowledge and try to memorize and reiterate those divisions and subdivisions.

This type of knowledge is actually meant for inducing people to look inward. Thereby, one should be led to ponder that he has been wandering in so many categories of life since infinite time and he should now endeavor to be free from that. But what is likely to happen is that, by knowing about the luxuries of the heavenly life, one may aspire to get such a life. In other words, he develops longing for a new worldly existence. Is it not pitiable that the scriptural knowledge of different types of existence should induce any one to desire the continuation of worldly existence?

He would also hold strong opinions about traditions and strictly adhere to the same. He would attach more importance to external clothing and insist that without being attired in a particular way or without holding some specific symbols, no one can attain liberation. He does not know that Jainism has laid down 15 categories of Siddhas, inclusive of those in non-Jain traditions. The poor fellow does not realize that liberation consists of getting rid of all sorts of attachment, dress code, craving, prejudices, etc. Where is the scope therein for clinging to this or that attire? Those people, however, remain stuck with such superficial, ephemeral considerations!

લહ્યું સ્વરૂપ ન વૃત્તિનું, ગ્રહ્યું વ્રત અભિમાન;
ગ્રહે નહીં પરમાર્થને, લેવા લૌકિક માન.

॥૨૮॥

Lahyun Swarup Na Vruttinun, Grahyun Vrat Abhimän;
Grahe Nahin Paramärthane, Levä Laukik Män.

He does not recognize the bent of his tendencies and stays arrogant of observing restraints; for the sake of gaining worldly esteem, he does not adopt the true path.

- 28 -

Explanation & Discussion:

The main factor that does not allow a sectarian to see the truth is his ego. This stanza explains how ego causes him to stay oblivious of his wrong tendencies. It is necessary that the spiritual aspirant remains aware of his tendencies, which govern most of his activities. There are mainly two types of tendencies, those leaning towards the soul and those leaning towards the worldly life. The spiritual endeavor consists of overcoming the latter type. Restraints and austerities are laid down for that purpose.

What is required is that one should first take cognizance of his wrong tendencies and resort to restraints and austerities for overcoming the same. If that aspect is not kept in view, the wrong tendencies would continue to prevail simultaneously with observance of restraints and austerities. In that case, the observance would not serve any purpose. Restraining the wrong tendencies is therefore the essence of spiritual pursuit.

Tattvärtha Sutra (VIII-13) states: "Nihshalyo Vrati." It means that restraints are meant for those who are free from faults. The scriptures lay down deception, wrong perception and expectation of reward as three faults that hurt the most and hence need to be overcome. Those faults are indicative of one's wrong tendencies. But a sectarian does not look at his wrong tendencies and remains proud that he has been observing the restraints and austerities. He does not recognize that the ultimate purpose of observing the restraints is to gain equanimity. As a matter of fact, that is the objective of all spiritual pursuits. Observance of restraints and austerities without awareness of that purpose constitutes a lifeless ritual.

Being ignorant of that purpose, a sectarian person feels elated that he has been observing restraints and austerities. As people know about his observance, they consider him a highly religious person and give him regard and respect as such. He too feels happy to get such esteem and stays satisfied with that. Hence, if he comes across a true Guru, he would not adopt his teaching. He would feel that if he gives up the traditional approach, he would lose the respect and regard that he has gained. Thus, for the sake of maintaining his ego, he abandons the real objective of observing restraints and austerities.

અથવા નિશ્ચય નય ગ્રહે, માત્ર શબ્દની માંય;
લોપે સદ્વ્યવહારને, સાધન રહિત થાય.

॥૨૯॥

Athavä Nishchay Nay Grahe, Mätra Shabdani Mäny;
Lope Sadvyavahärne, Sädhan Rahit Thäy.

Otherwise a sectarian mere verbally
resorts to the absolute point of view;
he thus forsakes the right practices
and stands deprived of the means.

- 29 -

Explanation & Discussion:

After explaining the characteristics of the
Vyavahäräbhäsi, Shrimad now turns to the Nishchayäbhäsi.
The term Nishchay Nay has been explained at the beginning
of this chapter. It means absolute point of view. There
are scriptures like Samaysär, which have been written from
that angle. They describe the inherent purity of the soul,
which cannot be corrupted. If one truly understands this with the
right perspective, such books are very useful for gaining
spiritual elevation. However, if those books are read by persons
without enough background to understand the absolute point of
view, they would simply assume that the soul is pure,
immutable, incorruptible, etc. Then they would think that
devotion, detachment, restraints, etc. are unnecessary and give
them up.

Nishchay Nay is for the aspirants who have reached a reasonable level of spiritual development. It is meant for realizing the true nature of the soul. Otherwise the knowledge of self remains only at information level.

The state of a person, who realizes the purity of the soul, would undergo radical change. Then it would be hard for him to indulge in any type of defilement or infatuation. But resorting to absolute purity of soul without adequate spiritual background is fraught with danger. That can lead to Nishchayäbhäs inducing the people to give up sound religious practices, which are helpful in spiritual pursuit. They stay bereft of the wholesome means like devotion, detachment, restraints, etc. By unduly resorting to only the absolute viewpoint, the sectarian thus stays deprived of the vital means of spiritual progress.

જ્ઞાનદશા પામે નહીં, સાધનદશા ન કાંઈ;
પામે તેનો સંગ જે, તે બૂડે ભવ માંહી.

॥૩૦॥

Jnänadashä Päme Nahin, Sädhandashä Na Känyi;
Päme Teno Sang Je, Te Boode Bhavamänhi.

He does not attain the state of enlightenment,
nor is he equipped with its means;
one who comes in contact with him gets
drowned in the sea of worldly existence.

- 30 -

Explanation & Discussion:

Acquiring knowledge is not the end of spiritual pursuit. It is merely a beginning. The objective is to gain the state of enlightenment, and that cannot be realized without applying scriptural knowledge to ones internal tendencies. The restraints and austerities are meant to help the process of changing the internal tendencies in line with the true nature of the soul. Since a Nishchayābhāsi exclusively resorts to only the absolute viewpoint, his understanding stays mostly at the verbal level. He tends to ignore the importance of detachment and other wholesome aspects and stays deprived of the right means for spiritual development.

Thus, standing devoid of enlightenment as well as of the right means, the sectarian stays far away from the path of liberation and remains engulfed in the vicious cycle of birth and death. However, the Nishchayābhāsi may speak very well. He might attract many people by his apparently strong logic. The unsuspecting ignorant people, who are so attracted, may be induced to adopt his one-sided view. Thus they also become liable to be drowned in the sea of worldly existence.

એ પણ જીવ મતાર્થમાં, નિજમાનાદિ કાજ;
પામે નહિ પરમાર્થને, અન્-અધિકારીમાં જ.

॥૩૧॥

E Pan Jiv Matārthamān, Nij Mānādi Kāj;
Pāme Nahin Paramārthane, An-adhikārimān Ja.

The bare knowledgeable also remains
sectarian on account of his ego, etc.;
he does not get the right path and
stays unworthy (of liberation).

- 31 -

Explanation & Discussion :

It was pointed out in stanza 28 that while observing restraints, etc. the lifeless ritualist cherishes the ego of being called a devotee. The same logic applies to the bare knowledgeable person. Such a person cherishes the ego of being called knowledgeable. If he accepts the truth, he has to admit that he was on the wrong path. That would hurt his ego. In order to preserve that ego, he shuns the right path and remains conceited. That is a wrong approach; it is Mithyätva. Hence, the bare knowledgeable person remains unworthy of liberation.

This is mainly on account of undue insistence on absolute viewpoint. He does not realize that a Nay presents only one viewpoint with partial truth. It can be right from some perspective, but at best it is a relative truth. In order to arrive at the overall truth, one needs to take into consideration all the viewpoints. The truth thus lies in a combination of absolute (Nishchaya Nay) and practical (Vyavhär Nay) points of view. That is Syädväd, Anekäntväd, or multiplicity of viewpoints. It gives due importance to partial truth, and is the Jain theory of relativity. Resorting to only one viewpoint is Ekänt, which leads to an illusory conclusion. Such a one-sided viewpoint cannot be true, nor can it lead to the whole truth. This stanza therefore conveys that those, who exclusively insist on only Nishchay Nay, are Ekänti. They are far from the truth and cannot be considered as treading on the right path.

નહિ કષાય ઉપશાંતતા, નહિ અંતર વૈરાગ્ય;
સરળપણું ન મધ્યસ્થતા, એ મતાર્થી દુર્ભાગ્ય.

॥૩૨॥

Nahi Kashäy Upashäntatä, Nahi Antar Vairägya;
Saralpanun Na Madhyasthatä, E Matärthi Durbhägya.

Unfortunate is the sectarian, who has
not calmed down the passions, does
not have inner detachment, and is
neither straightforward nor impartial.

- 32 -

Explanation & Discussion:

The spiritual level of an aspirant is governed by the presence of certain attributes, which a sectarian does not have. In order to avoid being caught within the sectarian net, one should know those attributes. This stanza therefore describes four principal attributes, which a spiritual aspirant must have and which a sectarian does not possess.

The first is pacification or calming down the passions. Anger, ego, deception, and greed are the main passions that need to be calmed down; but a sectarian does not heed to that aspect on account of insistence on his own viewpoint. The second is internal detachment, which a sectarian cannot cultivate because of the same reason. The third is straightforwardness, which can come forth only from the absence of vanity, deception, etc. The fourth is impartial attitude, which comes from an open mind. Only an open-minded person remains receptive to the truth, and that enables him to dispassionately evaluate different viewpoints. Dispassionateness is the antithesis of sectarianism. Hence a sectarian cannot resort to that.

It would be easy to understand that one, who calms down the passions, does not stay attached to the worldly aspects. Detachment is thus implied in a calmed-down state. Similarly straightforwardness and impartiality flow from such a state. Calming of the passions thus brings fourth other attributes. Unfortunately a sectarian does not possess these attributes and as such he cannot undertake real spiritual pursuit. Such a sectarian therefore continues the worldly cycle of birth and death.

લક્ષણ કહ્યાં મતાર્થીનાં, મતાર્થ જાવા કાજ;
હવે કહું આત્માર્થીનાં, આત્મ-અર્થ સુખસાજ.

॥૩૩॥

Lakshan Kahyän Matärthinän, Matärtha Jävä Käj;
Have Kahun Ätmärthinän, Ätma-artha Sukhasäj.

The characteristics of the sectarian
have been stated in order to avoid them;
now I am describing those of the truth
seeker for the sake of spiritual bliss.

- 33 -

Explanation & Discussion:

The description of sectarian people ends here. It is not meant to put down any one. The purpose is to show the drawbacks of sectarianism, so that the aspirants can avoid the same and come to the right path. This is done impartially and out of compassion.

If one avoids sectarianism, he can turn to the right way of seeking truth. The characteristics of such truth seekers are laid down in the next chapter. Its purpose is to draw the attention of the aspirants towards the path of unobstructed bliss. That bliss is inherent within the soul, but is not manifested at present. By developing the attributes of truth seekers, one can be equipped with the means to attain lasting happiness.

Chapter 3
Characteristics of Truth Seekers (Mumukshus)

The truth seekers are those who are primarily interested in gaining self-realization. The term used in the text for such people is Ätmärthi, which literally means one who seeks the well being of his soul. The worldly soul has been wandering, because it has never conceived of its true nature and well being. Of course, it is interested in gaining happiness. For that purpose, however, it looks towards worldly sources, which are incapable to provide happiness. When it realizes that happiness lies within and cannot be gained by looking out, it turns inward. Such turning indicates that it is intent upon seeking the truth. In other words, it has now oriented itself towards its true well being, or Ätmärth.

This chapter is expressly meant for laying down the characteristics of such truth seekers. It also outlines the chronological order of attaining liberation. That consists of recognizing a true Guru, carrying out his commands, and resorting to the activities that lead to the ultimate objective. The factors relevant for this purpose are: calming down the passions, aspiring for liberation, disaffection for the cycle of birth and death, and compassion for all living beings. These factors are the prerequisites for gaining right perception. It leads to right thinking and that in turn leads to liberation.

આત્મજ્ઞાન ત્યાં મુનિપણું, તે સાચા ગુરુ હોય;
બાકી કુળગુરુ કલ્પના, આત્માર્થી નહિ જોય.

॥૩૪॥

Ätmajnän Tyän Munipanun, Te Sächä Guru Hoy;
Bäki Kulguru Kalpanä, Ätmärthi Nahin Joy.

> *The self-realized are the*
> *ascetics, and they are the true Gurus;*
> *a truth seeker does not have any*
> *fancy about the family priests.*
>
> *- 34 -*

Explanation & Discussion:

We come across many monks, but not all of them can be true ascetics and therefore cannot be resorted to as Gurus. Five attributes of a true Guru were laid down in the 10th stanza. Of those five, the attribute of self-realization is the first and foremost. It is therefore said here that true asceticism abides in self-realization. Ächäräng Sutra (1-5-3) states: "Jam Sammanti Päsah Tam Monanti Päsah." It means that where there is right perception, there is monkhood.

Only such persons need be acknowledged as true Gurus. As stated in the previous chapter, there are people who attach importance to family priests, even though such priests may not have any concept of self-realization. But a truth seeker has no fancy for them. His purpose is to seek the true Guru, and does not therefore harbor any attachment to the family priests or to those belonging to any particular sect.

પ્રત્યક્ષ સદ્ગુરુ પ્રાપ્તિનો, ગણે પરમ ઉપકાર;
ત્રણે યોગ એકત્વથી, વર્તે આજ્ઞાધાર.

||૩૫||

Pratyaksha Sadguru Präptino, Gane Param Upakär;
Trane Yog Ekatvathi, Varte Äjnädhär.

Considering the direct access to
a true Guru as supremely beneficial,
one would act on his precepts with the
united energy of body, speech, and mind.

- 35 -

Explanation & Discussion:

The importance of a true Guru cannot be overemphasized. Looking at the characteristics of a true Guru, it is obviously very rare to have access to such Gurus. As such, if one gets that access, he should consider it supremely beneficial. In spiritual pursuit, there is no other means which is as helpful as a living Guru. The benefits that can be derived from such a Guru are incomparable to those derived from any other source.

The worldly soul has been wandering mainly on account of inaccessibility of a true Guru. If one had the contact of such a Guru, his wandering would have come to an end. The problems that an aspirant cannot solve by reading scriptures, etc. can be easily resolved by such a Guru. Similarly, the faults that the worldly soul has been indulging in cannot be eliminated without the right guidance. Therefore access to a true Guru should be considered as unprecedented. If one comes in contact with such a Guru, he should surrender to him with all his energy and stay in total obedience to him. Physical, vocal, and mental are the three faculties with which one can endeavor for gaining anything. The true endeavor consists of exercising all these faculties in staying obedient to the Guru.

The worldly soul has stayed ignorant of the path of liberation since infinite time. Such ignorance can be equated to darkness. As Shrimad wrote (Vachanāmrut # 211), "If darkness is divided into various grades, none of them can resemble the light." Similarly none of the concepts of the worldly soul, which has been groping in the dark, can be true or close to the truth. Hence it cannot get to the path of liberation by its own efforts. The self-realized Guru should guide it. That can happen only by surrendering to a true Guru and by carrying out all his commands, explicit as well as implicit.

એક હોય ત્રણ કાળમાં, પરમારથનો પંથ;
પ્રેરે તે પરમાર્થને, તે વ્યવહાર સમંત.

॥૩૬॥

Ek Hoy Tran Kālamān, Paramārathano Panth;
Prere Te Paramārthane, Te Vyavahār Samant.

> *There is only one path of supreme*
> *bliss for all the time;*
> *the practice, that leads to that*
> *bliss, is worth adopting.*
>
> *- 36 -*

Explanation & Discussion:

Supreme bliss lies in the state of liberation. One should therefore resort to the path of liberation. That path is the same at all times, but happens to be laid down in differing terms. For instance, Tattvärtha Sutra (I-1) states: "Samyagdarshanajnänacháritráni Mokshamärgah". It means that the path of liberation consists of right perception, right knowledge, and right conduct, all in unison. Another scripture states: "Jnänakriyäbhyäm Mokshah", which means that the liberation can be attained by knowledge and practice together. On the face of it, the two Sutras would look different. But there is actually no difference. The difference between the two appears only because the latter Sutra takes perception as implicit in knowledge. As such, the difference is only apparent. It is the scriptural style to put the same thing in different words for emphasis on a certain aspect.

The different theologies, however, prescribe the path of liberation differently. Vedänt, for example, lays down one path, while Buddhism lays down another. That happens on account of viewing the same objective from different perspectives. As such, an aspirant may wonder which one he should adopt. It is therefore said here that there cannot be different paths for attaining liberation. To know the soul, to become convinced of its existence, and to stay in tune with its nature constitute the path to liberation. That path has been laid down after taking into consideration all the various perspectives. As such, it remains the same all throughout.

In this connection, Shrimad observed (Vachanämrut # 54), "There are no different paths for liberation. Whoever experienced supreme bliss from liberation gained it through the same way. There is no difference of opinion about the path. That path is easy; it is the path of bliss, it is steady and prevails forever. No one has gained liberation without understanding the secret of that path."

Regarding the significance of rituals, etc. he said in the same letter (#54): "The omniscient Lords have laid down thousands of rituals and precepts to point out the path. Those rituals and precepts are fruitful if they are adopted with a view to proceed on that path; they are futile if they are resorted to while forsaking that path."

The absolute and practical viewpoints were explained earlier. This stanza lays down the importance of both of them. The absolute viewpoint (in the first line) focuses on the ultimate objective, while the practical viewpoint (in the second line) lays emphasis on the means for achieving that objective. Shrimad's observations in the first paragraph above are based on the absolute point of view, while those in the second paragraph are made from the practical point of view.

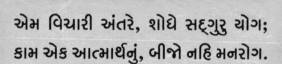

એમ વિચારી અંતરે, શોધે સદ્ગુરુ યોગ;
કામ એક આત્માર્થનું, બીજો નહિ મનરોગ.

॥૩૭॥

Em Vichäri Antare, Shodhe Sadguru Yog;
Käm Ek Ätmärthanun, Bijo Nahin Manrog.

> *Thinking as such, one seeks access*
> *to a true Guru; Self-realization is*
> *his only aspiration; his mind*
> *knows no other ailment.*
>
> *- 37 -*

Explanation & Discussion:

Once an aspirant understands what needs to be done for gaining lasting bliss and realizes the utmost importance of a true Guru in pursuing that objective, he would start seeking access to such a Guru. Since the well being of the soul remains his only objective, he is not concerned with any other aspect. By virtue of his advancement on the spiritual path, he may get respect and devotion from others, but a true aspirant would not give importance to that and would remain indifferent to all such aspects. If he gets elated thereby he would miss the real objective of his well being.

Shrimad has repeatedly emphasized the utmost importance of a Guru in spiritual pursuit. He has written (Vachanämrut # 76): "Do not seek anything else. Find out only one virtuous person and conduct yourself by surrendering every thing at his feet. If you do not attain liberation thereby, take it from me. The virtuous is the person, who stays continually soul-oriented, whose words can come to the experiential level, even though they are not available in the scriptures or not heard anywhere else, and whose innermost spirit is without any expectation."

Therefore if one wants his soul's well being, he must channel all his efforts to find a true Guru. All other desires or objectives such as worldly respect, home, family matters, wealth, and even his body must be subordinated to the primary goal of finding a true Guru. He should set aside all worldly desires and go for the well being of his soul with this single-minded purpose. Everything that does not lead to the well being of the soul needs to be treated as a disease. Just as we stay away from a disease, a spiritual aspirant would not covet any worldly aspect. His mind would not be inclined towards any such consideration.

કષાયની ઉપશાંતતા, માત્ર મોક્ષ અભિલાષ;
ભવે ખેદ, પ્રાણીદયા, ત્યાં આત્માર્થ નિવાસ.

||૩૮||

Kashäyani Upashäntatä, Matra Moksha Abhiläsh;
Bhave Khed, Pränidayä, Tyän Ätmärtha Niväs.

The state of truth-seeking arises
when passions are calmed down, liberation
remains the exclusive aspiration, there prevails
disaffection for the life cycle, and there is
compassion for all living beings.
- 38 -

Explanation & Discussion:

The scriptures lay down following five aspects as the prerequisites for seeking truth: (1) Sham, meaning calming down or pacification of the passions, (2) Samveg, meaning aspiring exclusively for liberation, (3) Nirved, meaning disaffection for worldly life, (4) Anukampä, meaning compassion, and (5) Ästhä, meaning faith. Of these, first four are specified in this stanza as the characteristics of a truth seeker. The fifth (faith) is not mentioned here, because it is implicit in the first four. Those four terms are briefly explained below.

Sham: Anger, ego, deceit, and greed are the four main passions that keep the worldly soul bound to the cycle of birth and death. In Jain terminology, they are known as Kashäys. The spiritual pursuit mainly consists of overcoming these Kashäys. It is, however, hard to do so, because the worldly soul has been used to indulging in Kashäys since infinite time. But one can try to calm them down by cultivating the opposite attributes. For instance, anger can be pacified by forgiving, ego by modesty, deception by straightforwardness, and greed by contentment. That calming down of Kashäys is called Sham.

Samveg: The worldly life is beset with longings, desires, and aspirations. Every one has various desires and aspirations. When some of these desires are unfulfilled, the soul is induced to take a new birth in a place where its desires are likely to be fulfilled. The life cycle thus continues as long as one harbors any desire. It means that a soul is going to wander until it gives up all worldly desires and aspires only for liberation. Such exclusive aspiration for liberation is called Samveg.

Nirved: The worldly soul has always remained attached to sensual objects and has been trying to feel happy by getting the same. It has never realized that lifeless objects have no capability to give happiness. Attachment to the worldly objects can be given up only when one realizes that the worldly life is beset with misery. Thereby he loses interest in seeking the worldly comforts and sensual pleasures. In other words, one is totally disaffected of the worldly life. Such disaffection is called Nirved.

Anukampä: During its infinite wandering, the worldly soul has thought of its own comforts and sensual happiness, and for maintaining that, it has not hesitated even from hurting other beings. When it turns introvert, it understands that every being wants to live happily and does not like to be disturbed in its quest for happiness. Thereby one feels that he should not hurt other beings. Moreover, he also realizes that every living being has an identical soul, which might be destined to gain liberation. As such, he learns to respect each and every being. If any of them is in trouble or afflicted, his heart would grieve for them. Such compassion is called Anukampä.

When an aspirant has developed these attributes, he is considered a truth seeker and can therefore proceed in search of truth.

દશા ન એવી જયાં સુધી, જીવ લહે નહિ જોગ;
મોક્ષમાર્ગ પામે નહીં, મટે ન અંતર રોગ.

॥૩૯॥

Dashä Na Evi Jyän Sudhi, Jiv Lahe Nahin Jog;
Mokshamarga Päme Nahin, Mate Na Antar Rog.

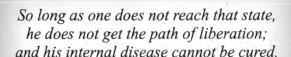

So long as one does not reach that state,
he does not get the path of liberation;
and his internal disease cannot be cured.

- 39 -

Explanation & Discussion:

The stipulations laid down in the last stanza are the prerequisites for seeking truth. In their absence a person cannot develop the receptivity of mind. As such he cannot derive the right benefit from the teaching of a Guru. Guru also knows that his teaching would not be effective unless the person has receptivity. He would not therefore like to waste his energy over the undeserving pupil. Moreover, the true Gurus are not easily found, because they prefer to stay away from worldly surroundings. One, who is not a truth seeker, is therefore not likely to get access to such a Guru and if he happens to get access, he would not be able to grasp the Guru's teaching.

It has been made clear in the first chapter that no one can get on the path of liberation without proper guidance. The person who does not have the above requisites stays bereft of the right guidance. As such he stays away from the path of liberation and continues to wander in the cycle of birth and death. That wandering is the lasting disease with which the worldly soul has been afflicted. Other diseases do not last very long. Even if there is an incurable disease, it disappears with the end of the life. The worldly wandering, however, continues from birth to birth and is therefore seemingly unending. That disease cannot be cured so long as the aspirant is unqualified or not prepared to receive the right guidance.

આવે જ્યાં એવી દશા, સદ્ગુરુબોધ સુહાય;
તે બોધે સુવિચારણા, ત્યાં પ્રગટે સુખદાય.

||૪૦||

Äve Jyän Evi Dashä, Sadguru Bodh Suhäy;
Te Bodhe Suvichäranä, Tyän Pragate Sukhadäy.

> *When that state is reached, the teaching*
> *of the true Guru shines out; and the blissful*
> *right thinking emerges from that teaching.*
>
> *- 40 -*

Explanation & Discussion:

When one attains the deserving state, the Guru is pleased to show him the right path. The pupil is then in a position to think correctly and his mind remains inclined towards the Guru's teaching. Since that teaching can penetrate the heart, the pupil is able to grasp and comprehend it. Such teaching pertains to the everlasting nature of the soul and impermanence of every worldly aspect; one therefore needs to be concerned only with the well being of the soul. As the pupil thus learns that he is the everlasting soul, he is induced to think about his own well being. That is termed here as the right thinking. That thinking is blissful and will lead to the knowledge of Self.

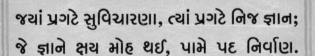

જ્યાં પ્રગટે સુવિચારણા, ત્યાં પ્રગટે નિજ જ્ઞાન;
જે જ્ઞાને ક્ષય મોહ થઈ, પામે પદ નિર્વાણ.

॥૪૧॥

Jyän Pragate Suvichäranä, Tyän Pragate Nij Jnän;
Je Jnäne Kshay Moh Thai, Päme Pad Nirvän.

> *Knowledge of Self is manifested by*
> · *emergence of right thinking; and*
> *getting rid of delusion by that*
> *enlightenment, one attains liberation.*
>
> *- 41 -*

Explanation & Discussion:

What makes the worldly soul wander? Obviously, the absence of right thinking. When an aspirant reaches the state of right thinking, he keeps pondering over the nature of the Self, and its potential to gain pure form. Thereby he overcomes delusive perception and gains the right one. It is called Samyag Darshan. He experiences the true nature of the Self, which gives rise to bliss. Once the aspirant gains that realization, his next and the only objective would be to get rid of the delusion pertaining to behavior.

One normally stays with delusion on account of ignorance of his true nature. As his perception becomes clear, he realizes that deluded behavior is not his nature. However, that may prevail on account of the previous Karma. By vigorously and vigilantly pursuing the objective of liberation, he gets enough vigor to overcome the behavior-related delusion and attains omniscience. It continues during that lifetime and at the end he rises to the ultimate state of liberation.

ઉપજે તે સુવિચારણા, મોક્ષમાર્ગ સમજાય;
ગુરુશિષ્યસંવાદથી, ભાખું ષટ્પદ આંહી.

॥૪૨॥

Upaje Te Suvichäranä, Mokshamärga Samajäy;
Gurushishya Samvädathi, Bhäkhun Shatpad Änhi.

The path of liberation can be comprehended
with the emergence of right thinking;
the six Fundamentals relating to that path
are laid down hereunder in the form of
dialogue between the preceptor and the pupil.
- 42 -

Explanation & Discussion:

This is the concluding stanza of this chapter. The reader might have noticed that all the phases of spiritual pursuit have been briefly laid down in this part. Emergence of right thinking is the most crucial phase. Thereby one earnestly intends to get on the path of liberation. Shrimad realizes that the aspirant is the truth seeker and is therefore willing to show that path. But he thinks that instead of directly laying down the path, it would be better to say it in the form of a dialogue between a pupil and a preceptor. That pattern enables one to anticipate the questions and doubts that arise to spiritual aspirants, and to answer and satisfy them in the replies. This generates interest among the seekers and the explanation becomes more comprehensible. The essence of truth was revealed by Lord Mahavir to Gautamswämi in the same manner.

Further, the pupil conceived of here is Ätmärthi, who is not going to ask the questions for the sake of mere curiosity. He is a real truth seeker who will present the issues that a seeker genuinely comes across during his search for truth. His purpose would be to get them clarified so that he can pursue the path of liberation with confidence. He also knows that the preceptor is enlightened, and is in a position to give satisfactory replies to all his questions.

Chapter 4
Statement of Six Fundamentals

Treading on the path of liberation involves a long journey. One has to advance on that path step by step. Such an advance can be compared to a ladder of elevation. Jainism conceives of such a ladder having 14 steps. They are called Gunasthänaks, meaning the stages of elevation. The initial three stages consist of wrong or semi-wrong perception. During those stages an aspirant is below the level of a truth seeker. Right perception emerges in the 4th stage. The actual and lasting spiritual advancement starts from that stage. Every activity, including the acute austerities, is considered futile in absence of this right perception. Since the aspirant is not in a position to observe restraints at this stage, it is termed as the stage of right perception without restraints.

While explaining the characteristics of truth seekers laid down in the last chapter, it was mentioned that the description therein presents the step by step advancement till the emergence of right thinking. By virtue of such thinking, one is induced to think of six basic aspects relating to the soul. Having unwavering faith in those six aspects constitutes right perception. Therefore the Letter of Six Fundamentals (Appendix-II), which was addressed by Shrimad to Laghuräjswämi, states that those six basic aspects are the abode of right perception.

Some people would contend that those Fundamentals are not found in Jain tradition; they have never even heard of them. As such, they fail to make out from where they have been brought forth. It would therefore be pertinent to point out that they are from the ancient scriptures. Of the original 12 scriptures, the last one, Drashtiväd, has been lost since more than 2000 years. But from its description in Samaväyäng and other texts, it is learnt that it contained 14 Purvas. The 7th Purva was designated as Ätmapraväd. These six Fundamentals deal with the subject of that Purva. They were described by Ächärya Siddhasen Diwäkar in Sanmati Prakaran about 1800 years ago. Comparatively recently they were included in Sadsathbolani Sajzäy by Upädhyäya Yashovijayji.

The existence of the soul, its permanence, its indulgence in Karma, bearing of consequences, the state of liberation and the method of attaining the same constitute the six Fundamentals. They are closely related to Nav Tattva comprising Jiv, Ajiv, Punya, Päp, Äsrav, Bandh, Samvar, Nirjarä, and Moksha. Jiv (soul) denotes a living being. Its animation subsists by virtue of its consciousness. Everything else that does not have consciousness is inanimate, which means Ajiv. As Kartä (doer, actuator) of its Karma, a soul acquires Punya (good or wholesome Karma) or Päp (bad or unwholesome Karma). The incoming of Karma is Äsrav. Bearing the consequences of Karma implies that there is bondage (Bandh) of Karma. The liberation is Moksha and the means thereof are Samvar (stoppage of Karma) and Nirjarä (annihilation of Karma). No one should therefore remain under the apprehension that Shrimad might have brought these six Fundamentals from nowhere. As a matter of fact, by explaining the same so simply and logically, he has brought to light the path of liberation, which was lying semi-dormant since long.

These six Fundamentals form the basis of Jainism. In this respect, Shrimad wrote (Vachanämrut # 493): "The enlightened entities have laid down the teaching of these six Fundamentals in order to remove the sense of ego and attachment arising from the dreaming state of the worldly soul, that has been prevailing since the time without beginning....The discernment arising from these six Fundamentals is meant to enable the soul to realize its true Self."

'આત્મા છે', 'તે નિત્ય છે', 'છે કર્તા નિજકર્મ ';
'છે ભોક્તા', વળી 'મોક્ષ છે', 'મોક્ષ ઉપાય સુધર્મ '.

॥૪૩॥

`Ätmä Chhe', `Te Nitya Chhe', `Chhe Kartä Nijkarma';
`Chhe Bhoktä', Vali 'Moksha Chhe', ` Moksha Upäy Sudharma'.

*'Soul exists', 'it is eternal', 'it is Kartä
of its own Karma', 'it bears
the consequences', also 'there is
liberation' and 'the means of
liberation constitute true religion'.* - 43 -

Explanation & Discussion:

The first Fundamental asserts the existence of the soul. That assertion is very vital. The existence of the soul makes the spiritual pursuit meaningful. If there is no soul, the question of spiritual pursuit would not arise. Many people tend to believe that soul does not exist. They contend that existence consists of the physical body and brain, and it is produced by procreation or by division of cells. The invalidity of such a contention will be explained later. For the time being, it is enough to assert the existence of the soul.

The second Fundamental states that the soul is eternal. That assertion is meant to overcome the contention of the non-believers. Most of them do not dispute the liveliness of all animate beings, but they contend that such liveliness arises at the time of birth and disappears at the time of death. As such, it is not eternal and does not last forever. Till recently, people with scientific approach used to hold such a belief. The trend, however, seems to be changing and many scientists, including a few well known neurologists, have started believing that there has to be something beyond the body and the brain.

The third Fundamental states that the soul is the Kartä (doer or actuator) of its Karma. This is primarily stated while keeping in mind the worldly soul. We all are in the midst of different situations, some favorable and some unfavorable. We are used to experience a sense of pleasure and happiness by the favorable situations and a sense of pain and unhappiness by the unfavorable ones. In reality, no situation is capable of giving happiness or unhappiness. We are merely used to reacting to different situations with a sense of craving or aversion. That reaction results in acquisition of Karma, and we ourselves are responsible for that.

The fourth Fundamental states that the soul bears the consequences. The Karma that the worldly soul acquires stays with it and gives its consequences at the appropriate time. Such consequences are in the form of getting various situations including the nature of species, type of body, and its surroundings. Different situations thus occur from time to time depending upon the type of Karma, which becomes operative. In those situations the soul reacts with either craving or aversion and thereby it acquires new Karma. The worldly cycle thus continues.

The fifth Fundamental states that there is liberation. It means freedom from the bondage of Karma. Since no situation stays forever, every soul should accept the given situations as consequences of its own Karma and should bear the same with equanimity without indulging in the sense of likes or dislikes. In that case, one would not acquire new Karma. Since old Karmas automatically fall off after their fruition, the soul eventually can become Karmaless. That state is liberation, the ultimate objective.

The sixth Fundamental states that there is a way to attain liberation and resorting to that path constitutes religion. The primary function of religion is thus to lead the worldly soul towards liberation. The purpose of composing this Ätmasiddhi Shästra is to show that path. It was therefore stated in the second stanza, that the path of liberation, which stands mostly forsaken at present, has been explicitly described here.

Every religion purports to lay down the right path for its followers. Some of them, however, have no concept of liberation. They do talk of salvation, but equate it with gaining the pleasure of an Almighty or some other deity, and enjoying the situation that He might extend by virtue of His pleasure. Such a state is termed as heavenly happiness. No state can, however, continue forever. It is conceivable that a time may come, when one would lose the favor of such a superhuman entity. Then the superhuman entity would throw him out with an appropriate punishment!

Jainism does not depict such a salvation. It lays down the state of ultimate liberation from which one does not come back. That is the perfectly blissful, eternal state. The liberated soul has not to take a new birth and stays forever in that blissful state. This concept is not aristocratic in the sense of reserving it for only a few selected souls. It is fully democratic. It not only states that every soul is equal, but also states that every soul has the potentiality to attain liberation. What needs to be done is to realize that potentiality and to manifest the true nature of the soul. All spiritual endeavors are meant for that purpose.

ષટ્સ્થાનક સંક્ષેપમાં, ષટ્દર્શન પણ તેહ;
સમજાવા પરમાર્થને, કહ્યાં જ્ઞાનીએ એહ.

॥૪૪॥

Shatsthänak Sankshepamän, Shat Darshan Pan Teh;
Samajävä Paramärthane, Kahyän Jnänie Eh.

*These are the six steps (Fundamentals) in brief
and they also constitute the six schools of
thought; the enlightened ones have described
them in order to elucidate the ultimate truth.*

- 44 -

Explanation & Discussion:

These six Fundamentals constitute the six steps on the path of liberation, which need to be approached one by one. First of all, one has to believe in the existence of the soul. When no doubt remains about that, he needs to consider that the soul is eternal; it is indestructible and stays forever. After being convinced of that, he would conceive of its continually acquiring Karma and realize how he has been undergoing birth after birth as a consequence. Thereby he would think of reaching the Karmaless state so as to be free from the cycle of birth and death. Then he needs to consider how to gain that state and resort to the path of liberation.

The six Fundamentals also constitute the six main ideologies or schools of thought, prevailing in the spiritual realm. They are collectively called Shaddarshan. Shad (a derivation of Shat) means six and Darshan means theological school of thought. Those six schools are presented differently by different people. The Vedäntist consider only those schools which are based on the Ved. Sänkhya, Yog, Purva Mimänsak, Uttar Mimänsak, Nyäy, and Vaisheshik are the six schools. The list obviously keeps Jainism and Buddhism out, because they do not subscribe to the Ved. In order to accommodate them, the schools are laid down a bit differently. Since Nyäy and Vaisheshik schools have much in common, they are grouped together under the title Naiyäyik. Similarly Purva Mimänsak and Uttar Mimänsak are grouped together under the title Vedänt. The six schools then consist of Sänkhya, Yog, Vedänt, Naiyäyik, Jainism, and Buddhism.

All these schools have the same common objective of liberation. The differences arise on the account of differing beliefs about the concepts of the creation, creator, soul, and liberation. Sänkhya, Jainism and Buddhism, for instance, do not believe in the creation of the world, while other schools believe in creation and a creator. Sänkhya, Yog, Naiyäyik, and Jainism believe in the endless number of individual souls. Vedänt believes in one single soul. Buddhism does not believe in the existence of an everlasting soul. Such differences arise, because most of the people tend to think from their own perspective. Jainism takes into consideration all possible perspectives. The six Fundamentals present the synthesis of all these different viewpoints. It is therefore said in this stanza that the Fundamentals constitute those six ideologies.

Some people like to accommodate even the atheist belief of Chärväk within the framework of six schools. For that purpose they group Sänkhya and Yog together, because their approach is more or less similar and treat Sänkhya, Naiyäyik, Vedänt, Jainism, Buddhism and Chärväk as six schools of thought. In the Stavan (adoration prayer) of Naminäth, the

21st Tirthankar, the great philosopher-poet-monk Änandghanji has treated Sänkhya, Yog, Buddhism, Mimänsak, Chärväk, and Jainism as the six schools and has presented a unique way of synthesizing them.

Änandghanji takes the detached Lord as personifying the spiritual realm and treats those six schools as constituting different limbs of the Lord. The concept of Sänkhya and Yog about the soul is somewhat analogous to the Jain concept. They are therefore treated as constituting the two feet of the Lord. Mimänsak (which is the same as Vedänt) believes in one single eternal soul, while Buddhism believes in ever-changing states. Thus they represent the Jain beliefs from the substantial (Dravyärthic) and variable (Paryäyärthic) points of view, respectively. From the Dravyärthic point of view, all souls are identical. As such, they can be treated as one single unit. That concept is analogous to the Mimänsak belief of only one Brahman pervading everywhere. From the Paryäyärthic point of view, however, every soul continues to assume a new state from time to time. That concept is analogous to the Buddhist concept of ever-changing states. Mimänsak and Buddhism are therefore treated as constituting two arms of the Lord. Chärväk is treated as representing the stomach of the Lord. The stomach accepts different types of food, but it distributes the same to various limbs and does not keep anything with it. Similarly, Chärväk took into consideration all the different theories about the soul, but did not adopt any of them. His view is therefore comparable to the stomach.

The last one, Jainism, represents the head, which is the highest limb of the Lord. In order to explain that status, the Stavan ends with the following summarization.

Jinvaramän Saghalä Darshan Chhe,
Darshane Jinvar Bhajanä Re;
Sägarmän Saghali Tatinä Sahi,
Tatinimän Sägar Bhajanä Re.

It means: All the schools of thought are covered within the school of the omniscient Lord, while the Lord's school of thought may or may not be covered completely in a particular school. This is comparable to the sea and a river. All rivers flow into the sea, while the flowing of the sea into the mouth of a river may or may not occur.

Änandghanji attributes the highest status to Jainism, not because he was a Jain monk. Jainism stands the highest, because it presents the whole truth after taking into consideration all the viewpoints. Jainism synthesizes all of them. This will be clear from the questions and answers that are going to follow. It will be seen that the pupil presents all possible questions that have been raised by different viewpoints and the Guru gives satisfying replies from the right point of view. The pupil is the real truth seeker, and the replies to his questions conclusively put his doubts to rest. It is therefore said here that these six Fundamentals have been described for explaining the truth.

Chapter 5
Pupil's First Doubt regarding Existence of the Soul

The questioning session starts from this chapter. Let us emphasize once again that the pupil is genuinely interested in seeking the truth. He is aware of the six Fundamentals, and seriously intends to undertake spiritual pursuit on that basis. But there are some doubts in his mind about the existence and nature of the soul and he wants to remove them. He knows that only an enlightened person can clarify the points that bother him. He therefore approaches an enlightened Guru and gently presents his doubts to him. His first doubt pertains to the existence of the soul. In this respect, Shrimad has said of (Appendix-II) the first Fundamental :

"As there is existence of physical objects like a pot, cloth, etc. so is there existence of the soul. As the properties of a pot, cloth etc. provide evidence of their existence, so the obvious property of consciousness, to manifest itself as well as others, is evidence of the existence of the soul."

The following are the questions that arise to the pupil in this connection.

નથી દૃષ્ટિમાં આવતો, નથી જણાતું રૂપ;
બીજો પણ અનુભવ નહીં, તેથી ન જીવસ્વરૂપ.

॥જપ॥

Nathi Drashtimän Ävato, Nathi Janätun Roop;
Bijo Pan Anubhav Nahin, Tethi Na Jiv Swaroop.

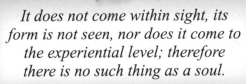

*It does not come within sight, its
form is not seen, nor does it come to
the experiential level; therefore
there is no such thing as a soul.*

- 45 -

Explanation & Discussion:

It will be noticed that the pupil here raises certain basic questions, which could arise to any thinking person. He has learnt that perceiving, knowing, and experiencing are the principal attributes of the soul. His doubts are centered on these. Perception implies visibility. Most of the worldly objects are visible. Our knowledge therefore generally rests on what we see. If something is not visible, we usually remain ignorant of it and if some one tells us about its existence, we have doubt about it.

The pupil doubts the existence of the soul, because it is not visible. Moreover, it is not possible to know it by any other means, because no form is attributed to it. The pupil argues that even if the soul is accepted as formless and shapeless and hence invisible to the eyes, it should be experienced by some other organ. We should be able to experience it by touch, taste, smell, etc. But it is not experienced by any organ. In that case how can it be identified and how is it possible to believe in its existence without identification? The pupil therefore argues that these are the reasons to think that the soul does not exist.

અથવા દેહ જ આતમા, અથવા ઈન્દ્રિય પ્રાણ;
મિથ્યા જુદો માનવો, નહીં જુદું એંધાણ.

॥૪૬॥

Athavä Deh Ja Ätamä, Athavä Indriya Prän;
Mithyä Judo Mänavo, Nahin Judun Endhän.

Or call the body itself as the soul,
or call it as senses or breath;
it is wrong to believe it is distinct,
because there is no differentiating sign.

- 46 -

Explanation & Discussion:

The pupil continues his arguments. After pointing out the invisibility of the soul, he argues that if there is anything like the soul, it should be the same as the body. We notice that a live body eats, drinks, walks, thinks, and undertakes other activities. Since all such activities are the signs of life, the pupil argues that the living body can be termed as the soul. Then considering the knowing capability of the soul, he remembers that knowledge is gained by different sense organs. We touch by skin, taste by tongue, smell by nose, see with eyes, and hear through ears. These sense organs are therefore the channels for knowing. If any of them stops working, knowledge pertaining to that sense is blocked. For instance, if one loses eyesight, he is unable to see. The pupil therefore argues that the sense organs can be termed as soul.

Then the pupil's attention turns to breath. Even if a man loses the vitality of every sense organ, he is still considered alive so long as respiration continues. The breath is thus an infallible sign of life. Therefore he suggests that respiration can be termed as the soul. According to his arguments, the soul can therefore be equated with body or senses or breath. Since there appears no sign of the soul apart from these three aspects, the pupil argues that it would be meaningless to talk of its existence, as different from the body.

વળી જો આત્મા હોય તો, જણાય તે નહિ કેમ ?
જણાય જો તે હોય તો, ઘટ પટ આદિ જેમ.

॥૪૭॥

Vali Jo Ätmä Hoy To, Janäy Te Nahi Kem?
Janäy Jo Te Hoy To, Ghat Pat Ädi Jem.

*Moreover, if there is a soul, why is
it not noticed? If it is there, it should
be noticed like a pot or cloth.*

- 47 -

Explanation & Discussion:

The pupil now elaborates his argument against the existence of the soul. In routine life existence denotes tangibility. An object comes to our knowledge by virtue of its tangibility. In the spiritual discussion, a pot and cloth are taken as representatives of tangible objects. The pupil makes use of that metaphor and argues that if the soul exists, we should be able to notice it like a pot or cloth.

This argument is based on visibility. Eye is an organ with which we can see everything that comes within eyesight, and we believe what we see. We are so accustomed to the concept of visibility that we hesitate to believe in what is not visible to us. The pupil intends to pinpoint that when we can see even far off things, how come we do not see the soul, which is so close to us? He forgets that the eye, which is capable of seeing distant objects, is not able to see those which are very close. For instance, it fails to see the ointment applied within the eye.

Our concept of visibility hardly permits us to think of an invisible object like soul. It would be interesting to cite one anecdote. Once a group of science students went to a learned man and asked him to provide proof of the soul. Their arguments were similar to those raised here by the pupil. The man told that the soul being formless and shapeless, it is invisible and intangible. As such it cannot be comprehended by sense organs. There are quite a few things that are beyond the capability of senses. One has therefore to keep faith in the words of the enlightened in such respects.

The students were not satisfied with the explanation and insisted upon some concrete proof. The man then said that he would show the soul to the most intelligent among them. The students brought forward one of them and said that he had the sharpest intellect. Thereupon, the man asked that student to first show his intellect and thereafter he would show the soul. The student was exasperated by that argument, and said that intelligence being intangible, it cannot be physically brought forth. The learned man then replied that the same logic applies to the soul. The students then had to admit the intangibility of the soul.

માટે છે નહિ આતમા, મિથ્યા મોક્ષ ઉપાય;
એ અંતર શંકા તણો, સમજાવો સદુપાય.

॥૪૮॥

Mäte Chhe Nahin Ätamä, Mithyä Moksha Upäy;
E Antar Shankä Tano, Samajävo Sadupäy.

Thus, there is no soul and therefore
the means of liberation are futile;
kindly show me the right way to
remove this internal doubt of mine.

- 48 -

Explanation & Discussion:

The pupil now concludes his arguments. He says, "I feel that there cannot be anything like the soul, separate from the body, brain, etc. If it is not there, where is the question of its bondage or liberation?" It is said that, "Mulo Nästi, Kuto Shäkhä?" This means, "If there are no roots, how can there be branches?" So there appears hardly any reason for pursuing the path of liberation.

The pupil does not really believe in what he is arguing out. He has resorted to it only for eliciting the right reply. He has faith in the Guru. He understands that if the Guru speaks of the soul, it must exist. Therefore he surrenders to him and says, "This is the doubt that has been plaguing my mind. Please give me satisfactory reply about the existence of the soul so that I can proceed on the path of liberation."

It should be noticed that the doubts of the pupil arise from the wrong concept of identifying the soul with the body. He raises the following points against the existence of the soul: (1) it is not seen, (2) it has no form, (3) it is not experienced, (4) it can be the same as body, senses, or breath, (5) there is no separate sign of its existence, and (6) it is not visible like a pot or cloth. The Guru will now clear these points one by one and establish the existence of the soul to the satisfaction of the pupil.

Chapter 6
Guru's Explanation about the Existence of the Soul
(First Fundamental)

The Guru patiently listens to the arguments of the pupil. He knows that the pupil is a truth seeker and presents the arguments merely to know the truth. In a way, the Guru is pleased to know about his mind. In order to remove the pupil's doubts, he takes his arguments one by one and explains in the following ten stanzas how his doubts are misplaced. He knows that basically all doubts arise from the identification of the soul with the body. Therefore he takes that aspect first.

ભાસ્યો દેહાધ્યાસથી, આત્મા દેહ સમાન;
પણ તે બન્ને ભિન્ન છે, પ્રગટ લક્ષણે ભાન.

||૪૯||

Bhäsyo Dehädhyästhi, Ätmä Deh Samän;
Pan Te Banne Bhinna Chhe, Pragat Lakshane Bhän.

The soul seems the same as the body
due to the illusory identification
with embodiment; but both of them
are different as can be evidenced by
their manifest characteristics.

- 49 -

Explanation & Discussion:

If we want to know about the existence of any object, we need to look for the properties of that object. Take the instance of milk. We know that the white color, liquidity, sweet taste, nourishment, transform ability to yogurt, etc. are the properties of milk. Whenever we come across all these properties, we can say that the object must be milk. Being composed of earth, metal, etc. and having some shape which can hold other materials, are the principal properties of a pot; while the capability to be worn, spread, washed, etc. are the properties of cloth. Similarly consciousness, which has the capability to experience itself and also to know other objects and situations, is the property of the soul.

However, due to wrong identification the soul seems like the body. The worldly soul has been staying in one body or another since the infinite time. That induces it to identify itself with the body. This happens on account of the ignorance about its own true self. In this connection, Shrimad has stated (Vachanämrut # 902) as follows:

Deha Jiv Ek Rupe Bhäse Chhe Ajnän Vade,
Kriyäni Pravrutti Pan Tethi Tem Thäy Chhe;
Jivani Utapati Ane Rog Shok Dukh Mrutyu,
Dehano Swabhäv Jiva Padamän Janäy Chhe;
Evo Je Anädi Ek Rupano Mithyätva Bhäv,
Jnäninä Vachan Vade Dur Thai Jäy Chhe;
Bhäse Jad Chaitanyano Pragat Swabhäv Bhinna,
Banne Dravya Nij Nij Roope Sthit Thäi Chhe.

It means: "Body and soul seem identical on account of ignorance, and thereby their activities also seem identical. Birth, disease, mourning, misery, and death, which are properties of the body, seem to be happening to the soul. That false identification, prevailing from infinity, disappears with the words of the enlightened. Then, the nature of the conscious soul and that of lifeless matter evidently look different and both those substances come to light as abiding in their own true nature."

Thus, this illusory concept leads to identifying the bodily activities with those of the soul. If one thinks properly, it can be easily seen that the soul and the body are distinct and different; they have different characteristics. The soul is pure consciousness, which is intangible, shapeless, and formless. It is inherently imbibed with awareness. That property enables it to comprehend and to know. That knowing property is the exclusive characteristic of the soul. No other substance possesses that property.

On the other hand, the body is the aggregation of lifeless matter called Pudgal. It does not have knowing capability. Touch, taste, sight and smell are its principal attributes. Heavy or light, rough or smooth, hot or cold, and sticky or dry are the eight types of touch, of which every Pudgal particle has four types. Sweet, sour, bitter, pungent, and acrid are the five types of taste, and every particle can have one or more of those tastes. Violet, indigo, blue, green, yellow, orange, and red are the seven colors (scriptures lay down white, black, yellow, red, and green as the main colors). Every particle has one of those or a color derived therefrom. Good odor and bad odor are two types of smell and every particle has one of them.

But soul does not have any of those attributes. Thus body and soul are totally different substances. They have distinctly different characteristics. During the embodied state, however, the soul has to stay within some body and occupies the same space that the body occupies. They thus stay together during the life span. That concurrent occupation creates the illusion of identification. That illusory approach is termed as Adhyäs. Under the influence of that Adhyäs, one thinks itself as the body and treats the comforts and discomforts of the body as its own. If there is some injury to the body, the soul feels as if it is experiencing the pain. If the body needs food for recouping its energy, the soul feels as if it is hungry. Such Adhyäs leads to desire, and any desire is the root cause of wandering from birth to birth. During that wandering, it migrates from one body to another. But its Adhyäs continues to stay and it tends to identify itself with the body that it gets from time to time. The purpose of religion is to convey that the soul is different from the body.

The identification of the soul with the body is comparable to the mixture of milk and water. In that mixture, water and milk are homogenized and they seem to have assumed one form; they also look as one substance. Actually, however, it is a mixture of the two substances, which can be separated by an appropriate process.

ભાસ્યો દેહાધ્યાસથી, આત્મા દેહ સમાન;
પણ તે બન્ને ભિન્ન છે, જેમ અસિ ને મ્યાન.

॥૫૦॥

Bhäsyo Dehädhyästhi, Ätmä Deha Samän;
Pan Te Banne Bhinna Chhe, Jem Asi Ne Myän.

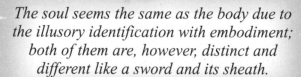

The soul seems the same as the body due to
the illusory identification with embodiment;
both of them are, however, distinct and
different like a sword and its sheath.

- 50 -

Explanation & Discussion:

This stanza once again states that soul and body seem identical only on account of false identification. That repetition is made in order to emphasize the difference between the two. But here, their separateness is compared with a sword and a sheath. When a sword is within its sheath, it does not come to the notice and both of them look as one object, but no one can deny the separate existence of the sword from its sheath. Similarly the soul, though unnoticeable, is separate from the body. Moreover, as the sword occupies the entire space of the sheath, the soul stays within every part of the body.

The Adhyäs pertaining to the body, which is called Dehädhyäs in these two stanzas, was discussed earlier. But there is also an Adhyäs relating to the senses. It is called Indriyädhyäs. The worldly soul is used to know through the senses and as such it remains attached to the objects of the senses. Under the impact of that attachment, the soul conceives of happiness as lying in the sense objects and tries to seek that from the external sources. Such attachment being too strong, the worldly soul remains involved with the sense objects and the circumstances associated with them. That extrovert state is termed as Bahirätmä. By virtue of that involvement, the soul does not find time to look inward to its own nature. That condition will change, when it comes in contact with a true Guru. Thereafter, it is awakened from the slumbering state of ignorance and turns inward. That introvert state is termed as Antarätmä.

જે દ્રષ્ટા છે દ્રષ્ટિનો, જે જાણે છે રૂપ;
અબાધ્ય અનુભવ જે રહે, તે છે જીવસ્વરૂપ.

||૫૧||

Je Drashtä Chhe Drashtino, Je Jäne Chhe Roop;
Abädhya Anubhav Je Rahe, Te Chhe Jiv Swaroop.

> *That, which is the seer of eyesight,*
> *which recognizes form, and whereby*
> *unobstructed experience is retained,*
> *constitutes the essence of the soul.*
>
> *- 51 -*

Explanation & Discussion:

The pupil had asked, "Why is the soul not visible to the eye?" The eye is the most vital sense organ. Other organs are also important; but losing any of them does not handicap a person to the extent he would feel handicapped by the loss of eyesight. If one loses, for instance, taste of the tongue or the tongue is somehow inoperative, he would feel less uncomfortable than the one who loses eyesight.

In reply to the pupil's question, the Guru asks him to figure out the element that actually sees when an object comes within eyesight. We normally conceive of two factors, which are involved in the act of seeing. One is the eye and the other is the object. The eye is the means with which it is possible to see and thereby the object is reflected to the eye. But the question is, "Who is the seer?" He must be different from the means as well as the sight. Another question is, "Who actually knows what is seen?" In other words, "Who knows the form?" The Guru states that whoever is the seer and the knower, is termed as the soul. Seeing and knowing are the properties of the soul. The eye is merely an instrument in the act of seeing. With that instrument, the objects become visible to the seer; but the seer itself, the soul, cannot be visible thereby.

For example, consider a person looking out from a window of his house. He sees the street, the houses, the people, and the vehicles passing by. If there are no obstructions, he can also see the trees or the lake and the hills that may be lying far beyond. But what is the role of the window in the act of seeing those objects? Does it see all that? No. The window is a means for seeing, while the person is the seer of the window as well as the scene. Moreover, the window cannot "see" the person inside, much like our eyes cannot "see" our soul. Thus, the soul is the seer of the eye as well as the sight.

Another question of the pupil was pertaining to experiencing the soul. By experiencing, we mean the feeling with which is associated the sense of `I' or `mine'. The Guru tells him to analyze his experience and to find out who experiences the sense of `I'. For instance, we walk with legs and undergo the experience of walking. That experience is thus associated with the ability of the legs to walk. Now let us analyze it. If, for instance, I lose the ability to walk on account of my legs being inoperative, can I still visualize the former experience of walking? Of course, yes. It means that the experience of `I used to walk' was not associated with the legs. We can therefore eliminate the legs as being 'I'. As another example, I might have an infection in a finger which needs to be cut off in order to prevent spreading the infection. Now after healing the wound, can I visualize how much pain I had experienced? Of course, yes. Thus we eliminate the finger as having the sense of 'I'.

If we continue that process of elimination, it would be found that none of the limbs or the body parts, with which we normally associate the sense of 'mine' is the experiencer. It means that the act of identifying `I' with the body is misplaced. The real `I' is the invisible experiencer that stays within, and which continues to function irrespective of any physical loss, handicap, or disability. That experiencer is the soul.

છે ઈન્દ્રિય પ્રત્યેકને, નિજ નિજ વિષયનું જ્ઞાન;
પાંચ ઈન્દ્રીના વિષયનું, પણ આત્માને ભાન.

||૫૨||

Chhe Indriy Pratyekane, Nij Nij Vishayanun Jnän;
Pänch Indrinä Vishayanun, Pan Ätmäne Bhän.

Each of the senses has the knowledge
of its own subject matter; but
the soul has the knowledge of the
subject matters of all five senses.

- 52 -

Explanation & Discussion:

The pupil had also pointed out that the soul can be analogous to the sense organs. That analogy arises, because the worldly soul is used to identifying itself with the sense organs. Different living beings can have one or more (up to five) senses. Humans are blessed with all five senses. But the capability of each sense organ is restricted to the object of that sense only. For instance, the tongue has the capability to taste, but it cannot smell, see, or hear. The nose can smell, but it cannot taste, see, or hear. Similarly the eyes can only see and ears can only hear. Moreover, such seeing or hearing capability is limited to specific wave lengths of light or sound. Thus every sense organ has limited capability, confined to its own subject and other conditions. If the soul is identified with the sense organs, it would also have limited capability to know, and that too, subject to possessing the sense organs.

That is, however, against the nature of the soul. It has an infinite capability to perceive and to know. Hence it has the capability to know the subjects of all five senses, individually or collectively, regardless of possessing the sense organs. That capability is not fully manifested at present, because it stands obscured and obstructed on account of the impact of various Karmas. The purpose of spiritual pursuit is to eradicate the bondage of that Karma so as to manifest the full capability of the soul.

દેહ ન જાણે તેહને, જાણે ન ઇંદ્રી, પ્રાણ;
આત્માની સત્તા વડે, તેહ પ્રવર્તે જાણ.

॥૫૩॥

Deh Na Jäne Tehane, Jäne Na Indri, Prän;
Ätmäni Sattä Vade, Teh Pravarte Jän.

The body does not know that, neither
do the senses, nor the breath;
the knowing capability prevails on
account of the presence of the soul.

- 53 -

Explanation & Discussion:

The pupil had suggested that the body or the sense organs or the breath could be treated as the soul. Since knowing capability is the basic attribute of the soul, the Guru asks him to examine whether any of the above three aspects has the capability to know. Every one has seen that at the time of death the body continues to exist without the capability to know. It does not have any sense of feeling and does not experience pain, even when it is cremated. Therefore the body cannot be the soul.

Now consider the sense organs. They experience the senses of touch, taste, smell, etc. when the body is alive. When it is dead, the sense organs continue to be in the same place, but they lose the capability to experience. If some food is put on the tongue, it cannot taste; if a flower is brought near the nose, it cannot smell; the eyes which used to see different objects even from a distance, can no longer see, even if the objects are brought close to them. The same is the case with sound and touch. The ears cannot hear and the skin cannot feel. All these organs used to function, while the soul was there in the body, but they stop functioning as soon as the soul leaves. Hence the sense organs cannot be the soul.

Now examine the breath. Breathing is an essential activity of a live body. It continues uninterrupted for the whole life. As soon as the body is dead, it stops breathing. One may therefore tend to equate breath with life. A study of the breathing mechanism would indicate that it is a device to provide oxygen to the body. But oxygen is not life. Had it been life, the longevity could be extended indefinitely with oxygen cylinders. The respiratory system is no doubt essential for life, but it does not constitute life. There are various other activities like metabolism, blood circulation, brain activity, etc. which are also essential for life. In fact, brain stoppage is considered the sure sign of death. All of these activities, including breathing, are incidental to the live body (body with the soul in it). None of these activities can be equated with the soul.

Thus neither the body nor senses nor breath can be the soul, since they function only when the body is alive. The movements of the body and the knowing capability of the senses prevail in the presence of the soul only and they stop functioning in its absence. Therefore it is only the soul that perceives, sees, knows, and experiences.

સર્વ અવસ્થાને વિષે, ન્યારો સદા જણાય;
પ્રગટરૂપ ચૈતન્યમય, એ એંધાણ સદાય.

॥૫૪॥

Sarva Avasthäne Vishe, Nyäro Sadä Janäy;
Pragat Roop Chaitanyamay, E Endhän Saday.

It is always seen as distinct during all the states; manifest consciousness is its ever present characteristic.

- 54 -

Explanation & Discussion:

The pupil had also raised the question of some sign or mark with which soul can be identified and had asked, how would it be possible to accept the existence of soul in the absence of any distinguishing mark. The Guru tells him that as long as there is a soul, all the parts of the body remain live and conscious. Awareness is evident in every part of the body. That is the sign of consciousness. That is experienced not only when one is awake, it prevails even during the sleeping, dreaming, or slumbering state. If a fly or mosquito sits on the body while one is asleep, he moves it away by waving the hand. Moreover, awareness continues to stay while undergoing changes in physical states. For instance, one grows from childhood to youth or to old age, his health may improve or deteriorate, but he remains aware of the changes taking place in such states.

Further, there is elegance in every part of the body. They look different from what they would look in absence of life. That difference is the sign of consciousness. Similarly, one usually remembers what he might have experienced during a dreaming state. When he wakes up after a sound sleep, he realizes that he had gone through sleep and experiences the freshness gained thereby. It indicates that consciousness, the knowing capability, prevails in such states. That is the sure and manifest sign of the existence of the soul. In fact, being alive or dead can be ascertained by the existence or non-existence of consciousness.

ઘટ, પટ આદિ જાણ તું, તેથી તેને માન;
જાણનાર તે માન નહિ, કહીએ કેવું જ્ઞાન ?

॥૫૫॥

Ghat, Pat Ädi Jän Tun, Tethi Tene Män;
Jänanär Te Män Nahi, Kahie Kevun Jnän.

> *You believe in the pot, cloth, etc.*
> *because you (see and) know them;*
> *what type of knowledge is it, that*
> *you do not believe in the knower?*
>
> - 55 -

Explanation & Discussion:

The pupil had said that if the soul exists, it should be apparent like a pot, cloth, and other material objects. In a way, the reply has been already given when it was explained that the soul is intangible, it has no form or shape and is therefore not visible like material objects. Here the Guru points out to the pupil, "You being the knower, you know pots, cloth, etc. and therefore believe in their existence. But then, why do you overlook the knower itself? Is it possible to know anything without existence of the knower? Since you know all those objects, it is clear that there is the knower. Is it not ironic that while believing in the objects that you know, you are hesitating to accept existence of the knower (soul) itself?"

પરમ બુદ્ધિ કૃશ દેહમાં, સ્થૂળ દેહ મતિ અલ્પ;
દેહ હોય જો આતમા, ઘટે ન આમ વિકલ્પ.

||૫૬||

Param Buddhi Krush Dehamän, Sthool Deh Mati Alpa;
Deh Hoy Jo Ätamä, Ghate Na Äm Vikalpa.

> *There may be sharp intellect in*
> *a frail body and poor intellect in an*
> *obese body; that cannot happen,*
> *if the body had been the soul.*
>
> - 56 -

Explanation & Discussion:

While reverting to the argument of the pupil about equating the body with the soul, the Guru asks him to examine the functioning of intellect. It is observed in many cases that a person may be having a very slim body, but he would be highly intelligent. Shrimad himself had a frail body, but how intelligent he was, is known to every one. This Ätmasiddhi Shästra itself is evidence of his intellect.

On the other hand, it is also observed that one may be having a fat bulky body, but he may be short of intelligence. If the body is the soul, the bulkier the body, the greater must be the soul and as a corollary, a bulkier person should be more intelligent than a slim one. However, our general experience is contrary. So there is no rationale in arguing that the body and the soul are the same.

જડ ચેતનનો ભિન્ન છે, કેવળ પ્રગટ સ્વભાવ;
એકપણું પામે નહીં, ત્રણે કાળ દ્વયભાવ.

॥૫૭॥

Jad Chetanano Bhinna Chhe, Keval Pragat Swabhäv;
Ekpanun Päme Nahin, Trane Käl Dway Bhäv.

Manifest properties of lifelessness and
consciousness are different; they can never
become one, duality prevails forever.

- 57 -

Explanation & Discussion:

It has been explained earlier that the basic properties of lifeless matter and consciousness are different and distinct. Their manifest characteristics are different. When two lifeless things come together, they can either form a homogenous mixture like that of milk and water or heterogeneous one like that of sand and sugar. In either of the cases, the things retain their own lifeless nature. Neither are they transformed into some different substance, nor do they become conscious matter.

If the things that come together are subject to a chemical reaction, a new substance can emerge out of their composition. For instance, the combination of hydrogen and oxygen can result in water vapor. But that composition also does not give the property of consciousness to water. Moreover, even in the composed form, hydrogen does not become oxygen nor does oxygen become hydrogen. The atoms of hydrogen retain their properties and the atom of oxygen retains its own. Those properties simply remain latent so long as the composition lasts. This becomes evident when hydrogen and oxygen are separated by the appropriate process. Then they again manifest their own distinct properties.

In this connection, it is worth pointing out what the great poet Banarasidas said about the soul and lifeless matter. He stated that equanimity, elegance, sublimation, knowing capability, happiness, experiencing, and consciousness are the seven manifest attributes of the soul. On the other hand, existence in the form of body, mind, speech, non-cognizance, aggregation, lightness, heaviness, etc. are the attributes of lifeless matter.

These attributes of the soul are explained by Shrimad in Vachanämrut # 436, 437, and 438. Moreover, he stated (Vachanämrut # 266):

Jad Bhäve Jad Pariname, Chetan Chetan Bhäv;
Koi Koi Palate Nahin, Chhodi Äp Swabhäv.

It means: Lifeless matter turns into lifelessness and the conscious soul into consciousness. No substance changes into something else and gives up its own original properties.

Every original substance thus retains its property and does not adopt the property of a different substance. Similarly, though the body and conscious soul happen to occupy the same space, they do not adopt the properties of each other and cannot be reduced to one matter. They were two separate substances in the past, they are separate in the present, and will remain so in the future.

આત્માની શંકા કરે, આત્મા પોતે આપ;
શંકાનો કરનાર તે, અચરજ એહ અમાપ.

॥૫૮॥

Ätmäni Shankä Kare, Ätmä Pote Äp;
Shankäno Karnär Te, Acharaj Eh Amäp.

The soul itself happens to be skeptical
of the soul; it is immensely amazing
that it is the doubter of itself !

- 58 -

Explanation & Discussion:

After presenting his doubts, the pupil said that there is no soul. The Guru successfully countered his arguments. After taking into consideration all the points underlying the pupil's arguments, he convincingly illustrated the existence of the soul in simple language which anyone can understand. The ability to explain the abstract nature of the soul in such simple terms is the commendable ability and characteristic of Shrimad.

Finally as a climax, the Guru tells the pupil, "You doubt the existence of the soul, but have you considered who actually doubts? Who thinks that I have doubt? Who is that 'I'? Do you know who has the capability to doubt?" Doubting is the property of the soul. Lifeless matter does not have that capability. Doubt presupposes the existence of the doubter. Thus doubt itself is the evidence of the soul's existence. To doubt such existence amounts to saying, "I do not exist". But unless one exists, how can he doubt? In the end the Guru states to the pupil, "By doubting the existence of the soul, you are doubting your own existence. Can there be anything more amazingly ironic than that?"

Chapter 7

The Pupil's Second Doubt regarding the Everlastingness of the Soul

The Guru's explanation about the existence of the soul was so complete that the pupil was fully convinced by it. He has no doubt in that connection and admits the existence of the soul. Now another doubt arises in his mind about the eternity or everlastingness of the soul. Based on biology and Buddhism he argues that life might be arising from birth and disappearing with death.

આત્માના અસ્તિત્વના, આપે કહ્યા પ્રકાર;
સંભવ તેનો થાય છે, અંતર કર્યે વિચાર.

॥૫૯॥

Ätmänä Astitvanä, Äpe Kahyä Prakär;
Sambhav Teno Thäy Chhe, Antar Karye Vichär.

You have explained various considerations about the existence of the soul; it is possible to believe in that by duly reflecting upon the same.

- 59 -

Explanation & Discussion:

The pupil contemplated at length over the clarifications given by the Guru regarding the existence of the soul. Such contemplation is very necessary, because in absence of that, the Guru's teachings would not have a lasting impact on the mind. If water is poured over a cloth or other porous objects it would percolate the same, but if it is poured over a hard stone it would simply make its surface wet and the rest of the water would flow away. Similarly if one contemplates about what has been taught, the teaching would penetrate his heart.

People often listen to sermons or lectures. If the speaker is an eloquent orator, the impression that arises in the mind is, "Oh, it was excellent." But if someone asks what the speaker had said, they usually scratch their heads, because they cannot remember or recollect what they had heard. This happens because people generally go to lectures for social reasons, for fun, for judging the eloquence of the orator, or for the sake of leisurely spending time. They may therefore enjoy the speech, but nothing worthwhile goes within or is retained.

It is therefore necessary to ponder over what one listens. The deeper the contemplation, the more durable the impact. The contemplation at length is particularly necessary in spiritual aspects. In fact, it is essential. In this case, the pupil has reflected deeply upon what the Guru had said and he feels convinced about the existence of the soul, separate from the body, sense organs, and breath.

બીજી શંકા થાય ત્યાં, આત્મા નહિ અવિનાશ;
દેહયોગથી ઉપજે, દેહવિયોગે નાશ.

||૬૦||

Biji Shankä Thäy Tyän, Ätmä Nahin Avinäsh;
Deh Yogathi Upaje, Deh Viyoge Näsh.

Now another doubt arises regarding the
indestructibility of the soul; it might
emerge with the formation of the body and be
destroyed when the body is decomposed.

- 60 -

Explanation & Discussion:

The pupil now contends that the soul is not everlasting. It is every day experience that whatever we come across is subject to wear and tear, and is ultimately destroyed. The pupil therefore argues that the soul also must be subject to the same process of destruction. He has now no doubt about its existence; but he feels that the soul might be arising with the formation of the body and might be destroyed at death.

The pupil's argument is similar to Chärväk's point of view. Chärväk was an atheist who did not believe in the existence of soul. He believed in living merrily as long as one survives. This can be seen from the following slogan of his philosophy:

Yävat Jivam Sukham Jivet, Runam Krutvä Dhrutam Pibet;
Bhasmibhutasya Dehasya, Punarägamanam Kutah?

It means, "Live happily as long as you are alive; enjoy the rich foods even by incurring debt; how is the body, that is turned into ashes, going to come back?"

But the pupil is not an atheist and does not believe in the philosophy of Chärväk. His purpose is to know the truth so that he can undertake the spiritual pursuit without having any doubt. He therefore presents the problems arising in the mind with a view to obtaining clarification.

અથવા વસ્તુ ક્ષણિક છે, ક્ષણે ક્ષણે પલટાય;
એ અનુભવથી પણ નહીં, આત્મા નિત્ય જણાય.

॥૬૧॥

Athavä Vastu Kshanik Chhe, Kshane Kshane Palatäy;
E Anubhavathi Pan Nahin, Ätmä Nitya Janäy.

Alternately, every thing is ephemeral and
undergoes change every moment; that
experience also precludes the eternity of soul.

- 61 -

Explanation & Discussion:

The pupil presents another argument based on every day experience. It is our experience that everything goes on changing. New things get old; they are torn, worn, broken, divided, decomposed, transformed, and so on. The change and transformation is thus the law of nature. Nothing stays in the same form and changes occur every moment. When that is the general experience, how is it possible to believe that the soul does not undergo change and stays in the same form forever? It must also be undergoing change.

This doubt of the pupil is similar to the belief of Buddhism. Lord Buddha laid down that everything is transitory; nothing stays forever and continual change is the order of the universe. He therefore argued against the eternity of anything and refused to accept the everlastingness of the soul. For most people that theory seemed reasonable and in accordance with every day experience. Millions of people therefore adopted it and became followers of Buddha.

Chapter 8

Guru's Explanation of the Soul's Everlastingness
(Second Fundamental)

In the last chapter, the pupil raised his doubts about the everlastingness of the soul. Of course, the Guru has heard such arguments before. They are therefore not new to him. He is aware of the philosophies of Chärväk (non-existence of the soul) and Buddhism (transient or non-permanent nature of the soul). He knows that Buddhism has apparently a strong case and most of the spiritual aspirants would stumble on that issue. He is therefore going to address all the relevant aspects to show where those philosophies are one-sided and incomplate. The following nine stanzas are meant to establish the eternity of the soul and to dispel all doubts about its impermanence.

દેહ માત્ર સંયોગ છે, વળી જડ રૂપી દશ્ય;
ચેતનનાં ઉત્પત્તિ લય, કોના અનુભવ વશ્ય?

॥૬૨॥

Deh Mätra Sanyog Chhe, Vali Jad Roopi Drashya;
Chetananä Utpatti Lay, Konä Anubhav Vashya?

The body is a mere composition; it is
lifeless, has a form, and is visible;
on whose experience do emergence
and extinction of consciousness rest?

- 62 -

Explanation & Discussion:

The pupil had contended that the soul might be emerging from the body and disappearing with death. In order to counter that, the Guru asks him to consider the nature of the body. It is basically a composition. It is composed of carbon, hydrogen, nitrogen, calcium, etc. Alternately it can be said that it is composed of the five main elements: earth, water, fire, air, and space, which are known as Panchmahābhoot. To describe it in physical terms, it can be said that it is an organized assemblage of blood, muscles, fat, bones, etc. all of which are covered by the skin.

Thus the body does not have its own substantial existence. Moreover, it is lifeless. Touch, taste, smell, and color, which are the attributes of the lifeless Pudgal, are present in the body. Being lifeless, it does not have knowing capability. Besides, it has some form. Its visibility is manifest to us, because we are able to see the body. In other words, the body is an inanimate subject of eyesight.

How can such a body be capable of knowing the emergence and the extinction of the soul? The attributes of the soul are completely different from those of the body. Soul is not a composition; it has its own substantial existence. It is full of consciousness; knowing and awareness are its inherent characteristics. Moreover, it has no form or shape; it is intangible and invisible.

If the soul is subject to emergence and extinction, then who knows about the same? Obviously soul cannot know its own emergence or extinction. Then, can the body know it? Here, the body means the lifeless one without a soul. It is plain that a lifeless body is incapable of knowing or experiencing. It does not even experience the pain when it is buried or cremated! In that case, how can it know that the soul emerges or is extinct? Hence the question is: What is the basis on which one can say that the soul arises and is destroyed?

In this respect Shrimad stated (Vachanämrut # 718) that the body cannot be the basis, because it is manifestly lifeless. If one says that consciousness itself knows its own emergence and extinction, that amounts to begging the question, because thereby one has to admit of the consciousness as knowing its own emergence and extinction! It is anomalous to say that, and such a statement merely amounts to a verbal aberration. To say that the soul knows its emergence and extinction, but it does not last, is analogous to someone saying that he has no tongue. Therefore, nobody knows about the emergence and extinction of the soul.

જેના અનુભવ વશ્ય એ, ઉત્પન્ન લયનું જ્ઞાન;
તે તેથી જુદા વિના, થાય ન કેમે ભાન.

॥૬૩॥

Jenä Anubhav Vashya E, Utpanna Layanun Jnän;
Te Tethi Judä Vinä, Thäy Na Keme Bhän.

The knowledge of such emergence
and extinction can in no way arise,
unless the agency experiencing that
knowledge is different from the object.

- 63 -

Explanation & Discussion:

After explaining that the body cannot know the emergence and the extinction of the soul, the Guru asks the pupil to consider who can know about it. It can be stated as a matter of principle that the agency, which knows the emergence and the extinction of an object, must be different from that object. It is therefore clear that only a substance, other than the soul, can experience the emergence and the extinction of the soul.

This concept may seem a little abstract. Let us therefore explain it with an illustration. Suppose the birth or death of a person is to be known. In that case, is it possible for that person to know his own birth or death? Obviously not. Only some one else can know that the person has come into being or that he has come to an end.

Now, if the soul emerges with the body and disappears with its death, as it has been argued, the question would be: "Who knows about such emergence and extinction?" It was explained above that the inanimate body is not capable of knowing anything and only the soul (consciousness) has the property of knowing. Further, there is no other agency that can know about it. Hence to contend the soul's emergence or extinction turns out to be merely imaginary. Thus, there is no emergence or extinction of the soul and it is everlasting.

જે સંયોગો દેખિયે, તે તે અનુભવ દશ્ય;
ઉપજે નહિ સંયોગથી, આત્મા નિત્ય પ્રત્યક્ષ.

॥૬૪॥

Je Sanyogo Dekhie, Te Te Anubhav Drashya;
Upaje Nahin Sanyogathi, Ätmä Nitya Pratyaksha.

> *Whatever compositions that we notice*
> *can come to the experiential level;*
> *no composition can, however, bring*
> *out the evidently everlasting soul.*

- 64 -

Explanation & Discussion:

After explaining that there is no agency to witness the emergence of the soul, the Guru suggests to examine the compositions that we come across and find out whether there can be any composition that can turn out the soul. With all the scientific developments and inventions at our command, no one has brought out such a composition.

When Dolly (the sheep) was cloned in Scotland, some people thought that it would be possible to create life. But what the scientists actually did was to discover a new mode of turning out a body, in which the soul could dwell. Such bodies are normally generated by cellular division or by fertilization of a female egg with a male sperm. Cloning merely provides a technique, whereby the male role in the process of procreation can be eliminated. That technique thus does not lead to the creation of the soul. If the soul could be created by composition or by any other technique, there are quite a few corporations that would produce it and the soul could then be purchased from the market. No one has, however, succeeded in doing that.

The commentary given under this stanza (Vachanämrut # 718) is pertinent in this connection. It states: "The compositions that we witness are visible tothe soul, which experiences everything. It means that the soul knows them. While examining the nature of such compositions there does not appear any composition that would result in a soul". The soul is thus not a product of any composition. It is an original, eternal substance on its own.

જડથી ચેતન ઉપજે, ચેતનથી જડ થાય;
એવો અનુભવ કોઇને, ક્યારે કદી ન થાય.

॥૬૫॥

Jadthi Chetan Upaje, Chetanthi Jad Thäy;
Evo Anubhav Koine, Kyäre Kadi Na Thäy.

No one can ever experience the emergence of consciousness out of lifeless matter; nor can one experience the consciousness turning into lifeless matter.

- 65 -

Explanation & Discussion:

Lifeless matter and the conscious soul are two distinct and separate substances. They are independent of each other and one cannot emerge or be created out of the other. The lifeless matter that is pertinent here is known as Pudgal. Whatever we see with the eyes or experience with the help of any other organ is termed as Pudgal. It is a composite of infinite Paramänus (the smallest particle), which are the most subtle, indivisible parts of matter. In scientific terms, subatomic particles may be treated as an approximation to Paramänus.

It is possible to bring about different articles by combinations of Paramänus or by composing them suitably. Such bringing about is called production. Actually, however, it is transformation, because what is being done is bringing out something by processing the articles that were already in existence. Thus what actually happens in the name of production is really transformation.

What we have to consider now is whether lifeless Pudgal can be transformed into the soul or, whether the soul can be transformed into Pudgal. Jainism states that such a transformation is not possible. With the help of science, we have brought out many lifeless objects by combination or composition of Pudgals. We have also been successful in producing robots and putting them to work, but no one could put life therein. No permutation, combination or composition of Pudgal can thus be visualized to bring about the conscious soul. On the same analogy, the conscious soul can never be reduced to lifeless matter.

કોઈ સંયોગોથી નહિ, જેની ઉત્પત્તિ થાય;
નાશ ન તેનો કોઈમાં, તેથી નિત્ય સદાય.

॥૬૬॥

Koi Sanyogothi Nahin, Jeni Utpatti Thäy;
Näsh Na Teno Koimän, Tethi Nitya Sadäy.

> *That which cannot arise out of any combination, cannot merge with anything else, and is therefore eternal.*
>
> - 66 -

Explanation & Discussion:

As stated above, all the objects that come to our notice have been continually undergoing transformation. It means that the old forms disappear and the new ones come into being. Similarly, the old compositions are decomposed and the new ones take their place. Every existing form thus gives place to a new one and no form stays forever. Some of the transformations, like withering of flowers, are evident; while others, like aging, come to our notice after a long time. But the process is continuing every moment. Jainism conceives of 'Samay' as the smallest unit of time, which is the infinitesimal part of a second. As such, it can be stated that every form gives place to a new one in each Samay.

Such transformation, however, occurs in the case of the objects, which are formed by composition or combination. It does not occur in the case of natural substances, which are not subject to composition or combination. Such substances cannot be produced, nor can they be destroyed. They can neither arise out of any combination, nor would they merge in anything else. The soul is such an original substance. It does not undergo any transformation and stays the same forever.

In this context, it would be of interest to refer to what Shrimad has said in the Letter of Six Fundamentals (Appendix-II). It is stated: "A pot, or cloth stays as such for some time only, but the soul stays forever. Pot, cloth, etc. are composed of some materials; but the soul is a substance on its own, because no composition can be envisaged for producing the soul. Consciousness cannot arise out of any composition, so it is not a product. Since it cannot be composed, it has to be imperishable, because what cannot be produced by any composition, cannot be decomposed, nor can it merge with anything else."

કોધાદિ તરતમ્યતા, સર્પાદિકની માંય;
પૂર્વજન્મ સંસ્કાર તે, જીવ નિત્યતા ત્યાંય.

||૬૭||

Krodhädi Tartamyatä, Sarpädikani Mäny;
Purva Janma Sanskär Te, Jiv Nityatä Tyäny.

Snakes and such other creatures have
varying degrees of fury, etc.; such traits
are derived from previous births,
that shows eternity of the soul.

- 67 -

Explanation & Discussion:

In this stanza, the Guru establishes the existence of previous births as evidence of the everlastingness of the soul. This aspect has now been scientifically explored and it has been found that in several cases the information about previous lives was incontrovertible.

Moreover, it is noticed that snakes, scorpions, and such other creatures are furious. Their fury is not learnt by them in the present life. Similarly who could have taught a dog to bark or a tree to extract the required nutrients from the soil or air? They obviously possess those traits from birth. As such, the same must have been brought forth from an earlier life. In other words, the soul concerned must have acquired those traits, while it was in another body during a previous life. That is the evidence of the soul migrating from one body to another. It can therefore be clear that while changing the body from birth to birth, the soul continues to exist.

There are many people who refuse to believe in a previous life. If, however, they try to observe nature, they can notice innumerable living beings with different forms and shapes, different aptitudes, having varying number of sense organs, undergoing different types and varying intensities of pain, and so on. Is it possible that all such differences and variations occur without any cause? Keeping aside other beings, even among human beings there is diversity. Some are black, some are white; some are poor, some are prosperous; some live longer, some shorter; some stay healthy, some are afflicted with disease, and so on.

Science would state that the physical variations are due to the differences in parental genes. But what about the differences and diversities prevailing among the members of the same family? How do children get diseases, which are not possessed by their parents? Even twins conceived at the same time and born of the same parents display much diversity! There has to be some reason for all that, because nothing happens without a cause. The only sensible reason is that such things happen on account of something that a soul might have indulged in an earlier life. It shows that the soul must have been existing earlier and once we accept that, it is easy to see that it would continue to exist in the future.

The explanatory note given (Vachanämrut # 718) under this stanza is pertinent in this connection. It states, "The fury is noticed among snakes by birth; absence of violence is noticed among pigeons. From the very birth, bugs and other insects have the fear complex of being caught, and hence they tend to escape when we try to catch them. By birth, some beings have greater tendency of love, some have higher equanimity, some are more fearless, some have higher fear complex, some have more serenity, some have greater detachment, and some have more attachment for food, etc. Since such differences are noticed as existing from the birth, the reason therefor must lie in the traits developed from earlier lives."

આત્મા દ્રવ્યે નિત્ય છે, પર્યાયે પલટાય;
બાળાદિ વય ત્રણ્યનું, જ્ઞાન એકને થાય.

||૬૮||

Ätmä Dravye Nitya Chhe, Paryäye Palatäy;
Bälädi Vay Tranyanun, Jnän Ekane Thäy.

*As a substance, the soul is eternal but
its states continue to change;
childhood, adulthood and old age are
experienced by the same person.*

- 68 -

Explanation & Discussion:

This and the subsequent two stanzas are in reply to the pupil's contention that the soul should be ephemeral or transitory. The reply in this stanza is based on Anekäntväd, meaning the multiplicity of viewpoints. Jainism considers every thing mainly from two points of view. One relates to the true nature of a substance and is known as the Dravyärthic viewpoint. From that viewpoint, a substance always remains the same and continues to hold its natural properties. Neither does its nature change, nor do any of its substantial properties disappear. Jainism lays down six original substances, of which soul and Pudgal are the most significant.

Take the instance of soul. Consciousness and knowing capability are its inherent properties, which always stay with it. Even when a soul is born as a one-sensed being, it is not entirely devoid of consciousness or of the knowing capability. This can be seen by the sense of pain and pleasure that is experienced even by plant life. As a substance, the soul thus continues to exist along with its inherent properties. From the Dravyärthic point of view, therefore, the soul stays forever.

The second viewpoint relates to its changing states. For instance, by virtue of Karma a human may be reborn as an animal, or a male as a female, but the soul remains the same. Those changes merely indicate its changing states. To take a familiar example, a child grows up to be a youth and then grows old. These changes occur in the same person.

Now let us consider Pudgal. Earlier, we had talked about transformation taking place in the worldly life. Every transformation involves a change from an old state to a new one. Natural forces are continually at work to bring about such changes. When water is turned into snow, its liquid form gives place to the solid one. The living beings too are instrumental in bringing about such changes. When a cow eats grass, the carbohydrate form of grass is destroyed and it assumes the form of blood, meat, milk, etc. When a goldsmith makes earrings out of a necklace, he destroys the necklace form of the gold and gives it the form of earrings. Thus, in every case of transformation, the old form disappears and the new form comes into being, but the matter, hydrogen and oxygen in the case of water, and gold in the case of jewelry, remains constant.

Changes occur every moment, but many changes become obvious after some time. The sea waves provide the example of the changes occurring every moment. The waves continue to rise and fall every moment, but the water remains the same. The waves merely present its changing states. In spiritual terminology this phenomenon of ever changing states is termed as Paryäy, and to consider anything from that point of view is called the Paryäyärthic viewpoint.

This stanza states that the soul stays constant like the water in the sea, but its states go on changing like the sea waves. Ignorance and enlightenment, for instance, represent two different states of the soul. Similarly, childhood, youth, old age, etc. are the changing states of an embodied soul. If one views the soul from that angle, it can be termed as transitory and ephemeral. Since, however, the soul knows all such changing states, it can safely be stated that the soul itself remains constant; it stays forever.

અથવા જ્ઞાન ક્ષણિકનું, જે જાણી વદનાર;
વદનારો તે ક્ષણિક નહિ, કર અનુભવ નિર્ધાર.

||૬૯||

Athavä Jnän Kshanikanun, Je Jäni Vadanär;
Vadanäro Te Kshanik Nahin, Kar Anubhav Nirdhär.

Or, one who talks of the transitoriness
after knowing it as such, cannot
itself be transitory; you can make
sure of this by experiencing it.

- 69 -

Explanation & Discussion :

Since the pupil had contended about the transitoriness of the soul, the Guru points out that one, who talks of the transitoriness, should be existing. It is a matter of principle that one cannot speak without existing. As such, he himself cannot be transitory. Let us make this point a little more explicit.

When we term any thing as transitory, we mean that it undergoes change every moment. Now if one, who knows something as transitory, is himself transitory, he ceases to exist the moment after knowing that. In that case, how can he express that a particular thing is transitory? For expressing that, he needs to exist and it means that he cannot be transitory.

The Guru intends to point out that the pupil's argument of the soul being transitory is meaningless. Without the soul there is no life and without life no one can speak. The fact that the pupil talks, indicates that there is a soul within him, and that soul continues to exist while he speaks. To call it transitory would mean that the existing soul itself states that it is transitory. Isn't it absurd to state that? The Guru therefore asks him to ponder over that and to find out and determine for himself that his soul is not transitory.

કયારે કોઈ વસ્તુનો, કેવળ હોય ન નાશ;
ચેતન પામે નાશ તો, કેમાં ભળે તપાસ.

॥૭૦॥

Kyäre Koi Vastuno, Keval Hoy Na Näsh;
Chetan Päme Näsh To, Kemän Bhale Tapäs?

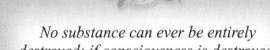

No substance can ever be entirely destroyed; if consciousness is destroyed, find out wherein it can merge.

- 70 -

Explanation & Discussion:

The Guru now turns to a scientific truth. Nothing that exists can be entirely destroyed. There can be alterations, whereby a substance would undergo changes in its states. In other words, while retaining its existence, the substance gives up the old state and assumes a new one. Jainism calls this

Utpäd-Vyay-Dhrauvya. Assuming the new state is Utpäd, giving up the old one is Vyay and retaining its own substance is Dhrauvya. No substance can thus be really destroyed. That is the scientific law of conservation of matter. Jain seers were aware of that, and therefore refused to admit the concept of Creation or a Creator.

Since the pupil had contended that the soul cannot be everlasting, the Guru states that as a substance, the soul cannot be destroyed. As such, if it ceases to exist in its present form, it must be assuming a new one. The Guru therefore asks the pupil to find out what new state the soul would assume, or wherein it would merge, if it ceases to exist.

The explanation given under this stanza (Vachanämrut # 718) takes the illustration of an earthen pot and points out, "When such a pot is broken, it is said that the pot is destroyed, but the earth of which it was made is not destroyed. Even if the pot is reduced to pieces, even if it is pulverized, the earth would stay as Paramänu, it cannot be entirely destroyed. Not a single Paramänu of the erstwhile pot can be lost, because it is of every one's experience that an object can be transformed, but it is not possible to conceive of its total destruction."

The Guru therefore tells the pupil that if by extinction of the soul he means its transformation similar to a pot, he should specify the form that a soul would assume after its extinction. In other words, as the Paramänus of the earthen pot are mixed with other earthly aggregates of Paramänus, he should explore with what matter consciousness can be mixed. He would then find out that consciousness is a substance that cannot mix with or merge into anything else. Therefore the only conclusion would be that the soul is everlasting consciousness.

Chapter 9
Pupil's Third Doubt regarding the Soul being Kartä

After learning about the existence and eternity of the soul, the pupil thinks that if the soul is inherently endowed with infinite enlightenment and happiness, why has the worldly soul been wandering from birth to birth undergoing unhappiness and distress? Moreover, why is there so much diversity in bodies and varieties in worldly situations? While pondering over that, the idea comes to his mind that Karma could be the reason, and if it is so, the question would be: "How does Karma arise?"

The theory of Karma is generally acceptable to almost all the Aryan philosophies, but Jainism has gone deeper into the matter. It states that by virtue of indulging in craving and aversion, the worldly soul continually acquires Karma. There are many types of Karma, but Jainism classifies them in eight broad categories. Four of them like age span, status, etc. do not affect the nature of the soul and therefore are treated as Aghäti or non-defiling Karma. The remaining four are called Ghäti or defiling ones. Of those latter four, Mohaniya or deluding Karma is considered the most harmful, because that Karma does not allow the worldly soul to perceive its true nature and is thus responsible for its wandering from birth to birth.

In addition to laying down the different types of Karma, which is called Prakruti, Jainism also specifies its duration known as Sthiti, its intensity known as Ras or Anubhäg, and the quantity or area of the bondage known as Pradesh. It says that Mithyätva, Avirati, Pramäd, Kashäy, and Yog are the five factors that lead to the acquisition of Karma. Mithyätva denotes wrong perception, Avirati denotes attachment and absence of restraint, Pramäd denotes indolence, Kashäy denotes passions, and Yog denotes invigilant indulgence of physical, verbal, and mental faculties. Of these five, Mithyätva is the most significant, followed by Kashäy.

The pupil has not gone that deep regarding the philosophy of Karma. It is, however, clear to him that either the soul might be acquiring bondage of Karma or it might not. If it acquires, the pupil wonders how it would be acquiring that bondage. Several alternatives occur to him in this respect. Would Karma be clinging on its own? Or could it be within the nature of the soul to acquire Karma? Or would God or Nature be prompting it to do so? He presents these alternatives (doubts) in the following stanzas.

કર્તા જીવ ન કર્મનો, કર્મ જ કર્તા કર્મ;
અથવા સહજ સ્વભાવ કાં, કર્મ જીવનો ધર્મ.

॥૭૧॥

Kartä Jiv Na Karmano, Karma Ja Kartä Karma;
Athavä Sahaj Swabhäv Kän, Karma Jivano Dharma.

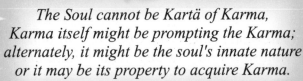

The Soul cannot be Kartä of Karma,
Karma itself might be prompting the Karma;
alternately, it might be the soul's innate nature
or it may be its property to acquire Karma.

- 71 -

Explanation & Discussion:

The pupil states that there is no evident reason for the soul itself to acquire Karma. When it knows that it has to bear the consequences of its Karma, why would it act in a way which would lead to the bondage of Karma? It is therefore possible that the existing Karma might be prompting new particles of Karma to turn towards the soul and they might be clinging to it. In that case it would not be possible for the soul to avoid the influx of Karma and it would helplessly remain bound to it.

Occurrence of the bondage that way, however, does not seem reasonable to him. Therefore he thinks that it could be the nature of the soul to act in a way that leads to bondage. In that case, the soul would be helplessly acquiring bondage. If it is the soul's natural property to acquire Karma, no one can prevent such nature from functioning, and the soul would forever continue to acquire Karma.

આત્મા સદા અસંગ ને, કરે પ્રકૃતિ બંધ;
અથવા ઈશ્વર પ્રેરણા, તેથી જીવ અબંધ.

॥૭૨॥

Ätmä Sadä Asanga Ne, Kare Prakruti Bandh;
Athavä Ishwar Preranä, Tethi Jiv Abandh.

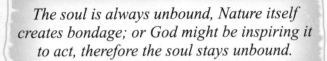

The soul is always unbound, Nature itself creates bondage; or God might be inspiring it to act, therefore the soul stays unbound.

- 72 -

Explanation & Discussion:

Another idea occurs to the pupil. He has learned that the soul is inherently unattached and unbound. As such, no bondage can arise and the acquisition of Karma is merely imaginary. In other words, the soul cannot indulge in anything that can lead it to bondage. Any activity is left to Nature or Prakruti, which consists of the three basic attributes of Satva, Rajas, and Tamas. Such an activity of Nature cannot bind the soul. Therefore it remains unbound.

The pupil might also be resorting to the Sänkhya philosophy, which provides a different connotation to the term Prakruti. That philosophy divides the entire universe into two parts. One is termed as Purush, which denotes the soul and the other is termed as Prakruti, which denotes every thing else. Prakruti is supposed to have 24 components. Of these, the first group consists of the five fundamental aspects of earth, water, fire, air, and space. The second group consists of the five sense organs of skin, tongue, nose, eyes, and ears. The third group consists of the five active organs of speech, hands, feet, anus, and genitals. The fourth group consists of the five sense objects of touch, taste, smell, sight, and sound. Mind, intelligence, tendencies, and ego are the remaining four. The worldly life consists of the interaction of those 24 elements, while Purush, the soul, stays unaffected by any of them.

After arguing from that Sänkhya philosophy, the pupil remembers the concept of God as the creator and regulator of the world. The Vedäntists and Naiyäyiks believe that every thing happens solely by the wish and inspiration of God. The pupil therefore thinks that the soul might thus be acting under the inspiration of God. In that case too, the soul does not do anything of its own and as such, it should not incur bondage.

માટે મોક્ષ ઉપાયનો, કોઈ ન હેતુ જણાય;
કર્મતનું કર્તાપણું, કાં નહિ, કાં નહિ જાય.

॥૭૩॥

Mäte Moksha Upäyano, Koi Na Hetu Janäy;
Karmatanun Kartäpanun, Kän Nahi, Kän Nahi Jäy.

As such, there is no purpose in
seeking the path of liberation;
either the acquisition of Karma does
not occur, or it stays forever.

- 73 -

Explanation & Discussion:

The pupil now concludes his arguments. He says that considering the above possibilities, it is clear that the soul cannot acquire the bondage of Karma. If the soul happens to acquire Karma by virtue of nature, it cannot escape from that. No substance can give up its properties. The soul will therefore continue to acquire Karma, if it happens to be its property. As such, there is no purpose in pursuing the path of liberation.

The concept of liberation is based on averting Karma. By virtue of acquisition of Karma, the soul has to take birth in order to bear the consequences. Since it is mostly involved in unwholesome Karma, it begets unfavorable situations and as such undergoes misery and pain associated with that. If it is to be freed from that, it needs to avoid acquiring Karma. However, if acquisition of Karma is not within its nature, the questions of avoiding it does not arise. Alternately, if the acquisition occurs on its own, the soul would be helpless in the matter. Therefore the pupil argues that there is no point in talking about liberation.

Chapter 10
Guru's Explanation about the Soul being Kartä
(Third Fundamental)

The Guru sees that the pupil is led by the considerations of Sänkhya and other beliefs and has not correctly grasped the theory of Karma. Therefore he has doubt about the soul being Kartä (doer or actuator) of Karma. He has presented the following four alternatives for the occurrence of Karma: (1) Karma itself may be actuating new Karma, (2) It may be the nature of soul to acquire Karma, (3) Every thing might be occurring by virtue of Prakruti, and (4) Karma might be acquired under the inspiration of God. He has, however, failed to consider the possibility of the soul inducing the activities of the body, speech, and mind. If such activities occur under the inspiration of the soul, it evidently becomes responsible for that.

In this connection, it is worth considering what Shrimad stated in the Letter of Six Fundamentals (Appendix-II). It states: "All objects are associated with purposeful activity. All of them are seen with some or other activity that causes change or alteration. The soul is also imbibed with activity. Being active, it is Kartä. The omniscients have described three types of its activities. In the absolute state when the soul stays tuned to its pure nature, it is Kartä of that nature; in terms of worldly activities, it is Kartä of the material Karma; and nominally it is Kartä of the physical objects like buildings, towns, etc."

Of these three types, the first type does not result in bondage of Karma, because the soul stays within its own nature. The second one does account for bondage. The third one is nominal and would result in Karma, only if the soul resorts to the sense of attachment or resentment, while being involved in such activities. In the following five stanzas the Guru explains how the soul behaves under the influence of considerations and hence incurs bondage.

હોય ન ચેતન પ્રેરણા, કોણ ગ્રહે તો કર્મ ?
જડસ્વભાવ નહિ પ્રેરણા, જુઓ વિચારી ધર્મ.

॥૭૪॥

Hoy Na Chetan Preranä, Kon Grahe To Karma;
Jad Swabhäv Nahi Preranä, Juo Vichäri Dharma.

If there is no inspiration from
consciousness, who would acquire Karma?
Examine the natural property, the lifeless
matter has no capability to inspire.

- 74 -

Explanation & Discussion:

Since the pupil suggested that the soul cannot be Kartä of Karma, the Guru asks him to figure out what induces Karma particles to be attached to the soul. Like other Pudgal particles, Karma particles also prevail everywhere and make movements of their own accord. Left to themselves, they would simply pass by without creating any impact on the soul. When, however, they pass by, the worldly soul happens to react to it with a sense of craving or aversion by virtue of his likes or dislikes.

Now, such craving or aversion is not the inherent part of the soul's property, but it has the capability of indulging therein. As the worldly soul has been used to indulge in craving and aversion, it happens to react to the Karma particles, which come within its proximity. Such indulgence motivates those particles to infiltrate the province of the soul. This is similar to a person smeared with oil being prone to attract dirt. As the dirt stays on the body until he cleans it, so do the Karma particles stay with the soul until maturity. That is called bondage. That bondage extends the appropriate consequences at the time of maturity. At that time, if the soul neither resents nor gets attached to any situation and bears the consequences with equanimity, it would not acquire new Karma and the existing bondage would be stripped off in due course.

However, the worldly soul is used to indulging in craving or aversion depending upon the types of consequences. If the soul considers them favorable, it would crave for their continuance, and if it conceives of them as unfavorable, the soul endeavors to avert the same. By virtue of such craving and aversion, the soul incurs new bondage. The earlier bondage is bound to extend its consequences. But by reacting to that with craving or aversion, the soul incurs new bondage. The cycle of old Karma leading to new Karma thus continues to operate.

Karma particles are lifeless. However intense the existing bondage of Karma may be, they have no capability to bring in new Karma on their own. It is entirely due to the wrong inclination of the soul that new Karma particles get into it. Let us take an example. By virtue of an earlier wholesome Karma, one may be blessed with a favorable situation. At the time of dinner, for instance, he may be served with relishing sweets. If he takes that as a result of his Karma and eats the same without any particular preference for the type of food, he can be considered as dispassionately availing the consequence of his Karma. Thereby he does not acquire new ones. However, being used to indulging in likes and dislikes, he may feel elated by the sweets and crave for getting more or getting the same again. That craving induces fresh Karma particles to enter the soul's province and stay with it. In other words, it acquires new bondage.

Here is an example of aversion. One gets into an unfavorable situation by virtue of an earlier unwholesome Karma. Suppose he gets an evil-minded neighbor, who starts abusing him for a wrongly perceived cause. Now if the person takes it as a consequence of his earlier Karma and bears it with equanimity, he does not acquire new Karma. However, being used to retaliating, he gets angry and fights back. That tendency to fight back induces new Karma particles to enter the soul's province. Thus the soul becomes the Kartä by virtue of its indulgence in craving or aversion.

Such a capacity to induce or inspire lies only with the soul. The lifeless Pudgal (Karma) cannot do that. It is therefore said in the second part of the stanza that lifeless objects do not have such capability. They can merely be instrumental to what happens. They can neither induce nor inspire any one to behave in a particular way. Suppose, in the above illustration, the person hits the neighbor with a stick. In that case the stick is no doubt instrumental in giving vent to the anger, but if the person keeps his anger under control, the stick is not going to prompt him to hit, nor is it going to hit the neighbor on its own accord.

As another example, suppose a watch is lying on the ground. If someone picks it up, its lying in that condition becomes instrumental in being picked up. But if the person is not inclined to pick it, the watch is not going to tell him to pick it up. Therefore the Guru here states that it is not the property of lifeless objects to induce or to inspire.

જો ચેતન કરતું નથી, નથી થતાં તો કર્મ;
તેથી સહજ સ્વભાવ નહિ, તેમ જ નહિ જીવધર્મ.

||૭૫||

Jo Chetan Karatun Nathi, Nathi Thatän To Karma;
Tethi Sahaj Swabhäv Nahi, Temaj Nahin Jiv Dharma.

> *If consciousness does not induce, no Karma*
> *occurs; as such, that is neither the innate*
> *nature nor the property of the soul.*
>
> *- 1 -*

Explanation & Discussion:

As one of the alternatives, the pupil had suggested that the incurring of Karma could be the innate nature of the soul. In other words, it could be the nature of the soul to acquire Karma. The Guru therefore points out that if the soul does not indulge in craving or aversion, it does not induce the Karma particles to infiltrate. They would continue to move according to their own nature without causing any impact on the soul. Therefore, if the soul stays equanimous in all the situations, no bondage would occur.

The inherent property of an object cannot be separated therefrom. Wherever there is an object, its property is bound to be there. If such property can be separated, the object itself would cease to exist. For instance, sweetness is the inherent property of sugar. We cannot come across any sugar which is not sweet. If there is some object that looks like sugar, but does not taste sweet, it could be salt or something else, but not sugar. As such, if acquisition of Karma had been the property of the soul, it would never stop acquiring Karma. In that case, it can never reach the Karmaless state. It is, however, known that innumerable souls have attained that state and have been liberated. Therefore acquisition of Karma is not the property of the soul.

કેવળ હોત અસંગ જો, ભાસત તને ન કેમ ?
અસંગ છે પરમાર્થથી, પણ નિજભાને તેમ.

||૭૬||

Keval Hot Asang Jo, Bhäsat Tane Na Kem?
Asang Chhe Paramärthathi, Pan Nij Bhäne Tem.

Had the soul been entirely unbound,
why do you not experience that?
In absolute sense it is unbound, but that
is only subject to self-realization.

- 76 -

Explanation & Discussion:

In chapter two, we discussed the Nishchay Nay or the absolute point of view. From that point of view, the soul is unbound and stays pure forever. The Sänkhya and Vedänt philosophies are based on that. While presenting the case of the soul not being the Kartä, the pupil resorted to that viewpoint and argued that the soul embodies total purity; it always remains spotless and unadulterated. It cannot therefore be involved in anything that would attract Karma particles. As such, it should stay unbound. It should be noted that this argument is analogous to the stand point of the bare knowledgeable persons.

The Guru now points out that what the pupil said is correct from the absolute point of view. But that is the ideal state, which denotes the state of liberation. Liberated souls are pure and stay pure forever. The worldly soul, however, remains attached to worldly involvement. It feels elated when the situation is favorable, and gets depressed when it is not. Thus it indulges in craving and aversion.

Had the worldly soul been unbound and unadulterated, the pupil should have been able to experience the purity within himself. The fact that he does not experience it, shows that his inherent pure state is not manifest at present. Similarly other worldly souls are far from purity. The Guru therefore states that the soul is inherently unbound, but currently that state is dormant within him. One therefore needs to make effort for manifesting that state. If one can abide within his inherent purity, he stays unbound, otherwise he has to strive for gaining perfect purity. For that purpose, one has to understand his present limitations. If he ignores that aspect, he would not get to the right path, and will continue to wander in the worldly life.

કર્તા ઈશ્વર કોઈ નહિ, ઈશ્વર શુદ્ધ સ્વભાવ;
અથવા પ્રેરક તે ગણ્યે, ઈશ્વર દોષપ્રભાવ.

॥૭૭॥

Kartä Ishwar Koi Nahi, Ishwar Shuddha Swabhäv;
Athavä Prerak Te Ganye, Ishwar Doshprabhäv.

There is no creator God, God denotes
perfect purity; if God is conceived of as being
an inspirer, he would be subject to impurity.

- 77 -

Explanation & Discussion:

The pupil had argued that God might be prompting the souls to behave in a way that would lead to Karma. Most religious philosophies conceive of God as the creator, regulator, or motivator and as a dispenser of justice. People like to believe in such a concept, because they feel that if they keep Him pleased, God would provide for them, and make them happy and comfortable. Moreover, if they remain devoted to Him, the kind and merciful God would also forgive their faults.

The psychologists believe that the concept of a protective God has arisen from childhood. Children remain scared of unknown situations, and like to rely upon their parents or other elders to protect them. Similarly many people like to believe in God who can protect them from evils. Moreover, as children are brought into this world by the interaction of parents, people tend to think of a creator, who must be producing the universe and everything else within it.

If one thinks deeply, it would be easy to see that there is no basis for the concept of creation or a Creator. The Guru therefore states that there is nothing like God as the creator or the prompter. It is, however, perfectly reasonable to conceive of Godhood that connotes dignity and greatness born of total purity. This state denotes perfection. Such perfect purity is therefore equivalent to Godhood. That purity lies latent in every soul and one should endeavor to manifest the same.

Such a state is beyond all desires and aspirations. Now if God is considered the Creator, He must have the desire to create. Such desiring does not befit those who have attained perfection. As such, by being the Creator, God stands to lose. Instead of His dignity being elevated, it would actually be lowered. It is therefore stated that by treating Him as the Creator, God would be subject to impurity. Moreover, if God is conceived of as the prompter, why would He prompt one person to undertake wholesome Karma and another to undertake unwholesome one?

There are thus many problems in treating God as a Creator or prompter.

The explanation of this stanza (Vachanāmrut # 718) points out that if God or other agencies tied Karma to living beings, there would be no scope for justifying the existence of the soul. Its existence was accepted on the basis of the properties of inspiration, etc. If that property is attributed to God, what are the properties by which the soul can be identified? Therefore Karma is not inspired by God. That function has to be attributed to the soul itself.

ચેતન જો નિજ ભાનમાં, કર્તા આપ સ્વભાવ;
વર્તે નહિ નિજ ભાનમાં, કર્તા કર્મ-પ્રભાવ.

॥૭૮॥

Chetan Jo Nij Bhānmān, Kartā Āp Swabhāv;
Varte Nahi Nij Bhānmān, Kartā Karma-Prabhāv.

If the soul remains conscious of its true
self, it acts in tune with its nature;
if it does not remain conscious,
it would become Kartā of Karma by
virtue of its involvement.

- 78 -

Explanation & Discussion:

Earlier, the Guru had pointed out that the soul acquires Karma by virtue of its motivating the Karma particles to infiltrate within. But that happens only when the soul is extrovert. The situation starts changing when it turns introvert. Then it realizes that craving and aversion are not part of its nature. It therefore strives to avoid the same by staying within itself. This consists of right perception, right knowledge, and right conduct. As this happens to an ever increasing extent, its inherent purity starts manifesting and it remains absorbed therein. That is the soul's true nature and staying that way forever constitutes liberation.

The question may arise as, "How staying within itself could be the activity in the liberated state?" The liberated soul is supposed to be inactive. How can any activity be attributed in that state? In this respect, the explanation of this stanza in Vachanämrut (#718) mentions the following:

"The pure soul is not Kartä of any external, extrovert, or defiling activity and can therefore be termed as inactive. However, if it is said that it does not have the activity of its inherent nature and properties like consciousness, that would amount to the non-existence of its own nature. The pure soul does not have embodiment and as such it is inactive; but it is active by virtue of having the activity of consciousness, etc. which are inherent within its nature."

In short it is the nature of consciousness to remain active. Its activity in the worldly state comes to the experiential level in the form of craving, aversion, delusion, etc. Similarly, staying tuned to its nature is its activity in the liberated state. If it had no activity in that state, it would turn out to be a lifeless inanimate object.

Chapter 11
Pupil's Fourth Doubt regarding Bearing the Consequences of Karma

After realizing that the soul acquires the bondage of Karma by its own indulgence, the pupil comes to the next aspect of bearing the consequences of those Karma. Here he comes across the problem of the agency or the mechanism that can extend the consequences of Karma. The soul is no doubt the Kartä, but who is going to judge its activities and hand down the appropriate consequences? There does not appear to be any agency that would function as the dispenser of justice. His problems in this respect are presented in the following three stanzas.

જીવ કર્મ કર્તા કહો, પણ ભોકતા નહિ સોય;
શું સમજે જડ કર્મ કે, ફળ પરિણામી હોય?

॥૭૯॥

Jiv Karma Kartä Kaho, Pan Bhoktä Nahi Soy;
Shun Samaje Jad Karma Ke, Fal Parinämi Hoy?

The soul may be the acquirer of Karma,
but it is not the bearer of consequences;
how can the lifeless Karma be intelligent
enough to provide the consequences?

- 79 -

Explanation & Discussion:

The pupil admits that the soul acquires Karma on account of its craving and aversion, but how does it bear the consequences? There are two problems in admitting that the soul bears the same: Who is going to decide the right consequences and who would hand down the same to the souls? Had there been some living entity involved, then he may take such decisions and provide the right consequences. In this case, however, there is the soul on one hand, which acquires the bondage, and being the subject of that activity, it cannot, on its own, decide to bear the consequences. On the other hand, there is lifeless Karma, which is not capable to know anything. It does not even know that a particular soul has acquired certain bondage. How could it then decide about extending the consequences? Since it has no intelligence, it cannot make any decisions.

———————

ફળદાતા ઈશ્વર ગણ્યે, ભોક્તાપણું સધાય;
એમ કહ્યે ઈશ્વરતણું, ઈશ્વરપણું જ જાય.

||૮૦||

Faldätä Ishwar Ganye, Bhoktäpanun Sadhäy;
Em Kahye Ishwartanun, Ishwarpanun Ja Jäy.

If God is conceived of as the provider
of consequences, there could be a case
for bearing the consequences;
but by conceiving that way, the very
Godhood of God would be at stake.
- 80 -

Explanation & Discussion:

Most people believe in an almighty God, who would judge the activities of every being and would dispense justice. If one subscribes to that belief, then He is a suitable agency that can provide the appropriate fruits of Karma. God being impartial, He can properly judge every case and hand down the appropriate consequences to every being. But as stated in the last chapter, there is no valid case for believing in the existence of God as the Creator or the dispenser of justice. There are innumerable living beings who acquire Karma every moment. If we admit the existence of God in this way, He would not be in a position to judge all the cases, even if He is equipped with a supercomputer or with superhuman capability.

Moreover, sitting in continuous judgement presupposes the propensity to act and that itself would lead to the acquisition of Karma. It means that God would be subject to acquiring Karma Himself. Since Godhood denotes unadulterated purity, conceiving of Him as being the judge amounts to the negation of that purity. Thus by being a judge, He would stand to lose Godhood. Therefore, the existence of God as the dispenser of justice is ruled out.

ઈશ્વર સિદ્ધ થયા વિના, જગત નિયમ નહિ હોય;
પછી શુભાશુભ કર્મનાં, ભોગ્યસ્થાન નહિ કોય.

॥૮૧॥

Ishwar Siddha Thayä Vinä, Jagat Niyam Nahi Hoy;
Pachhi Shubhäshubh Karmanän, Bhogyasthän Nahi Koy.

> *Without the existence of God, there cannot be
> any order in the world; nor can there be
> places for bearing the consequences of
> wholesome and unwholesome Karma.*
>
> *- 81 -*

Explanation & Discussion:

Just as there is the necessity of some agency to dispense justice, it is necessary to have the right places where different souls can bear the appropriate consequences of their Karma. For instance, there is a need for heavenly abodes, where virtuous souls can reap the fruits of their wholesome (Shubh) Karma and also for infernal (hell) abodes, where the vicious ones can bear the evil consequences of their unwholesome (Ashubh) Karma.

The provision and maintenance of such locations necessitates the assumption of God. Without Him, who can maintain such places and who would regulate life and other forces operating in the world? By presenting this question, the pupil contends that since there cannot be such a God, there is no case for souls to bear the consequences of Karma. He does not want to contend that the soul does not have to bear the consequences. He is aware that if the soul acquires Karma, it has to bear the consequence. However, he is not clear about the mode of its operation and has raised these questions for seeking clarifications.

The readers are in a position to note that the pupil has been raising very vital questions on all issues. They may also feel that he is actually giving vent to their own minds. That happens because these questions and answers are actually presented by Shrimad himself. In order to make the presentation meaningful and interesting, he presented the six Fundamentals in the form of dialogue between the pupil and the preceptor. Since Shrimad had pure self-realization, he knew what type of questions would occur to the truth seekers and presented the same accordingly.

Chapter 12
Guru's Explanation of the Soul bearing the Consequences (Fourth Fundamental)

Jainism is very specific on one point. Every one has to bear the consequences of his own Karma. That is the universal, inexorable rule. Heavenly beings also cannot escape from that. Even the soul of Lord Mahavir had to live in the lowest infernal level for bearing the consequences of the acutely unwholesome Karma that it had acquired during the life of Triprushta Väsudev. There is no exception to that rule. In order to bring home that truth, Shrimad has observed the following in the Letter of Six Fundamentals (Appendix-II).

"All activities are fruitful; they are not futile. It is the evident experience that whatever is done has its consequence. Consumption of poison or sugar and contact with fire or snow do not fail to produce their consequences. Similarly if the soul indulges in defiled or undefiled mode, that mode is bound to be fruitful and that produces its consequences. Thus being the Kartä of such activity, the soul bears the consequences as well."

In the following stanzas, the Guru takes up the points raised by the pupil against the concept of the soul having to bear the consequences and puts his doubts to rest.

ભાવકર્મ નિજ કલ્પના, માટે ચેતનરૂપ;
જીવવીર્યની સ્ફુરણા, ગ્રહણ કરે જડધૂપ.

॥૮૨॥

Bhäv Karma Nij Kalpanä, Mäte Chetan Roop;
Jivviryani Sfuranä, Grahan Kare Jad Dhoop.

> The tendency to react is a propensity
> of the soul and is therefore conscious;
> the vibrations in the soul's vigor cause the
> lifeless particles to penetrate within.
>
> *- 1 -*

Explanation & Discussion:

The major question that normally arises in the minds of thinking people is: "How can lifeless particles of Karma be attached to the conscious soul?" This stanza is meant to explain that. Implicit in the concept of intangibility is that the soul is not capable of doing anything tangible. It can merely remain aware of what happens. But it is capable of inclination, because inclination and disinclination are intangible. In the perfected state, the soul does not have any inclination. The worldly soul, by virtue of its ignorance, is used to being inclined or disinclined towards different objects and situations. Such inclination or propensity, though not inherent in the soul, is a conscious property and is therefore known as Bhäv Karma.

If the soul does not have any inclination towards situations arising as a result of its previous Karma, it would not give rise to Bhäv Karma. By virtue of its inclination the Bhäv Karma arises, and that leads to likes or dislikes for the situations concerned. The soul's vigor is thereby directed towards or against such situations. In other words, it indulges in craving or aversion and that leads the Karma particles to infiltrate. That is known as material or Dravya Karma. That phenomenon can also be presented by saying that Bhäv Karma causes vibrations within a soul, and those vibrations attract the Karma particles inward and get attached to the soul. In other words, one's Bhäv Karma leads to the bondage of Dravya Karma.

Inclination or disinclination arises by the consciousness getting involved with the mental apparatus. Most worldly souls behave instinctively. This means that the soul loses its vigor to the extent of such instinctive behavior. It is therefore easy for the mind to drag consciousness the way it likes. In the case of spiritual aspirants too, when their mind exercises too much force, the consciousness may fail to exercise enough countervailing spiritual force to withstand it, and may remain subservient to it. The mind is thus primarily responsible for the acquisition of Karma. Therefore, during the spiritual pursuit, the emphasis rests on overcoming mental defilement, regardless of whether that actually leads to physical acts or not.

The anecdote of King Prasenjit is relevant here. On listening to Lord Mahavir's discourse, he gained detachment from worldly life. Hence entrusting the interests of his young son to his trusted counselors, he became a monk. In that capacity, once while meditating, he happened to hear from passers-by that he was a fool to entrust the interests of his son to the said counselors, who were conspiring to kill him and to take over the throne (kingdom). Thereby, he got concerned about the well being of his son. By thinking about the disloyalty of his counselors, he became so agitated that he forgot his state of monkhood and his mind became engrossed in fighting against those conspirators. Slowly, he reached a height of rage that would have led him to hell, if he had died at that moment. Of course, he turned back from those evil thoughts and overcame those defilements with deep repentance, and attained omniscience. This story emphasizes that the mental state prevailing from time to time makes all the difference.

ઝેર સુધા સમજે નહીં, જીવ ખાય ફળ થાય;
એમ શુભાશુભ કર્મનું, ભોક્તાપણું જણાય.

||૮૩||

Zer Sudhä Samaje Nahin, Jiv Khäy Fal Thäy;
Em Shubhäshubh Karmanun, Bhoktäpanun Janäy.

Poison and nectar do not understand, but
one who consumes them gets their results;
similarly a soul bears the consequences of its
wholesome or unwholesome Karma.

- 83 -

Explanation & Discussion:

The pupil had pointed out that Karma is lifeless, and does not understand how to extend the right consequences. Here the pupil's concept about the incapability of lifeless matter may, prima facie, seem reasonable, but it is not true. If we minutely observe, it can be noticed that every object is imbibed with some visible or invisible activity. All the objects that we come across are seen as undergoing change. New ones get old and worn; they change in size, shape, color, odor, and taste; they break, crack, and collapse. Visible and invisible forces are continually at work for bringing out such changes.

Lifeless objects do not have a specific plan to bring out any particular change. For instance, a flowing river does not have any plan to give the round shape to a rough stone. Being in the stream, however, the stone becomes round by the impact of the flowing water. In Jain terminology, it can be stated that the stone was to get a round shape and the flowing water was instrumental in bringing about that change. Therefore, it can be said that every object is imbibed with activity.

Here, the Guru explains that phenomenon with the illustration of poison and nectar. Those two substances are lifeless, and do not have any concept about their properties. Neither poison has any plan to kill nor does nectar have any plan to rejuvenate. But the person who consumes the poison would die, and the one who takes the nectar would be rejuvenated. Those outcomes occur on their own without those objects having any plan or intention to provide such results. Similarly the wholesome Karma does not have a plan to give good consequences, nor has the unwholesome Karma a plan to provide bad ones. But those fruits automatically come as a result of their inherent properties at the time of maturity. Thus, the pupil's contention that in the absence of God, there is no dependable mechanism that can provide the consequences of one's Karma is misplaced.

એક રાંક ને એક નૃપ, એ આદિ જે ભેદ;
કારણ વિના ન કાર્ય તે, તે જ શુભાશુભ વેધ.

॥૮૪॥

Ek Ränk Ne Ek Nrup, E Ädi Je Bhed;
Käran Vinä Na Kärya Te, Te Ja Shubhäshubh Vedya.

One becomes a king and another a pauper;
such differences cannot occur without cause;
that indicates bearing the consequences of
wholesome and unwholesome Karma.

- 84 -

Explanation & Discussion:

There are innumerable living beings in the world, but they are not identical. When we see insects like ants, or birds like crows, we tend to think that those of the same flock are identical, but they are not. All crows, for instance, look alike; but that impression arises because we get only a fleeting image and do not have the opportunity to observe them properly. If we examine closely, it could be seen that no crow is exactly similar to another.

This becomes clear when we observe the domesticated animals like cows or horses. In case of human beings, that becomes even more obvious. No person looks exactly similar to any one else. They differ in height, complexion, strength, facial features, etc. Even the functioning of their minds is different. One's concepts, sentiments, emotions, aspirations, etc. are bound to be different from those of others.

Even their intelligence and spiritual inclinations are different. If two persons pray to the same deity at the same time, the mode and depth of their devotion would be different. If they simultaneously undertake Samayik, one can gain equanimity quicker than the other; he may dwell therein deeper and longer than the other. Moreover, the level of equanimity in the same person also varies from time to time. Sometimes he gains it easily, while on another occasion he fails to gain it in spite of repeated efforts.

There has to be some reason for all such differences and variations. The spiritual science states that they are outcomes of previous wholesome or unwholesome Karma. One person tries to change his job for the better and succeeds in his endeavor, but another person resorting to the same process may fail to get a better job. We generally call it his bad luck. But we overlook the fact that the good or bad luck arises on account of one's Karma. By virtue of his wholesome Karma one may become a president or a king, and another with identical caliber might have to wander in the streets. It is therefore said here that good or bad situations arise as a result of the wholesome or unwholesome Karma, and every one has to bear its consequences.

ફળદાતા ઈશ્વરતણી, એમાં નથી જરૂર;
કર્મ સ્વભાવે પરિણામે, થાય ભોગથી દૂર.

||૮૫||

Faldätä Ishwar Tani, Emän Nathi Jaroor;
Karma Swabhäve Pariname, Thäy Bhogathi Door.

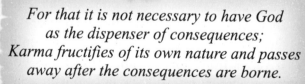

For that it is not necessary to have God
as the dispenser of consequences;
Karma fructifies of its own nature and passes
away after the consequences are borne.

- 85 -

Explanation & Discussion:

The pupil had pointed out the necessity of God as a dispenser of good or bad consequences and had asked, "Who would extend the appropriate consequences in absence of such a dispenser?" As a matter of fact, every action has its outcome, and no dispenser is required for that purpose. Whatever is being done, the consequences follow automatically. If one consumes poison, he faces the consequence of death; while by consuming sugar, he gets consequent energy. As another illustration, if one touches fire, he gets burnt; and if he touches snow, he would feel the sense of cold. These illustrations pertain to the objects of taste and touch, but the rule applies to every object and every situation. It can therefore be said that every conscious or unconscious activity has its consequence. The only difference is that the lifeless matter does not have the capability to experience the consequences, while the conscious soul does.

If one minutely observes, he can make out that every situation is the consequence of some operative Karma, and such Karma is stripped off after the consequences have been borne. If one keeps that in mind, he would bear those consequences with equanimity and would thereby avoid the new bondage of Karma. Attainment of the right perception would then be within easy reach. If consequence is kept in view, it would be hard for any one to indulge in vile thinking or wicked activities. The resultant consequence would scare him away from that. People would then tend to be virtuous, and happiness would prevail everywhere.

તે તે ભોગ્ય વિશેષનાં, સ્થાનક દ્રવ્ય સ્વભાવ;
ગહન વાત છે શિષ્ય આ, કહી સંક્ષેપે સાવ.

॥૮૬॥

Te Te Bhogya Visheshnän, Sthänak Dravya Swabhäv;
Gahan Vät Chhe Shishya Ä, Kahi Sankshepe Säv.

There are places for bearing the respective
consequences, depending upon the nature of
the Karma. O' pupil, this is rather an intricate
phenomenon and has been stated here in brief.

- 86 -

Explanation & Discussion:

Every living being is seen as undertaking some activity. As such, there are innumerable activities and infinite Karma. The question may therefore arise whether there could be so many places where the fruits of all such Karma can be extended to different souls. Are there abodes like heaven and hell, where different souls can bear the consequences of their wholesome and unwholesome Karma?

The explanation of this stanza in Vachanämrut (# 718) points out that there is no scope for apprehension that if God is not accepted as the dispenser of consequences and as the Creator, how can there be special locations like heaven and hell, where the consequences can be borne? One need not be skeptical on such grounds, because the best wholesome inclination constitutes the highest heaven, the worst unwholesome inclination constitutes the lowest infernality, and the mixed inclination of the wholesome and the unwholesome constitutes the human life and animal life.

As such, the highest form of inclination is the supreme abode, the worst form is the lowest abode, and the mixed form is the middle abode. Thus the destination corresponds to the established and lasting traits of a soul. It is natural that the wholesome inclination leads upward, the unwholesome leads downward, and the mixed inclination leads to the middle level. This requires detailed understanding of the properties of sentient and Karmic matter, the situations, and such other subtle aspects. For that one needs to study the philosophy of Karma in depth. This is a very intricate subject, and is thus stated here in brief.

Chapter 13
The Pupil's Fifth Doubt regarding Liberation

Here, the pupil raises the fundamental question of liberation. Most religions do not believe in ultimate liberation. Some religions treat heavenly life as a goal, but that life does not last forever. It can be retained only for a limited period. Some others consider abiding in proximity with God as liberation. Vedänt lays down the ultimate liberation, but that consists of the soul merging in the all-pervading Brahman. It means that the soul ceases to have its individuality in that state. Seeking such liberation thus amounts to seeking one's own extinction. In that case, why would any one be inclined to seek it?

By now, the pupil has grasped the philosophy of Karma and stands convinced that the soul acquires Karma and bears the consequences. He is now concerned about liberation, which can free the soul from the misery and unhappiness of worldly existence. The question that arises in his mind is that, "If the soul goes on acquiring Karma, how can it be liberated?" It is observed that while bearing the consequences of earlier Karma, the worldly soul reacts favorably or unfavorably to those consequences and thereby begets new Karma. In that case how can there be any end to it? As such, the pupil feels that there cannot be any possibility of its liberation from the cycle of birth and death. That problem is presented in the following two stanzas.

કર્તા ભોક્તા જીવ હો, પણ તેનો નહિ મોક્ષ;
વીત્યો કાળ અનંત પણ, વર્તમાન છે દોષ.

॥૮૭॥

Kartä Bhoktä Jiv Ho, Pan Teno Nahi Moksha;
Vityo Käl Anant Pan, Vartamän Chhe Dosh.

> *The soul may be the acquirer of Karma*
> *and bearer (of consequences), but it*
> *cannot be liberated; infinite time has*
> *elapsed, but the flaw (of acquisition of*
> *Karma) still continues to prevail.*
>
> *- 87 -*

Explanation & Discussion:

The pupil states that the worldly soul has been acquiring Karma, and bearing its consequences since time immemorial. While bearing the consequences, it reacts favorably or unfavorably to the situations that it gets from time to time, and thereby acquires new bondage. Since it is conditioned to react that way, the cycle of birth and death is going to continue forever. As such, it would be futile to think of liberation.

The worldly soul has always been smeared with Karma. It has been under its impact since infinite time, and has been taking birth after birth to bear its consequences. Though this has been going on since infinity, the cycle of birth and death has not yet come to an end. As the soul cannot refrain from indulging in craving or aversion, it would continue to acquire the bondage of Karma. It is therefore not possible to visualize the time when that cycle would come to an end. Hence it is contended that the cycle is going to continue forever, and there is no possibility of the soul being freed from it.

શુભ કરે ફળ ભોગવે, દેવાદિ ગતિ માંય;
અશુભ કરે નરકાદિ ફળ, કર્મ રહિત ન ક્યાંય.

॥૮૮॥

Shubh Kare Fal Bhogave, Devädi Gatimäny;
Ashubh Kare Narkädi Fal, Karma Rahit Na Kyäny.

If one does wholesome work, he would enjoy
its fruits in heaven or such other states; if he
does unwholesome, the fruits would be in hell,
etc. but nowhere can he be Karmaless.

- 88 -

Explanation & Discussion:

The pupil contends that whatever the worldly soul has been doing is either good or bad, and as such, it has been acquiring wholesome or unwholesome Karma. The bondage of wholesome Karma would lead to heaven or such other happy life, where it can avail of highly comfortable situations. If it were unwholesome, that would lead to infernal or such other unhappy life, where it has to bear evil consequences. As such, there is no scope for getting rid of Karma, and the soul can therefore never reach the Karmaless state.

By saying that the soul can get to heaven or some other happy life by virtue of wholesome Karma, the pupil has hinted at a very pertinent point. Many people believe that by undertaking wholesome activities, they would be able to attain liberation. Most religions support that view. But Jainism specifically states that however wholesome the activities, they cannot lead to liberation. Its concept of liberation is the Karmaless state, where the soul stays in a totally unadulterated and pure state forever.

As unwholesome activities lead to bondage, so do wholesome ones. The difference lies in the nature of the consequences. The wholesome activities lead to a superior type of life, while the unwholesome ones lead to an inferior one. Since both of them cause continuation of the worldly life, they are not useful in proceeding towards liberation. The wholesome bondage is differentiated from the unwholesome one by calling the former as "shackles of gold", while the latter as "shackles of iron". In order to gain liberation one has to break both the types of shackles.

Chapter 14
Guru's Explanation of Liberation
(Fifth Fundamental)

Every living being has desires, and undertakes some activity for satisfying the same. That activity is its pursuit, which is termed as Sädhanä. One who undertakes this pursuit is Sädhak, and the object of desire is Sädhya. These three aspects are present in every activity. That holds true even in the case of apparently insignificant activities of insects. If there is a sugar grain lying somewhere, an ant would smell it even from a distance and would want to get it. For that purpose it would come out of its hole, and carry away the grain. In this case, the ant is Sädhak, its coming out and carrying the sugar grain is Sädhanä, and the sugar grain is Sädhya. These three aspects are thus inherent in every type of pursuit, whether it be spiritual or worldly.

Here we are concerned with spiritual pursuit. In the present case, the pupil is the Sädhak. He wants to undertake the Sädhanä for gaining liberation, which is his Sädhya. But he is still not sure about the feasibility of the Sädhya (liberation) and has therefore raised questions about its attainment.

He has taken into consideration the activities with good or bad inclination, but has not thought of retreating from both these modes and of staying neutral or indifferent. This is mainly due to the fact that the worldly soul undertakes every activity with a biased mind. There is a sense of attachment or resentment associated with every activity. That leads to wholesome or unwholesome bondage. Hardly any one conceives of a state where one does everything with a detached mind, and therefore does not acquire new bondage. Since old bondage is going to be stripped off in due course, one can reach the Karmaless state by resorting to detachment in every situation. The Guru now explains that state.

જેમ શુભાશુભ કર્મપદ, જાણ્યાં સફળ પ્રમાણ;
તેમ નિવૃત્તિ સફળતા, માટે મોક્ષ સુજાણ.

॥૮૯॥

Jem Shubhäshubh Karmapad, Jänyä Safal Pramän;
Tem Nivrutti Safalatä, Mäte Moksha Sujän.

As you came to know about the fruitfulness
of the wholesome and unwholesome Karma,
so is their cessation fruitful; O' seeker,
there is therefore liberation.

- 89 -

Explanation & Discussion:

It is admitted that the activities of worldly souls are mostly wholesome or unwholesome. They are usually undertaken with a sense of attachment or resentment. That sense invariably bears fruits. If the activity is wholesome, it provides fruits in the form of good consequences; if it is unwholesome, it provides fruits in the form of bad consequences. There is, however, a third approach, which can be termed as pure. If one withdraws from the sense of attachment as well as resentment, his activity remains pure and thereby he does not acquire new Karma.

The term Nivrutti in this stanza is in the sense of such withdrawal (or detachment). Nivrutti does not mean inactivity, as some people might think. As long as one is alive, he is going to be involved in some mental or physical activity. It is therefore not possible to remain totally inactive. One can, however, remain detached, while undertaking any activity. Such activity amounts to Nivrutti.

The worldly soul thus needs to cultivate a sense of detachment so as to avert the bondage of Karma. One may logically ask, "When every activity is supposed to be fruitful, how can retreating from attachment (or resentment) remain without fruits?" The answer is that retreating from attachment would be fruitful in the form of gaining equanimity and thus not leading to any bondage. Since old Karmas are extinguished by bearing their consequences and since no new bondage occurs, one can reach the Karmaless state. That itself is liberation. The attainment of the Karmalessness can therefore be termed as the fruit of such retreating.

વીત્યો કાળ અનંત તે, કર્મ શુભાશુભ ભાવ;
તેહ શુભાશુભ છેદતાં, ઉપજે મોક્ષ સ્વભાવ.

॥૯૦॥

Vityo Käl Anant Te, Karma Shubhäshubh Bhäv;
Teh Shubhäshubh Chhedatän, Upaje Moksha Swabhäv.

Infinite time has elapsed while
maintaining the mode of good or bad;
the state of liberation arises by
uprooting those good and bad modes.

- 1 -

Explanation & Discussion:

The pupil had pointed out that as the worldly soul has been wandering since infinite time, it is not possible to visualize the end of that wandering. The Guru explains that infinite wandering has occurred, because during that entire time the soul has been living with a sense of good or bad. If it perceives some object or situation as good, it gets attached to that; and if it considers it as bad, it resents the same. This amounts to indulging in craving and aversion, and that has led to its wandering from birth to birth.

If the soul now realizes that attachment as well as resentment are not in tune with its true nature and are the causes of continuing birth and death, it would change its attitude. It would cultivate a sense of detachment. Than it would not react to any situation with attachment or resentment and would remain equanimous in every situation. Thus it would not incur new bondage. Such equanimity leads to the state of liberation.

દેહાદિક સંયોગનો, આત્યંતિક વિયોગ;
સિદ્ધ મોક્ષ શાશ્વત પદે, નિજ અનંત સુખભોગ.

।।૯૧।।

Dehädic Sanyogano, Ätyantic Viyog;
Siddha Moksha Shäshvat Pade, Nij Anant Sukh Bhog.

> *With the ultimate dissociation of the*
> *soul from connection with the body, etc.*
> *it eternally stays in the liberated state and*
> *experiences its own infinite bliss.*
>
> *- 91 -*

Explanation & Discussion:

Liberation literally means freedom from bondage. Attachment for worldly situations constitutes bondage and that bondage leads to different situations of happiness or unhappiness, pleasure or pain, etc. As the worldly soul reacts to such situations with a sense of craving and aversion, it acquires new bondage of Karma. Liberation means freedom from all such bondage so that the soul can experience its true state of infinite perception, infinite knowledge, and infinite bliss.

Liberation is the utmost abstract state, which is nearly impossible to put into words. Shrimad has described it in two stanzas of Apoorva Avasar (Vachanämrut # 738). Stanza 17 describes it as, "Free from mental, verbal, and physical particles of Karma and from all connections with lifeless objects, so that the highly graceful, blissful, and totally unbinding state may prevail without any interaction". In stanza 18 it is described as, "The state where there is no contact with a single lifeless particle, which is free from all faults and is unoscillating, pure, immaculate, full of consciousness, unique, unalterable, intangible, and innate". In the Letter of Six Fundamentals (Appendix-II), the state of liberation is stated as under.

"The soul is described as being Kartä of material Karma and thus subject to the consequences. Those Karmas can, however, be terminated as well; because even if the prevailing passions, etc. are very acute, they can be reduced by discontinuing their practice, by avoiding their contact, and by calming them down. They are reducible and can be destroyed. The state of bondage thus being destructible, the pure nature of the soul, devoid of bondage, is the state of liberation."

Of the three types of activities of the soul described in the third Fundamental, the second one associated with defiling instincts results in the bondage of Karma. The worldly soul is used to indulging in anger, arrogance, etc. whenever the circumstances arise. Such indulgence can be reduced, if one tries to calm down those passions by cultivating the sense of forgiving, modesty, etc. Thus the defiling instincts can go down by averting the same and by avoiding their repetition.

What can be reduced can also be destroyed. If the soul stays perfectly vigilant, it can avoid new bondage. Since the old Karmas get automatically stripped off after extending their consequences, its bondage can come to an end. The soul acquires the embodiment in order to bear the consequences of its Karma. If there were no bondage of Karma, there would be no need for embodiment. Such a pure, unembodied state of the soul is liberation. In that state, the soul ceases to be Kartä of any Karma, because being fully enlightened, it does not indulge in any passion or defilement. Thus, it retains its purity and stays in perfect bliss forever.

Liberation has been described in this stanza as the state where there is total dissociation of the soul from embodiment and related matter. Since this denotes the Karmaless state, the liberated soul does not have any bondage and is dissociated from all worldly aspects. It is the state where there is no connection with any lifeless particle. It is the ultimate disconnection, which means that reconnection is never going to take place. That state is eternal and it will never end. It is with infinite happiness. The liberated soul enjoys its inherent bliss forever.

Chapter 15
The Pupil's Sixth Doubt regarding the Means of Liberation

Now we come to the sixth Fundamental, which deals with the path (and means) of liberation. By treading on that path one can attain liberation, specified in the fifth Fundamental. Since the path of liberation is a prerequisite for the attainment of liberation, the question may arise, "Why has this Fundamental been kept last?" The reply is obvious. Unless one is clear about the objective of a pursuit, how would he be inclined to pursue it? For instance, if people know that there is a gold mine somewhere, they would come there even from far off places and try to explore that possibility. When it is known that crude oil is below a certain surface, people will drill there to get the oil. Thus if we know about anything valuable, we make efforts to get the same. Liberation is the most precious treasure that can be conceived of. We would therefore endeavor to attain it, if we know about it and know how to attain it.

Thus it was first necessary to show the pupil the impact of Karma on the worldly soul and explain that liberation is the only way to avoid the same. Now the pupil is convinced about the soul, its everlastingness, its acquisition of Karma, and about bearing its consequences. He is also sure that he can be free from misery and unhappiness of the worldly life by attaining liberation, and is therefore keen to know how to attain it. He does not have any doubt about the necessity of gaining liberation, but he is not sure about the right path and proper means. His purpose is to proceed on that way as quickly as possible. With that end in view, he presents his problems in the following five stanzas.

હોય કદાપિ મોક્ષપદ, નહિ અવિરોધ ઉપાય;
કર્મો કાળ અનંતનાં, શાથી છેદ્યાં જાય?

||૯૨||

Hoy Kadäpi Mokshapad, Nahi Avirodh Upäy;
Karmo Käl Anantnän, Shäthi Chhedyän Jäy?

Even if there be liberation, there
are no incontrovertible means.
How can Karma, prevailing since
infinity, be eradicated?

- 92 -

Explanation & Discussion:

It has been laid down that the worldly soul has been living with the bondage of Karma since infinite time. The problem therefore arises. "How can such a long-standing bondage be destroyed?" The pupil thinks that perhaps it may not be possible to destroy all of them within one lifetime. In that case no end can be seen to the bondage of Karma, because no one knows what type of life one would get next and who knows whether he would be able to continue the spiritual pursuit at that time?

Further, the worldly soul is conditioned to react favorably or unfavorably to situations that it gets from time to time. Thereby it continues to acquire new bondage. The pupil therefore states that unless there is some incontrovertible way to eradicate that long-standing bondage and to overcome the soul's conditioning, it is not possible to gain liberation. Merely knowing about liberation would thus be of little avail.

અથવા મત દર્શન ઘણાં, કહે ઉપાય અનેક;
તેમાં મત સાચો કયો, બને ન એહ વિવેક.

||૯૩||

Athavä Mat Darshan Ghanän, Kahe Upäy Anek;
Temän Mat Sächo Kayo, Bane Na Eh Vivek.

Or, multiple opinions and schools
of thought lay down the path in
numerous ways; it is not possible to
discern which one of them is right.

- 93 -

Explanation & Discussion:

There are many religions and schools of thought that describe the path of liberation, but they all prescribe it differently. Even within a religion there are various sects holding different views. Some state that acquiring right knowledge is the path of liberation; some believe that it can be gained by renouncing the worldly life. Some hold that austerities lead to the eradication of Karma, and therefore insist upon observing the same to the furthest extent possible. Some consider devotion to be the reliable way, while some contend that propitiating a particular deity is the way.

There are multiple views. The pupil has learnt about such views and knows that every one claims its point of view to be right. It is therefore a problem for him to figure out which view is correct. It seems as if he is in the midst of an intricate thicket and does not know how to come out of it. He therefore says that it is beyond his intelligence to decide which one of those views is right and should be adopted.

કઈ જાતિમાં મોક્ષ છે, કયા વેષમાં મોક્ષ;
એનો નિશ્ચય ના બને, ઘણા ભેદ એ દોષ.

||૯૪||

Kai Jätimän Moksha Chhe, Kayä Veshamän Moksha;
Teno Nishchay Nä Bane, Ghanä Bhed E Dosh.

Which creed leads to liberation
and which attire (dress) leads to it?
It is not possible to decide that
because of the multiplicity of views.

- 94 -

Explanation & Discussion:

The pupil continues to state his problem. There are too many sects, and each of them states that the path of liberation lies within its perimeter. Some lay down that aspirants belonging to a particular caste or creed are eligible for liberation. Some restrict the eligibility to males only. Many of them also insist upon a particular dress for the spiritual aspirants. There are also different opinions about the color of the dress. Hindu monks insist on saffron color, Buddhists insist on a yellowish tinge; Jain Shwetambars insist on a white garb, while Digambars insist upon nakedness. Since there are too many differences on such issues, it is not possible to decide which belief is right and which needs to be followed.

તેથી એમ જણાય છે, મળે ન મોક્ષ ઉપાય;
જીવાદિ જાણ્યા તણો, શો ઉપકાર જ થાય?

॥૯૫॥

Tethi Em Janäy Chhe, Male Na Moksha Upäy;
Jivädi Jänyä Tano, Sho Upakär Ja Thäy?

It therefore seems that we cannot get
to the means of liberation;
then what purpose is served by knowing
about the soul and related matters?

- 95 -

Explanation & Discussion:

The pupil feels that it may not be possible to figure out the right path and means of liberation. Then one cannot pursue the objective of liberation, and will therefore have to stay in the worldly life. As such, knowing about the soul, its acquiring of Karma, bearing the consequences etc. would be of no use. That knowledge would be worth while, only if it can be used for attaining liberation; otherwise it is not going to serve any useful purpose.

This does not mean that the pupil seriously thinks that there is no reliable way of attaining liberation. After learning about liberation, he feels sure that there must be a path of attaining the same. He is intent upon pursuing that path, and therefore, in the next stanza requests the Guru to indicate the true path.

પાંચે ઉત્તરથી થયું, સમાધાન સર્વાંગ;
સમજું મોક્ષ ઉપાય તો, ઉદય ઉદય સદ્ભાગ્ય.

॥૯૬॥

Pänche Uttarthi Thayun, Samädhän Sarväng;
Samjun Moksha Upäy To, Uday Uday Sadbhägya.

> *The first five replies have entirely*
> *cleared my doubts; now if I make out*
> *the right means of liberation, it*
> *would be my good fortune.*
>
> – 96 –

Explanation & Discussion:

The pupil states that he is completely satisfied by the replies to the questions that he had raised regarding the first five Fundamentals. He is now confident that the Guru's explanation about the path and means of liberation would also be equally satisfactory. He therefore states that if he understands the path of liberation, he would consider it his good fortune and would earnestly proceed on that path.

The pupil knows that the opportunity to understand the right path comes forth very rarely. By virtue of wholesome Karma, one may get health, wealth, good family, etc. But all such aspects are temporary; none of them remains forever. Only the conviction of truth at the bottom of the heart stays and is carried to the subsequent life. It is due to the rise of very wholesome Karma that the pupil has received the opportunity to learn the truth. He therefore feels excited that his present life could be put to use for realizing that truth. For that purpose, he requests the Guru to show the right path and proper means of liberation.

Chapter 16
Guru's Exposition about the Path and Means of Liberation (Sixth Fundamental)

The Guru has noticed that the pupil earnestly desires to proceed on the path of liberation. When a Guru gets such a pupil, he is pleased and is willing to teach him. Actually, the truly knowledgeable ones are usually looking for the right pupils to whom they can pass on their knowledge. The fountain of knowledge spontaneously starts flowing towards the deserving pupils. The Guru is therefore ready to show the right path to this pupil. That path has been laid in the Letter of Six Fundamentals (Appendix-II) as follows :

"There are means for attaining liberation. If the bondage of Karma continues to occur, its cessation would never be possible. But there are evident means like knowledge, conviction, soul-oriented life, detachment, devotion, etc., which are the opposites of that bondage. By the intensity of those means, the bondage of Karma becomes slack, is calmed down, and is destroyed. So knowledge, conviction, restraint, etc. are the means of liberation."

For gaining liberation, one should avoid whatever results in bondage. The first step is to avoid ignorance. All living beings instinctively tend to identify themselves with the body. But human beings are endowed with discernment (Vivek). By exercising it, one can learn that the embodiment and its surroundings are temporary phenomena, while the soul stays forever. Such learning is termed as right knowledge.

That learning, however, may not enable him to undertake right activity, because he would be lacking conviction. He therefore needs to acquire firm faith about the true nature of the soul. Thereby he gains the insight to understand what is right and what is wrong. That is called right perception. He then realizes that passions are unbecoming to him. For overcoming them, he tries to restrain them, develops detachment towards the worldly phenomena, contemplates about the true nature of the soul, and increasingly stays tuned to it. That leads to the devotion towards the omniscient Lords as well as to the Gurus. It is therefore said that knowledge, conviction, restraints, detachment, devotion, etc. constitute the path of liberation.

However, the Guru is aware that a brief explanation would not serve the purpose of the pupil. It may not be enough for him to undertake the journey on the road. The pupil may stumble somewhere on account of the inadequate knowledge and understanding. The path of liberation is therefore described at length in the following 22 stanzas. These stanzas can be divided in three groups. The first group consists of 11 stanzas that explain the concept of liberation, types of Karma, and how the same can be overcome. The second group consists of the subsequent six stanzas that lay down the stages on the road to liberation. The remaining five stanzas mainly relate to the process of attaining purity of the soul.

પાંચે ઉત્તરની થઈ, આત્મા વિષે પ્રતીત;
થાશે મોક્ષોપાયની, સહજ પ્રતીત એ રીત.

॥૯૭॥

Pänche Uttarni Thai, Ätmä Vishe Pratit;
Thäshe Mokshopäyani, Sahaj Pratit E Rit.

As you are convinced at heart about the five
replies, so will you be easily convinced
about the means of liberation.

- 97 -

Explanation & Discussion:

From the questions of the pupil, the Guru figures out that the pupil has become impatient to understand the path of liberation. He therefore advises him to calm down. The real problem was at the stage of the earlier Fundamentals. Most of the aspirants generally get stuck at those stages. Here, the pupil is entirely convinced of the first five Fundamentals. Shrimad has therefore used the phrase, "Thai Ätmä Vishe Pratit." It means that the conviction has reached the deep level within; and not merely at the superficial level. That happens only if one contemplates at length about what he has heard or read. The pupil has contemplated at length about what the Guru has said. Thereby the conviction of the first five Fundamentals has reached deep in his heart.

This type of conviction indicates the worthiness of the pupil. It shows that he was not asking the questions for the sake of curiosity, nor was he inquiring as a leisurely pastime. He is serious about spiritual pursuit. When a Guru notices such sincerity, he feels pleased. His mind opens up and what he says comes from his soul. The Guru has noticed that the pupil deserves to be taught, and therefore explains the path and means of liberation with utmost clarity.

In the beginning, the Guru tells the pupil that since he has been fully convinced of the first five Fundamentals, it would not be hard for him to understand the sixth (last). The term used here is `Sahaj', which means that the conviction will occur easily and naturally. Since the pupil has now no doubt about those first five fundamentals, he is in a position to understand the path easily. The verb `Thäshe', which means will happen, is meant to assure him about understanding the path.

કર્મભાવ અજ્ઞાન છે, મોક્ષભાવ નિજવાસ;
અંધકાર અજ્ઞાન સમ, નાશે જ્ઞાનપ્રકાશ.

॥૯૮॥

Karmabhäv Ajnän Chhe, Mokshabhäv Nijväs;
Andhakär Ajnän Sam, Näshe Jnänaprakäsh.

The state of Karma is ignorance, while abiding
in the Self is liberation; ignorance is darkness
and is destroyed by the light of knowledge.

- 98 -

Explanation & Discussion:

Here Shrimad has described two opposite states. One relates to staying identified with worldly situations resulting from Karma. That is termed here as Karmabhäv. The other relates to abiding in the true state of Self. That state leads to liberation, and is therefore termed as Mokshabhäv. So long as one remains inclined towards the state of Karma and its consequence, the state of liberation cannot arise. Those two are mutually exclusive states. On account of one's Karma one gets a body, sense organs, etc. But all those aspects are temporary; they do not form the parts of the true Self. For instance, if some one asks me: "Who are you?" I would reply that, "I am Manu". That reply is right to the extent it shows my worldly identification, but that is not my true and lasting identification. Identification with the body arises out of ignorance about my true Self. Such ignorance constitutes Karmabhäv, which is considered here as comparable to darkness.

While giving that reply, I should really keep in mind that the body, which is known as 'Manu', is a temporary phenomenon by virtue of some Karma. That is not the real me. I am the everlasting soul imbibed with infinite perception, knowledge, etc. If I stay with that concept, it is called Mokshabhäv. That is the right sense and is compared here with light. Darkness cannot be removed by hitting it with a club or any other instrument. It can be easily removed by lighting a lamp. Similarly, the darkness of ignorance can be removed by lighting the lamp of enlightenment (right knowledge).

Karmabhäv can also be interpreted differently. Many people contend that they would like to avoid all sorts of passions and proceed on the path of liberation, but previous Karma comes in the way and that does not allow them to go ahead. Such contention also amounts to Karmabhäv. They overlook the fact that the soul is imbibed with infinite vigor. The strength of Karma, however intense it may be, cannot stand against the rightly exercised vigor of the soul. Not to exercise that vigor on the pretext of Karma is also Karmabhäv.

On the other hand, some people are too sure of their

capability and remain action-oriented. They think that they can do whatever they like. They try to go by the slogan "Nothing is impossible". It is true that the soul has infinite capability, but that is lying latent at present. One therefore needs to endeavor for manifesting the same. To talk of overcoming Karma, without manifesting the latent vigor, is to overlook the present state. Such undue reliance on one's latent capacity can be termed as a different type of Karmabhäv.

Shrimad has virtually explained the entire path of liberation in this stanza. It states that the identification with the body is the ignorance of the soul. That Karmabhäv is the root cause of worldly life. What is therefore required is to light the lamp of enlightenment, with which the darkness of ignorance can be eradicated. The rest of the description in this chapter is an elaboration of what has been said in this stanza.

જે જે કારણ બંધનાં, તેહ બંધનો પંથ;
તે કારણ છેદક દશા, મોક્ષપંથ ભવઅંત.

॥૯૯॥

Je Je Käran Bandhnän, Teh Bandhno Panth;
Te Käran Chhedak Dashä, Mokshapanth Bhav Ant.

Whichever are the causes of bondage, they constitute the road to bondage; the state that uproots those causes constitutes the path of liberation and the end of embodiment.

- 99 -

Explanation & Discussion:

If some thing is to be accomplished, one has to avert the factors that might be coming in the way. The bondage of Karma operates as an impediment to the attainment of liberation. It is therefore obvious that one needs to avert the factors that cause that bondage.

Wrong perception, absence of restraint, indolence, passions, and undue exercise of the body, mind, and speech are the five main causes that lead to bondage. Of those five types, wrong perception is the first and foremost. It does not allow the worldly soul even to look towards its true nature.Wrong perception is removed with the emergence of right perception. That can arise by destroying the three subcategories of wrong perception, and by overcoming the four intense subcategories of anger, arrogance, deception, and greed, which are the infinitely lasting passions. Since right perception cannot emerge so long as these seven categories prevail, one should try to get rid of the same in order to gain right perception.

Thereafter one has to adopt restraints to overcome the other categories of passions and avert indolence to the furthest extent possible. The restraints are also helpful in regulating physical, mental, and verbal activities. All these factors can be brought under control by enlightenment and the endeavor in light thereof. As such, the enlightened state and the right endeavor constitute the path of liberation. That leads to the end of the cycle of birth and death.

રાગ, દ્વેષ, અજ્ઞાન એ, મુખ્ય કર્મની ગ્રંથ;
થાય નિવૃત્તિ જેહથી, તે જ મોક્ષનો પંથ.

।।૧૦૦।।

Räg, Dwesh Ajnän E, Mukhya Karmani Granth;
Thäy Nivrutti Jehathi, Te Ja Mokshano Panth.

> *Craving, aversion, and ignorance*
> *constitute the principal knots of Karma;*
> *receding therefrom constitutes the*
> *definitive path of liberation.*
>
> *- 100 -*

Explanation & Discussion:

Staying under the influence of deluding Karma is the principal cause of bondage. Craving, aversion, and ignorance of the Self are the main constituents of deluding Karma, which is the toughest of all Karmas. It is relatively easy to overcome the bondage of other Karmas that obscure and obstruct. The deluding Karma remains hard on account of the above three factors. They are therefore mentioned here as knots of bondage. It is easy to see that bondage can be removed by breaking the knots.

Everything moves smoothly if there are no knots. For instance, when we undertake sewing, the thread moves smoothly as long as there are no knots. As soon as a knot occurs, the sewing stops. One has to remove the knot before going ahead with the work. In routine life too, we can maintain good relations with others, so long as there are no knots in the mind. Once there is a knot, the relations get strained. In order to make them smooth again, we need to get rid of the knot.

Similarly, the task of overcoming Karma could be smooth, but for the three knots of craving, aversion, and ignorance. We need to strive hard to remove those knots. Since time immemorial we are used to having likes and dislikes for different individuals, different objects, and different situations.

That happens even when we come across some one for the first time. It shows that we have harbored a good or bad impression at the internal level. If the impression is favorable, we start liking him, and that can lead to an attachment for him. If the impression is unfavorable, we despise and try to avoid him. Such attachment and resentment constitute the knots that lead to the bondage of Karma.

Likes and dislikes occur in the case of other situations as well. We get various types of favorable or unfavorable situations as the result of our previous Karma. None of those situations is going to last forever. If therefore we stay equanimous in all situations, we do not acquire new Karma. But by virtue of our conditioning, we happen to crave for the situations that we perceive as favorable, and detest those which we perceive as unfavorable.

The third factor is ignorance. The term ignorance is not used here in the sense of being devoid of knowledge. No soul can be entirely devoid of knowledge. What we call absence of knowledge really means the shortage of it. Such shortage occurs on account of the influence of knowledge -obscuring Karma, which can be overcome by making more efforts. But that Karma is not relevant in the present context.

Here, ignorance denotes wrong or misleading knowledge, which is expressed in spiritual terminology as Mati-Ajnän, Shrut-Ajnän, etc. It means that the person concerned is intelligent enough to learn, and he might also have studied scriptures. But what he has learnt does not lead him to the truth or to the right path. In other words, he has not correctly understood or perceived what he has learnt. The bare knowledgeable person, whose state has been discussed in the first and second chapters, mostly belongs to this category.

Such ignorance arises on account of perception-deluding Karma, and in turn it becomes instrumental in acquiring new deluding Karma. Because of delusion, one forsakes his true nature and identifies himself with the conditions that he gets from time to time. That false identification leads him to do what is not in the interests of his true well being. Such activity results in the acquisition of Karma. As long as one thus practices craving, aversion, and ignorance, he is going to acquire new deluding Karma and the cycle of embodiment will continue to operate. When these three factors are overcome and removed, one gains right perception. Thereby he is induced to overcome the character-related deluding Karma, and will adopt restraints. That certainly is the path of liberation. This is the heart of Karma philosophy, which Shrimad has presented in this stanza.

આત્મા સત્ ચૈતન્યમય, સર્વાભાસ રહિત;
જેથી કેવળ પામિયે, મોક્ષપંથ તે રીત.

।।૧૦૧।।

Ätmä Sat Chaitanyamay, Sarväbhäs Rahit;
Jethi Keval Pämiye, Mokshapanth Te Rit.

The way one can realize the pure,
everlasting, conscious soul,
devoid of all illusions, constitutes
the path of liberation.

- 101 -

Explanation & Discussion:

Staying within the true nature of the soul constitutes liberation. Here, Shrimad pinpoints "Sat" and "Chaitanya" as the main attributes of the soul. "Sat" means everlasting. Whatever stays forever is therefore called "Sat". It denotes eternal existence. Jainism describes six basic substances which stay forever. Of these, we are concerned here with "Jiv" or soul. It always continues to exist and retains its inherent nature. This is true even for the worldly souls. Such souls appear to be contaminated by Karma, but that contamination is a superficial, temporary phenomenon. It is a Paryäy, a continually changing state, and does not affect the basic purity and inherent nature of the soul. If the nature of the soul could be contaminated, it could never get rid of it and hence can never be liberated. Since infinite souls have attained liberation by eradicating the bondage of Karma, it is clear that the inherent nature of the soul remains the same forever.

"Chaitanya" is the inherent property of the soul. It denotes consciousness, which indicates the knowing capability. By virtue of consciousness, the soul can exercise its vigor to know, and remains aware of itself as well as of others. Of all the six substances, only the soul has this property of knowing. That property stays with it forever, because no substance can be devoid of its inherent property. In the case of the worldly souls, this property remains obscured on account of the impact of Karma. As such, its capability to know infinitely is not manifested. Every living being, however, possesses some degree of knowing capability. This is true even of one-sensed beings. If a soul could lose this capability altogether, it would turn into a lifeless substance.

Thus, every soul is imbibed with the properties of everlastingness and consciousness; no soul can be devoid of that. The worldly soul is not conscious of its capabilities, because those capabilities are not manifest at present and stay latent. The soul seems to have forsaken the same and stays with the illusion of being devoid of those capabilities. Illusions are, however, not true. If a traveler, for instance, pursues a mirage in search of water, he will never get it. The earlier he gets disillusioned, the better will it be for him.

Similarly, the worldly soul stays in illusion about itself. By its wrong perception and identification with the body, it considers itself as mortal and devoid of knowledge. As such, it tries to gain knowledge from external sources. Even those, who look for the soul, tend to identify it with the sense organs or with the breath, etc. Only a few go ahead and undertake meditation for realizing the soul. During meditation, if they happen to see a "bright light" or such other phenomena, they may think of having realized the soul. Most of such experiences, however, occur out of fantasy.Such fantasies cannot lead toward the true objective. One should therefore be careful and not be carried away by any fantasy. He should make every possible effort to stay away from all the illusory impressions and try to realize the true properties of the soul. To be awakened to the natural properties and to stay constantly aware of it amounts to liberation. Therefore it is said here that the way one realizes his true properties of everlastingness, consciousness, purity, etc. without any illusion, constitutes the path of liberation.

કર્મ અનંત પ્રકારનાં, તેમાં મુખ્યે આઠ;
તેમાં મુખ્યે મોહનીય, હણાય તે કહું પાઠ.

॥૧૦૨॥

Karma Anant Prakärnän, Temän Mukhye Äth;
Temän Mukhye Mohaniya, Hanäy Te Kahun Päth.

> *Karmas are of infinite types, of these there are mainly eight; deluding (Karma) is the principal of them. Let me show how to destroy it.*
>
> *- 102 -*

Explanation & Discussion:

Every activity, whether it be physical, mental, or verbal, results in Karma. Since each activity has its own peculiarity, there can be as many types of Karma as the number of activities. Thus, there are infinite types of Karmas. The seers have laid down 148 (another version states 158) categories of Karma. All of them can, however, be classified in 8 broad divisions. Four of them are called Ghāti, in the sense that they adversely affect the capability of the soul. The remaining four are called Aghāti, because they do not adversely affect the soul. Knowledge-obscuring, vision-obscuring, deluding, and obstructing are the four defiling (Ghāti) categories. Of these, all except deluding can be overcome by putting in enough efforts. In other words, it is not too hard to overcome the impact of obscuring, and obstrucing Karmas.

The deluding category, as the name suggests, is delusive. That deludes the worldly soul, whereby it thinks and perceives wrongly. This is comparable to the situation of a drunkard. If one has too many drinks, he loses his common sense and judgement. He thinks of different persons and various objects the way they are not. He loses his discernment and may even think of his wife as being his mother or vice-versa. He thus remains under delusion on account of the impact of the drink. Similarly, under the impact of deluding Karma, the worldly soul fails to have right understanding of the Self. Under that impact it forsakes its true nature and identifies itself with the body. Thereby it tends to overlook its true nature, and considers the well being of the body as the only objective.

Under the influence of deluding Karma, one tries to look for happiness where it does not lie. He does not realize that different worldly situations arise as consequence of his earlier Karma, and none of them is the real source of happiness. He therefore indulges in the sense of attachment for situations that he thinks are the sources of happiness, and in the sense of resentment for those he considers otherwise. Thereby he acquires new Karma and continues to wander in the cycle of birth and death. It is therefore said here that deluding Karma is the most hurtful, and one needs to make all possible efforts to overcome it. The way to overcome the same is laid down in the next stanza.

કર્મ મોહનીય ભેદ બે, દર્શન ચારિત્ર નામ;
હણે બોધ વીતરાગતા, અચૂક ઉપાય આમ.

॥૧૦૩॥

Karma Mohaniya Bhed Be, Darshan Chäritra Näm;
Hane Bodh Vitarägtä, Achook Upäy Äm.

Deluding Karma is of two kinds,
pertaining to perception and practice;
they can be invariably destroyed by
enlightenment and detachment.

- 103 -

Explanation & Discussion:

The deluding Karma is of two types. One pertains to perception, which is termed as Darshan Mohaniya; the other pertains to practice which covers character and behavior. That is termed as Chäritra Mohaniya. The perception-deluding Karma does not allow one to perceive correctly. Thereby one stays devoid of right understanding and as such he cannot exercise the discernment to make out what is right and what is wrong. That is termed as Mithyätva, which is the root cause of worldly wandering. That situation changes when one knows about the truth from a right entity. For that purpose he should be eager to know the truth, and be lucky enough to come across a true Guru. If he recognizes the importance of such a Guru, he would develop reverence and respect for him. Only in that case, he would listen to and ponder over what the Guru states. The light may thereby dawn upon him, and he may realize that what he had been thinking until then was wrong.

Such realization leads him to rightly understand that he is not the body, which is an ephemeral and ever-changing apparatus. He realizes that he is a pure, everlasting soul, imbibed with infinite knowledge and infinite perception. Such enlightenment is termed in this stanza as "Bodh". That can come only from a true Guru. The words of the Guru emanate from the soul and are capable to penetrate the heart of the aspirant. That can awaken the worldly soul from the deep slumber that he has been indulging in since time immemorial. That enables him to discern right and wrong, and such discernment itself is right perception. Thereby he overcomes perception-related deluding Karma and comes to the right path. All possible emphasis has therefore been laid in the scriptures on the necessity of gaining right perception.

Thereafter, one has to deal with Chäritra Mohaniya, or character-deluding Karma. As explained above, perception-deluding Karma perverts thinking and creates delusion about the soul's own properties. The soul is inherently imbibed with infinite happiness, but the impact of the said Karma does not allow it to perceive that, and leads it to look for happiness from worldly objects. That situation changes with the overcoming of wrong perception. One is now in a position to understand the truth. He realizes that he is not the continually changing body, but he is the everlasting soul. He therefore sets the well being of his soul as the objective.

The built-in prejudices, conditioning, addictions, etc. may, however, come in his way. But he makes out that such factors operate as the consequence of the character-related delusive Karma that needs to be steadily overcome. By virtue of right perception, he recognizes those factors as hurting his own Self and tries to overcome the same. As the perception becomes increasingly clear, he realizes that his getting attached to or resenting any worldly situation is the principal cause of acquiring the bondage of Karma. Thus he develops detachment to an ever increasing extent. Ultimately, his detachment reaches a level, when he can stay free from all sorts of attachment or resentment. It is therefore said here that enlightenment and detachment are the infallible ways to overcome perception-related and character-related deluding Karmas, respectively.

કર્મબંધ ક્રોધાદિથી, હણે ક્ષમાદિક તેહ;
પ્રત્યક્ષ અનુભવ સર્વને, એમાં શો સંદેહ ?

||૧૦૪||

Karmabandh Krodhädithi, Hane Kshamädic Teh;
Pratyaksha Anubhav Sarvane, Emän Sho Sandeh?

The bondage of Karma arising from anger,
etc. can be destroyed by forgiveness, etc.
That is the evident experience of every one;
how can there be any doubt about it?

- 104 -

Explanation & Discussion:

The pupil had raised the question as to how the infinitely prevailing Karma can be uprooted. One should, however, remember that though the worldly soul has been bonded with Karma since infinite time, there is not a single Karma that prevails infinitely. The bondage of Karma has a time limit, and is stripped off after extending the consequences. But while bearing such consequences, the worldly soul happens to acquire new Karma and that way the bondage continues. If one does not acquire new Karma, the old Karmas will be extinguished on their own in due course.

The Guru here points out how the character-related deluding Karma can be overcome. The impact of that Karma is experienced in the form of passion, which is termed as Kashäy. Craving and aversion are the two basic Kashäys, and are known as Räg and Dwesh, respectively. Jain tradition divides them in four categories of anger, arrogance, deception, and greed. They can be overcome by developing the opposite attributes. Anger for instance, can be overcome by forgiveness, arrogance by modesty, deception by straightforwardness, and greed by contentment. Thus the surest way to overcome those passions is to resort to their respective opposites.

Some people may doubt whether those passions can be effectively overcome by developing the above mentioned attributes. For explaining the effectiveness, let us take the instance of anger, which includes the sense of jealousy, animosity, vengeance, ferocity, etc. That generally arises when we find someone not behaving properly or something not happening to our expectation. But becoming angry for that does not serve any purpose. Instead, if we forgive the person concerned and calmly explain how he was wrong, he may realize his mistake and may remain careful not to repeat it. On the other hand, when we become angry, not only do we hurt the person with whom we might be angry, but we hurt ourselves also by defiling our mind. We lose our own peace of mind and feel unhappy. If one realizes that, it would not be hard for him to practice forgiveness. Similarly it is possible to overcome ego and arrogance by developing modesty, deception by straightforwardness, and greed by contentment.

છોડી મત દર્શન તણો, આગ્રહ તેમ વિકલ્પ;
કહ્યો માર્ગ આ સાધશે, જન્મ તેહના અલ્પ.

॥૧૦૫॥

Chhodi Mat Darshantano, Ägrah Tem Vikalpa;
Kahyo Märga Ä Sädhashe, Janma Tehanä Alpa.

Giving up strong opinions and view
points about beliefs and ideology,
one, who follows the above mentioned
path, shall have to take few births.

- 105 -

Explanation & Discussion:

Worldly souls have been holding different opinions and beliefs about true well being. Most of them hold very strong attitude and insist that their viewpoints are right. However, if one tries to find out why he has been subject to wandering and analyzes all the relevant factors, he can make out that his insistence on the wrong viewpoint has been the most important factor. Though the worldly soul has never learnt the truth, every one usually holds his own concept as true. When such a concept is not well based, it is termed as Vikalpa. This needs to be given up, if one wants to get to the truth.

It was pointed out in the second chapter how sectarian persons stick to their own viewpoints and stay away from the truth. Such sticking to one's own views and holding strong opinions amount to self-indulgence, and is not helpful in spiritual pursuit. If one gives it up and follows the path indicated by a true Guru, he would come to the right path. He, who is on the right path, is going to reach the destination sooner or later. He would thus be absolved from taking infinite births. Hence it is said here that such an aspirant would have only a few births remaining before liberation.

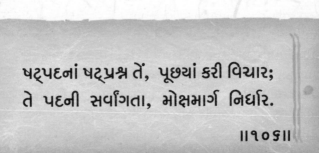

षट્પદનાં ષટ્પ્રશ્ન તેં, પૂછ્યાં કરી વિચાર;
તે પદની સર્વાંગતા, મોક્ષમાર્ગ નિર્ધાર.

॥૧૦૬॥

Shatpadanän Shatprashna Ten, Poochhyän Kari Vichär;
Te Padani Sarvängatä, Mokshamärga Nirdhär.

> *Contemplating about the six*
> *Fundamentals, you raised six questions;*
> *the totality of those Fundamentals*
> *constitutes the sure path to liberation.*
>
> *- 106 -*

Explanation & Discussion:

The pupil was desirous to learn the truth, and had therefore raised questions pertaining to the six Fundamentals. Since they have now been satisfactorily explained, he can make out that all six of them are essential for spiritual upliftment. Not a single one is to be left out. If one does not believe in the existence of the soul or its eternity, there would not be a reason to seek anything. Similarly if one does not believe in Karma and its consequences, he would not be required to do anything to be freed from it. The same way, one has to believe in liberation and the way to attain it. Thus the six Fundamentals together constitute the path to liberation.

The Letter of Six Fundamentals (Appendix-II) therefore states in the beginning that those Fundamentals have been termed by the enlightened entities as the abode of right perception. Towards its end, it is again emphasized that spiritually-oriented people would find them accurate and totally convincing. These Fundamentals are beyond doubts, and the discernment arising therefrom is meant for realizing one's true nature. The deeper one dwells, the more would he realize the truth underlying them. That would give rise to right perception, and by resorting to that one can proceed on the path of liberation.

જાતિ, વેષનો ભેદ નહિ, કહ્યો માર્ગ જો હોય;
સાધે તે મુક્તિ લહે, એમાં ભેદ ન કોય.

॥૧૦૭॥

Jäti Veshano Bhed Nahi, Kahyo Märga Jo Hoy;
Sädhe Te Mukti Lahe, Emän Bhed Na Koy.

There is no discrimination of caste
or attire (dress) in the said path;
whoever pursues it, attains liberation,
without any discrimination or difference.

- 107 -

Explanation & Discussion:

The pupil had raised the issue of caste, creed, and attire in which one can attain liberation. The Guru tells him that all those aspects are immaterial. Even a person belonging to a so-called lower caste can attain liberation. For instance, Metäraj Muni, who was a Ganadhar of Lord Mahavir, was raised in a very low family. Harikeshi Muni (Ref. Uttarädhyayan Sutra) also came from a very low caste.

In this connection, it would be interesting to point out that Jainism admits the possibility of attaining liberation in different traditions. Sthänäng Sutra mentions 15 types of liberated souls, depending upon their last life. One of them relates to those coming from the female sex, another from a house holder life, and still another from the non-Jain tradition. Shrimad has stated on several occasions that one should not insist on being a Jain.

What is really required for liberation is to know and adopt the right path. There need not be any difference of opinions or views about that. The first part (11 stanzas, # 97-107) of this chapter dealing with the path of liberation ends here.

કષાયની ઉપશાંતતા, માત્ર મોક્ષઅભિલાષ;
ભવે ખેદ અંતર દયા, તે કહીએ જિજ્ઞાસ.

॥૧૦૮॥

Kashäyani Upashäntatä, Mätra Moksha Abhiläsh;
Bhave Khed Antar Dayä, Te Kahie Jijnäs.

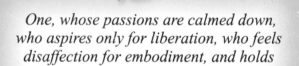

One, whose passions are calmed down,
who aspires only for liberation, who feels
disaffection for embodiment, and holds
compassion within, is called a truth seeker.
- 108 -

Explanation & Discussion:

Now starts the second part (6 stanzas) that describes the stages on the path of liberation. The first stage consists of being a truth seeker. This stanza states four characteristics for that purpose. Pacification or calming down the passions, aspiration for liberation, and disaffection towards the worldly life are the first three of them. It would be noticed that these three are the same as were given in stanza 38. This is mainly to emphasize the vital importance of these characteristics in spiritual pursuit. Moreover, this stanza is meant to set the first stage on the path of liberation. Since that path starts from the earnestness to learn the truth, the characteristics of truth seekers have to be specified as the requisites for the purpose.

The fourth characteristic is presented a little differently. Instead of compassion for all living beings as in stanza 38, this one specifies compassion within. This can be interpreted in two ways. One way is to interpret it as compassion lying within one's heart for all beings. The other way is to interpret it as compassion for oneself which is more relevant here. It needs to be borne in mind that the worldly soul has been wandering on account of his own faults. If one thinks about the pain and distress that he might have suffered during the innumerable births that he has taken, it would cause him to shudder. It is rightly said that the bones of all the embodiments of one soul would make a mountain higher than the Himalayas. Similarly, the tears shed on the occasions of the departure of his relatives during different births would exceed the quantity of water in all the oceans. What a pitiable condition arising out of one's own fault! It is therefore necessary that one should take pity upon oneself, and decide to undertake what is required for averting the pain and distress of the worldly life.

It should be noted that the above two interpretations are in no way contradictory to each other. As a matter of fact, one who has compassion for all beings, would surely have compassion for the Self. Similarly one, who has true compassion for oneself, is bound to extend the same to others.

There is also a difference of terminology between the two stanzas. In place of specifying those four aspects as the state of Ätmärthi (as in stanza 38), this stanza calls them the attributes of Jijnäsu, which means one who is intent to know the truth. However, for all practical purposes, Ätmärthi and Jijnäsu convey the same sense, and both are therefore termed here as truth seeker.

તે જિજ્ઞાસુ જીવને, થાય સદ્‍ગુરુબોધ;
તો પામે સમકિતને, વર્તે અંતરશોધ.

||૧૦૯||

Te Jijnäsu Jivne, Thäy Sadgurubodh;
To Päme Samakitne, Varte Antarshodh.

If such a truth seeker gets enlightenment
from a true Guru, he can acquire right
perception and would turn introvert.

- 109 -

Explanation & Discussion:

Once a person qualifies to be a truth seeker and becomes worthy, he understands what the true Guru teaches. It should be noted that the worldly soul must have come across true Gurus during its infinite wandering. He might have been in the assemblies of the omniscient Lords as well. However, the teachings of the Gurus and the sermons of the Lords did not help, because the soul did not have the background (that is, the four characteristics as discussed in the preceding stanza) to grasp the truth. It did not have the receptivity for the purpose.

The aspirant, who has the receptivity, can get enlightenment from the teaching of the true Guru. That would lead him to think that till now he had wrongly identified himself with the body, and failed to see the truth on account of his ego and attachment for worldly objects. He would therefore rely

Amal Shah

upon the Guru and follow his precepts. This is termed here as Samakit. That is the first phase of right perception, which can also be termed as Vyavahär Samakit.

મત દર્શન આગ્રહ તજી, વર્તે સદ્‌ગુરુલક્ષ;
લહે શુદ્ધ સમકિત તે, જેમાં ભેદ ન પક્ષ.

॥૧૧૦॥

Mat Darshan Ägrah Taji, Varte Sadgurulaksha;
Lahe Shuddha Samakit Te, Jemän Bhed Na Paksha.

Giving up beliefs, ideology, and strong opinion, if one acts as directed by a true Guru, he attains pure perception. This is beyond all differences and disputes.

_- 110 -_

Explanation & Discussion:

Worldly souls have been living with different beliefs and ideologies that they might have inherited or gained from sectarian or wrong gurus. Therefore the concepts that they might have formed about spiritual pursuit or about the nature of omniscient and liberated souls are not likely to be true. People, however, tend to hold traditional aspects very strongly. This shows the conceited mentality that constitutes the major obstruction in getting to the right path. Sticking to one's own viewpoint keeps the person away from the truth, and that is the main hurdle in getting to the path of liberation. One therefore needs to give up his beliefs, opinions, etc. and resort to the right Guru in order to learn the truth.

Here the pupil has adopted that approach. He has given up his earlier concepts and beliefs, and has gone to the shelter of the true Guru. He has pondered over the Guru's teaching, and has realized that true nature is beyond the physical state. As such, he tries to stay away from likes and dislikes, from the sense of exultation or grief from any worldly object or situation. He contemplates about true nature. Such contemplation can lead to a glimpse of the pure, unadulterated consciousness. That is, of course, a momentary experience, but the aspirant can never forget its taste. That constitutes the second phase of right perception.

વર્તે નિજસ્વભાવનો, અનુભવ લક્ષ પ્રતીત;
વૃત્તિ વહે નિજભાવમાં, પરમાર્થે સમકિત.

॥૧૧૧॥

Varte Nij Swabhävano, Anubhav Laksha Pratit;
Vrutti Vahe Nij Bhävmän, Paramärthe Samakit.

When there prevails experience, awareness and conviction of one's own nature; and when the tendency flows inward, it is termed right perception in the absolute sense.

- 111 -

Explanation & Discussion:

As the aspirant progresses on the spiritual path, he may increasingly experience the consciousness flowing within. That experience of true nature is identical to all spiritual aspirants, irrespective of the creed they may belong to. That is the blissful experience from which one would not like to turn back. Because of the limitations of embodiment, however, one's attention would be drawn towards the physical needs of the body. But he does not forsake the taste of the truthful state, while attending to the physical aspects. He remains aware of the blissful state even while undertaking activities like eating, making movements, etc. His involvement in all such activities is analogous to an actor playing a given role on stage. In other words, the aspirant continues to remain aware of his true state.

Being the embodied soul, he may, at times, be more involved in physical aspects. He needs to sleep, and therefore, the experience and awareness of the Self may not be maintained at that time. But his conviction about being the soul would not disappear. It is a fact that we remember our name even during sleep. As such, if some one calls that name, we wake up and respond to the call. That happens because our identification with the body remains during sleep. Similarly, a spiritual aspirant with pure perception stays convinced of his true nature during sleep.

A spiritual aspirant of that caliber therefore maintains three streams (Dhäräs) within himself. While staying tuned with the soul, he experiences his true nature; while being involved in physical activities, he remains mindful of his true nature; and during sleep, he retains its conviction. In spiritual terminology, these three streams are called Anubhavdhärä, Lakshadhärä, and Pratitidhärä, respectively. The first stays while one remains absorbed within the self, the second stays during the period he is awake, and the third stays all the time. In other words, he never forsakes his true nature and his tendency continually remains towards that nature. That is termed here as Paramärtha Samakit, meaning right perception in the absolute sense. That is the third phase of right perception, which is also known as Nishchay or experiential Samakit.

વર્ધમાન સમકિત થઈ, ટાળે મિથ્યાભાસ;
ઉદય થાય ચારિત્રનો, વીતરાગપદ વાસ.

॥૧૧૨॥

Vardhamän Samakit Thai, Täle Mithyäbhäs;
Uday Thäy Chäritrano, Vitarägpad Väs.

As the perception enhances, the illusion comes
to the end; with the advent of right conduct,
one abides in the totally detached state.

- 112 -

Explanation & Discussion:

From the time one gains right perception, he starts losing interest in worldly activities and tries to stay away from indulging in defiling instincts. As such, the bondage of Karma continues to be steadily eradicated. The impact of the character-related delusive Karma is mainly experienced in the form of anger, ego, deception, and greed. But there are varying levels of those Karma. The most intense and grossest is Anantänubandhi, meaning the infinitely lasting category, which is overcome at the time of initial right perception. With that perception, as the soul's purity increases, one starts overcoming the less gross forms of that Karma. When one reaches the state described in the last stanza, he gains effective control over all of them except the very subtle one known as Sanjwalan. It virtually means that the aspirant has overcome all defiling instincts. Such a person is in a position to reach the stage that the worldly soul has never attained before. It is called the stage of Apoorvakaran, meaning the unprecedented one. That stage has been described by Shrimad (Vachanämrut # 738) in stanza 13 of Apoorva Avasar (Unprecedented Occasion) as follows:

Em Paräjay Karine Chäritramohano,
Ävun Tyän Jyän Karan Apoorva Bhäv Jo;

Shreni Kshapakatani Karine Äroodhatä,
Ananya Chintan Atishay Shuddha Swabhäv Jo.

It means: "By overcoming the character-related delusion, I may come to the stage of unprecedented mode, and climbing over the (Karma) annihilating ladder, I may undertake the unique contemplation of intensely pure nature."

The spiritual path, beyond the unprecedented stage, is divided into two directions. One way is to go ahead by pacifying the extant Karma, and is known as the pacifying ladder or Upasham Shreni. The other way is to advance by destroying the Karma. That is called the annihilating ladder or Kshapak Shreni, which is referred to in the above verse. The progress on that ladder is swift and steady. By virtue of the destruction of Karma, the perception of such a person becomes perfectly clear and he becomes totally disillusioned of all worldly aspects. All sorts of defiling instincts come to an end, and he reaches the stage known as Kshinamoh, meaning the state devoid of all delusions. The remaining subtle forms of the obscuring and obstructing Karma are overcome at the end of that stage, and the person reaches the state of total detachment and omniscience. This has been termed as Vitarägpad.

કેવળ નિજસ્વભાવનું, અખંડ વર્તે જ્ઞાન;
કહીએ કેવળજ્ઞાન તે, દેહ છતાં નિર્વાણ.

||૧૧૩||

Keval Nij Swabhävanun,   Akhand Varte Jnän;
Kahie Kevaljnän Te, Deh Chhatän Nirvän.

When there prevails uninterrupted awareness of one's nature exclusively, that is termed as omniscience which is liberation despite embodiment.

- 113 -

Explanation & Discussion:

The state of total detachment laid down in the last stanza enables the person to stay aware of his true nature. When such awareness becomes exclusive and remains uninterrupted, that itself is termed as Kevaljnän or omniscience. Thus total detachment is the precursor of omniscience. Here the question may arise, "The Jain tradition conceives of Kevaljnän as a totally blissful state with the capability to know infinitely, to perceive infinitely, and be illumined of everything in the universe, past, present, and future. As such, would the concept laid here not be at variance with that traditional concept?"

By its own nature, the pure soul is inherently imbibed with infinite knowledge, infinite perception, and infinite bliss. But those properties are implicit in remaining aware of its true nature. The question therefore remains of illumination. For that purpose, let us first understand how the illumining capability operates. Its functioning is comparable to that of a mirror. As a mirror presents the image of everything that is lying in front of it, so the knowledge of everything in the universe shines out within omniscience. As the mirror does not take cognizance of the image that it presents, the omniscient Lords also merely stay aware of the Self and remain indifferent to everything else that reflects in their omniscience. Thus the attribute of knowing everything in the universe relates to the capability, not to the actual use of it. The emphasis on that capability is placed in order to point out the magnificence of omniscience to the laymen. The true magnificence, however, lies in the purity of the soul itself.

It is pertinent here to quote Ächäräng Sutra (1-3-4-122). It states: "Egam Jänai Se Savvam Jänai", which means, "He who knows One (Soul), knows all". When a person knows the soul in every respect, it means that his knowing capability has attained the perfect level. Nothing can remain beyond the purview of that capability. It is analogous to switching on a light in order to find something lying in the dark. Suppose we switch on a light to locate a ring that might have slipped from a finger. In that light not only does the ring become visible, but other objects in that area become visible as well. Similarly the state in which one remains fully aware of the Self, also enables him to be aware of everything else. The all-illumining capability is implicit in that state. The state of uninterrupted awareness thus covers all the attributes of omniscience.

But that state is still embodied, and does not therefore represent liberation. However, the omniscient Lords have the same level of perception, knowledge, and bliss that the liberated Lords possess, and since the state of liberation automatically emerges at the end of that life, the omniscient state can be termed as liberation or Nirvän despite embodiment. Thus all the stages from being a truth seeker to the ultimate state of liberation are described in these six (# 108-113) stanzas.

કોટિ વર્ષનું સ્વપ્ન પણ, જાગ્રત થતાં શમાય;
તેમ વિભાવ અનાદિનો, જ્ઞાન થતાં દૂર થાય.

॥૧૧૪॥

Koti Varshnun Swapna Pan, Jägrat Thatän Shamäy;
Tem Vibhäv Anädino, Jnän Thatän Door Thäy.

As a dream lasting even millions of years
subsides at the instance of waking;
the delusion prevailing since infinity
disappears with the advent of enlightenment.

- 114 -

Explanation & Discussion:

The worldly soul has been staying, since time immemorial, with the false identity of the body. As explained earlier, that false identity arises out of ignorance of its own nature. The fact that the said ignorance persists, even though the soul is inherently knowledgeable, shows that the worldly soul does not realize its consciousness and therefore continues to look for happiness from the worldly life. Its indulgence in such a wrong mode is comparable to a dream in which one envisions unreal and imaginary situations.

Sometimes a dream may seem to prevail for an inordinately long period. One can even fantasize to have passed millions of years. All such things seem to happen during a dream. But as soon as one awakes, the dream comes to an end, and with it ends everything that seemed to happen in that state.

Similarly, false identification with the body and other delusions, that have been prevailing since time immemorial, also come to an end, when one becomes aware of his true nature as a result of enlightenment.

છૂટે દેહાધ્યાસ તો, નહિ કર્તા તું કર્મ;
નહિ ભોક્તા તું તેહનો, એ જ ધર્મનો મર્મ.

॥૧૧૫॥

Chhoote Dehädhyäs To, Nahi Kartä Tun Karma;
Nahi Bhoktä Tun Tehano, E Ja Dharmano Marma.

If false identification with the body
ceases, you are no longer Kartä of Karma,
nor do you have to bear the consequences;
that is the essence of religion.

- 115 -

Explanation & Discussion:

As stated earlier, the identification of the soul with the body is the root cause of acquiring Karma. That false identification generates the sense of 'I', 'Me', and 'Mine' with different worldly connections and situations. The activities undertaken with that false identification therefore induce the Karma particles to penetrate and stay with the soul.

That situation would change if the soul realizes its true nature. Then it would automatically come out of false identification. Worldly activities would still take place thereafter, as long as the embodiment continues. But such a soul would not feel attachment for any of them. It would remain an indifferent spectator of whatever happens, and would not indulge in craving or aversion for any situation that may arise from time to time. Thereby it ceases to be Kartä or actuator of Karma and as such, it would not have to bear the consequences.

It is easy to understand that since such a soul does not acquire new Karma, it does not have to bear new consequences. But the question would arise about earlier Karmas that might still remain in balance. How can any soul be absolved from bearing the consequences of old Karma? Does the inexorable law of Karma and its consequences cease to operate in that case?

The law does continue to operate, but it should be remembered that the consequences of Karma are always extended to the body, not to the soul. It is only false identification that leads the soul to identify itself with the body, and to feel that it experiences the said consequences. When such identification falls off, the soul simply perceives and knows what happens to the body but stays free from the pain or pleasure associated with it. It merely remains an indifferent observer. As such, it does not bear those consequences.

Moreover, there is also the possibility of mass scale destruction of the extant Karmas. As a huge stack of cotton can be quickly burnt to ashes by a little spark, most of the Karmas are also extinguished with the spark of enlightenment. As such, getting freed from false identification is the gist of spiritual pursuit. It is therefore termed here as the essence of religion.

એ જ ધર્મથી મોક્ષ છે, તું છો મોક્ષ સ્વરૂપ;
અનંત દર્શન જ્ઞાન તું, અવ્યાબાધ સ્વરૂપ.

||૧૧૬||

E Ja Dharmathi Moksha Chhe, Tun Chho Moksha Swaroop;
Anant Darshan Jnän Tun, Avyäbädh Swaroop.

Only that religion leads to liberation,
you are liberation personified;
you are infinite perception, infinite
knowledge, and unobstructed bliss.

- 116 -

Explanation & Discussion:

The purpose of spiritual pursuit is to seek liberation. But liberation is not to be sought from the outside; it abides within and can be manifested by Self-realization. Since Self-realization can be gained by giving up identification with embodiment, it is stated here that giving up that identification leads to liberation. Self-realization is liberation incarnate. By virtue of that realization, one can experience infinite knowledge, infinite perception, and unobstructed bliss. Those attributes are inherent within the soul, but are simply not manifest at present. One can manifest the experience thereof by Self-realization.

શુદ્ધ બુદ્ધ ચૈતન્યઘન, સ્વયંજ્યોતિ સુખધામ;
બીજું કહીએ કેટલું ? કર વિચાર તો પામ.

||૧૧૭||

Shuddha Buddha Chaitanyaghan, Swayam Jyoti Sukhdhäm;
Bijun Kahie Ketalun? Kar Vichär To Päm.

You are pure, enlightened, consciousness
incarnate, self-radiant, and abode of bliss.
What else can be said? If you rightly
contemplate ~~... realize it.~~

- 117 -

Explanation & Discussion:

The Guru points out that it is really hard to describe the state of liberation. But everything can be identified by its attributes. He therefore lays down five vital attributes of the liberated soul as being pure, enlightened, full of consciousness, self-illuminating, and blissful. Let us consider them one by one.

Purity: The soul is inherently pure. It seems stained by the impact of Karma, but that is only superficial, not real. A pure crystal assumes the color of the object lying within its proximity but does not adopt that color. Similarly, the worldly soul assumes the phenomena of being a male or female, or having a heavenly, human, or animal embodiment, etc. by virtue of its Karma. These merely represent temporary states, which are termed as Paryäy. All the worldly states are thus ever-changing

Paryäys. None of them can alter the inherent purity of the soul. That purity remains latent in the worldly state, and becomes manifest in the liberated state.

Enlightenment: Infinite knowledge is a property of the soul. It has the inherent capability to know everything. For that, it does not need to go to the objects to be known. Those objects themselves are reflected in its knowing capability. It also does not need any external means for exercising its capability. That capability remains obscured by the knowledge-obscuring Karma. Thereupon the soul conceives of itself as devoid of knowledge and tries to gain it with the help of sense organs. It tries to know a surface by the sense of touch, taste by the tongue, odor by the nose, sight by the eyes, and sound by the ears. This happens because the worldly soul has forsaken its infinite capability to know. That capability, however, stays within and can be experienced by getting rid of the impact of the obscuring Karma.

Consciousness: This denotes the capability to remain aware. Awareness is the attribute that belongs only to the soul. No other substance has awareness. Here the term used is Chaitanyaghan, which literally means concrete consciousness. The use of the term "concrete" may seem contradictory since consciousness is intangible and cannot be concrete. However, the word "concrete" is used here to convey that consciousness is pure, perfect, complete, solid (no room for impurity to get in), and abides in every part of the soul. We become aware of whatever happens in any part of the body, because the soul pervades the entire body. The ability of awareness is not fully manifest at present because of the impact of Karma; but it can be fully experienced in the liberated state.

Self-illumination: What shines by itself and does not need any other means for cognition, is called self-illuminating. For instance, the sun is self-illuminating, no lamp is required to see sunshine. We can make it out even from a corner of our house. Similarly the soul is capable to know itself as well as other objects by virtue of its self-illumination.

Abode of bliss: Happiness and bliss are the inherent characteristics of the soul. No other substance has that. True happiness lies within. Since it is not presently experienced, we try to get that happiness from outside. But such happiness is temporary and depends upon external factors. It would disappear when those factors disappear or are removed. True happiness is transcendental. As such, one should stay away from all external factors and cultivate detachment towards all worldly objects. That is the prerequisite for obtaining transcendental happiness. This way, one abides in its own purity and that is the abode of bliss.

No one can accurately describe the state of liberation. It is a subject of experience and not of words. However, these five attributes can give some idea of that state. After describing the same, the Guru therefore says that one has to experience it in order to know it, and the way for that is to contemplate at length about one's true nature. Contemplation is a superb means, which can lead to the depth of the soul. All the latent capabilities of the soul would be awakened thereby.

નિશ્ચય સર્વે જ્ઞાનીનો, આવી અત્ર સમાય;
ઘરી મૌનતા એમ કહી, સહજસમાધિ માંય.

||૧૧૮||

Nishchay Sarve Jnänino, Ävi Atra Samäy;
Dhari Maunatä Em Kahi, Sahaj Samädhi Mäny.

*Conclusions of all the enlightened
ones are covered herein;
so saying, the Guru assumed silence
and got absorbed in innate ecstasy.*

- 118 -

Explanation & Discussion:

Whatever the Guru has said is based on the precepts and doctrines laid down by all the enlightened entities. He has neither added nor subtracted therefrom. As a matter of fact, there is only one path of liberation. It is therefore said here that all the enlightened ones have only one opinion. Their knowledge converges in what has been said here. The Guru has now nothing more to say. As an enlightened entity, he is used to staying within himself. He had opted to speak only for the sake of the pupil. That work now being over, he has adopted silence and assumed the state of innate ecstasy.

Ecstasy denotes the state of beatitude. There are various levels of that state. When one experiences peace of mind on account of health, or freedom from worry, etc., that can also be termed as ecstasy. Such ecstasy is, however, dependent upon some external factors and is not therefore innate. When ecstasy prevails of its own accord without any specific reason, it is termed as innate. That automatically occurs in the delusion-free state. Here the Guru assumes such innate ecstasy. This completes the third and final group of this chapter, containing five stanzas (# 114-118) describing the purity of the soul and liberation.

Chapter 17
Statement of the Pupil's Enlightenment

As mentioned in the last chapter, the dialogue between the preceptor and the pupil came to an end, when the Guru assumed silence and ecstasy. By watching him, the pupil is also induced to turn introvert. Thereby he could experience his soul abiding within. What he had heard from the Guru regarding the six Fundamentals now comes to his experiential level.

In stanza 117, the Guru stated that the pupil can realize his true nature, if he contemplates over it. The pupil did accordingly and thereby realized his true nature. In other words, he got enlightened. Now he does not need to know anything more. However, in order to be sure that what he has realized is right, he likes to state how the concept underlying the six Fundamentals has been assimilated by him.

સદ્ગુરુના ઉપદેશથી, આવ્યું અપૂર્વ ભાન;
નિજપદ નિજમાંહી લહ્યું, દૂર થયું અજ્ઞાન.

॥૧૧૯॥

Sadgurunä Upadeshthi, Ävyun Apoorva Bhän;
Nijpad Nijmänhi Lahyun, Door Thayun Ajnän.

I gained unprecedented sense
by the teaching of your honor;
I realized the true Self within
myself and got rid of ignorance.

- 119 -

Explanation & Discussion:

The pupil acknowledges his debt to the Guru, by whose teaching he attained enlightenment. As a matter of fact, enlightenment abides within and is not to be gained from outside. One has to create the background in which it can be manifested. In other words, one has to be worthy of such manifestation. Such worthiness is termed as Upädän. Since the pupil's Upädän was ready, the teaching of the Guru became instrumental in bringing it out. The pupil is, however, aware that but for the Guru, he could not have manifested it. As such, he acknowledges allegiance to the Guru for gaining enlightenment.

He starts with the first Fundamental relating to the existence of the soul. But humble as he is, he does not state that he is enlightened. He uses the term "Bhän", meaning the sense of Self. Until how, he was groping in the dark and was moving about without knowing the right path. He was trying to comprehend the Self by external modes. That was his ignorance. That ignorance has been removed by the instructions of the Guru and now he has been able to realize that the soul abides within the body. It has come to his experiential level that the relation of the soul to the body is comparable to that of a sword to its sheath or that of a coconut kernel to its outside shell. He had never gained this sense before, so he calls it the unprecedented sense.

ભાસ્યું નિજસ્વરૂપ તે, શુદ્ધ ચેતનારૂપ;
અજર, અમર, અવિનાશી ને, દેહાતીત સ્વરૂપ.

॥૧૨૦॥

Bhäsyun Nij Swaroop Te, Shuddha Chetanä Roop;
Ajar, Amar, Avinäshi Ne, Dehätit Swaroop.

I can visualize my nature as pure
consciousness, which is ageless, immortal,
imperishable, and transcendental.

- 120 -

Explanation & Discussion:

He now turns to the second Fundamental relating to the everlastingness of the soul. For that purpose, he presents the four attributes of the pure soul as being ageless, immortal, indestructible, and transcendental. As stated earlier, the soul is an original substance, which cannot be made by any composition or combination. This is in contrast to the body, which is a composition and is subject to decomposition. No original substance can decompose or perish, thus the soul is imperishable and immortal.

All compositions are subject to wear and tear. It is our experience that the body continues to wear. It grows old, ages, and goes on losing its vitality. This represents the process of a slow but steady decomposition, and the body eventually gets decomposed entirely. The soul is not subject to any such processes. It stays the same forever. During its infinite wandering, it has adopted the shapes of various bodies. It has faced pain and misery, which the bodies have been subjected to in different births. Regardless of all this, none of its (soul's) parts have been worn, damaged, mutilated, or fallen apart. Thus, not being subject to wear and tear, it is ageless and indestructible. Though abiding in the body for the time being, it is not a part thereof. Thus being different and distinct from the embodiment, the soul is transcendental.

Most people detest the impact of aging and therefore try to cover its symptoms of graying hair, wrinkles, etc. by dyeing, cosmetics, etc. Moreover, they generally remain scared of impending death. Thus almost every living being lives in fear relating to old age, disease, death, loss of wealth, loss of respect and status, etc. These fears arise out of considerations for the body. However, after realizing the true nature, one can make out that he is a soul, which is ageless, indestructible, and immortal. It is unbreakable, indivisible, inviolable, and non-combustible. No external situation is capable of afflicting it. As such, he feels free from fright. He has nothing to fear. Such a person stays fearless and indifferent to all states, which are subject to continual changes.

The phrase "Shuddha Chetanä Roop" used in this stanza needs some explanation. It refers to awareness, which is the main attribute of the soul. When one merely stays aware of what happens and remains indifferent to everything else, he can be said to be experiencing pure consciousness, which is the same as Shuddha Chetanä. This is awareness incarnate, and it is also known as Jnän Chetanä. In that state, it is possible to experience infinite bliss that is inherent in the soul. The pupil has now realized his own nature as being such consciousness imbibed with the above-mentioned four attributes.

કર્તા ભોકતા કર્મનો, વિભાવ વર્તે જ્યાંય;
વૃત્તિ વહી નિજભાવમાં, થયો અકર્તા ત્યાંય.

||૧૨૧||

Kartä Bhoktä Karmano, Vibhäv Varte Jyäny;
Vrutti Vahi Nij Bhävmän, Thayo Akartä Tyäny.

When delusion prevails, one is the Kartä
of Karma and bears the consequences;
but when the tendency flows within one's
own nature, he ceases to be the Kartä.

- 121 -

Explanation & Discussion:

Now the pupil talks about the third and fourth Fundamentals of being the Kartä or actuator of Karma and the bearer of its consequences. Karma occurs when one behaves beyond his nature. To know and stay aware is the nature of the soul. If one stays true to that nature, he does not acquire Karma. By virtue of delusion and the impact of Karma, one acts beyond his nature. This action is termed Vibhäv and thereby he acquires Karma. Thus, he becomes Kartä and has to bear the consequences.

Literally, Vibhäv is the opposite of Swabhäv. Since Swabhäv denotes one's nature, Vibhäv would stand for unnatural and is generally interpreted as such. But that is not the interpretation here. Had it been that interpretation, the soul could not be conceived of indulging in Vibhäv, because nothing can go against its nature. Vibhäv is therefore interpreted here as an attribute of the soul, which is beyond (not against) its nature and which the soul is capable of indulging in. If one does not go beyond, he stays within his nature. In other words, his tendency flows within and it does not result in the acquisition of Karma. This was pointed out in stanza 78, where the Guru had said that if the soul stays vigilant about its property, it acts in tune with its nature; and if it does not remain so vigilant, the sense of Kartä and Karma would prevail.

અથવા નિજપરિણામ જે, શુદ્ધ ચેતનારૂપ;
કર્તા ભોક્તા તેહનો, નિર્વિકલ્પ સ્વરૂપ.

||૧૨૨||

Athavä Nij Parinäm Je, Shuddha Chetanä Roop;
Kartä Bhoktä Tehano, Nirvikalpa Swaroop.

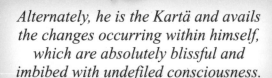

Alternately, he is the Kartä and avails the changes occurring within himself, which are absolutely blissful and imbibed with undefiled consciousness.

- 122 -

Explanation & Discussion:

The pupil continues with the third and fourth Fundamentals. He says that the soul can be treated as the Kartä in some respect. The pure soul is absolute consciousness, which stays tuned to its nature of knowing and witnessing. If the soul had been devoid of any activity in its pure state, it would be turned into a lifeless substance. Staying tuned to its nature is therefore the lasting activity of the soul.

Since every activity can be termed as "Karma" in a special sense, the unimpassioned knowing and witnessing by a pure soul can also be considered "Karma". In that sense, even the liberated soul can be treated as Kartā of such "Karma". Logically therefore it should "bear" the consequences, which it actually does in a way, by experiencing bliss. But "bearing" is a misnomer here. We can talk of the worldly soul as bearing the consequences, because it has the sense of doing something and of bearing the comforts or discomforts arising as the consequence of its Karma. The liberated soul, however, stays in perfect bliss. That results in experiencing pure consciousness.

In other words, bliss is the consequence of remaining within true nature, which is availed by the pure soul. But availing of that bliss is non-conceptual. While availing that, the liberated soul has no concept of `I', `me', or `mine'. That non-conceptuality is the essence of absolute bliss. Thus the question of bearing the consequence does not arise here. Since the liberated soul forever stays blissfully aware of its consciousness, it would simply be a formality to state that such a soul avails of the said consequence.

મોક્ષ કહ્યો નિજશુદ્ધતા, તે પામે તે પંથ;
સમજાવ્યો સંક્ષેપમાં, સકળ માર્ગ નિર્ગ્રંથ.

॥૧૨૩॥

Moksha Kahyo Nij Shuddhatä, Te Päme Te Panth;
Samajävyo Sankshepamän, Sakal Märga Nirgranth.

> *Liberation is self-purification;*
> *the way it is attained is the path;*
> *the entire path of the disentangled*
> *has thus been explained in brief.*
>
> *- 123 -*

Explanation & Discussion:

Now the pupil turns to liberation and its path, which are the fifth and sixth Fundamentals. The Guru said in stanza 113 that uninterrupted awareness of the Self is omniscience. Since liberation necessarily follows it, that itself was termed as liberation. The pupil has correctly grasped this concept, and therefore states that the purity of the soul is liberation. In other words, the infinite purity of knowledge, perception, and bliss, which are the inalienable attributes of the soul, constitutes liberation. As such, it is obvious that the way such purity can be achieved, is the path of liberation. The pupil feels exhilarated that the Guru has explained in brief, the entire path of liberation, which was laid down at length by the omniscient Lords.

The term Nirgranth denotes one who is disentangled or who has no knots. Knots can be external as well as internal. The inclination towards and attachment to the body, relatives, and other situations are the external knots; while anger, ego, deception, greed, etc. are the internal ones. All such knots constitute bondage, and a spiritual aspirant should endeavor to get extricated therefrom. The omniscience emerges only when all types of bondage are eradicated. This obviously involves uprooting the knots. Since the omniscient Lords have already accomplished this, they are free from the knots or any other entanglement. They are therefore termed here as "disentangled". The pupil thus concludes his understanding of the six Fundamentals.

અહો ! અહો ! શ્રી સદ્‌ગુરુ, કરુણાસિંધુ અપાર;
આ પામર પર પ્રભુ કર્યો, અહો ! અહો ! ઉપકાર.

॥૧૨૪॥

Aho! Aho! Shri Sadguru, Karunäsindhu Apär;
Ä Pämar Par Prabhu Karyo, Aho! Aho! Upakär.

Oh! Oh! the blessed Guru! the
unfathomable ocean of compassion!
you have immensely obligated this
down-trodden and miserable being!

- 124 -

Explanation & Discussion:

The pupil now feels elated for the true knowledge that the Guru has passed on to him. How could that be done, unless one is equipped with perfect knowledge and wisdom? The pupil is awe-struck by the way he gained internal peace by listening to the Guru. His state could be compared to a thirsty traveler coming across a clear lake. How would the traveler feel, when he quenches his thirst with the cool water, especially if he had been traveling for long under the hot sun?

However, the traveler's case relates to physical thirst, which is going to arise again even after being quenched. The pupil's was the spiritual thirst, which has been so quenched that it would not arise again. In other words, he has been led to the path of liberation, which he no longer has to seek. He therefore feels immeasurably obligated to the Guru, and experiences an incomparable level of contentment.

A question arises here for our consideration, "The pupil heard from the Guru about the six Fundamentals that we so often listen or recite. Then, how come we do not get enlightenment?" One reason is our unworthiness, and the other is the absence of personal contact with a Guru. Being in the physical presence of a Guru makes a big difference. There have been instances when people experienced realization merely by being in the presence of a Guru. This could happen, even if the Guru does not utter a single word; the accomplishment occurs merely by his presence!

Here, the pupil does not merely have access to a true Guru, but he has actually had the opportunity to listen and have his doubts clarified. It can be imagined how much benefit he may have gained. Therefore, the pupil is overcome by the grace of the Guru. But he does not know how to express his gratitude. As a mark of his esteem for the blessed Guru, only the utterance of "Oh! Oh!" comes out of his mouth.

Then he reflects that the uninterrupted stream of knowledge that he experienced can come out only from a high level of compassion. He remembers that compassion lies at the heart of enlightened entities. The entities live only for undergoing the ordained fate and for the sake of benevolence. That gives the pupil an idea of the level of compassion in the heart of the Guru. He finds it beyond his capacity to measure it, and feels content by devoutly addressing him as the unfathomable ocean of compassion.

The pupil also remembers how ignorant he was prior to the teaching of the Guru. Out of humility, he terms that state as utterly down-trodden. This shows his modesty and humbleness, without which he would not have been receptive to the teaching of the Guru. He feels awe-inspired as he compares his former miserable position to the highly enlightened level of the Guru. He realizes the world of difference between the two, but does not have the words to express it.

While composing Raghuvansh, the great poet Kalidas stated, "How high stands the Lord Raghu's family and how low is my intellect to describe it!" Ächärya Mäntungsuri also states in Bhaktämar Stotra, "I have very little knowledge and happen to be the source of ridicule for the learned; my devotion to You, however, forces me to utter the words of adoration!" The pupil also feels the same way, and stands in utter amazement, which he could express only by uttering "Oh, Oh" once again.

શું પ્રભુચરણ કને ધરું, આત્માથી સૌ હીન;
તે તો પ્રભુએ આપિયો, વર્તું ચરણાધીન.

॥૧૨૫॥

Shun Prabhu Charan Kane Dharun? Ätmäthi Sau Heen;
Te To Prabhue Äpiyo, Vartun Charanädhin.

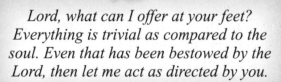

Lord, what can I offer at your feet?
Everything is trivial as compared to the
soul. Even that has been bestowed by the
Lord, then let me act as directed by you.

- 125 -

Explanation & Discussion:

The Guru has given instructions to the pupil out of innate compassion. He does not expect something in return. However, if someone does anything good for us, it is customary to reciprocate. This is normal courtesy. In ancient times, the pupils used to go to the preceptor's hermitage for learning. At the end of the study, they would offer something to their Guru, which was known as Daxinä.

Here the pupil achieved self-realization from the teaching of the Guru, and feels that he should offer something in return. But he cannot think of anything that can be commensurate to the teaching of the Guru. After realizing the significance of the soul, he has lost the importance of everything in the world. As such, he cannot conceive of any worldly object worth offering to the Guru.

As the pupil reflects over the soul, he realizes that it is unique; nothing is comparable to it. Since he realized the existence of the soul by virtue of the Guru's teaching, he feels as good as the soul having been granted by the Guru. Of course, that can not be returned; but he understands that the Guru would feel happy if he follows his precepts. To attach all possible importance to the soul, to consider everything from the point of view of its well being, and thereby to reach an ever increasing purity, constitute the right way of following the Guru. The pupil therefore makes up his mind to pursue that mode.

In spiritual pursuit, acting according to the guidance and instructions of a Guru is vital. Achäräng Sutra therefore states, "Änäe Dhammo, Änäe Tavo". It means that carrying out the instructions of the Guru and omniscient Lords obediently is real religion and penance. It is also said that the continual adoration of the innate compassion of the Guru leads to the realization of the soul. The scriptures even go to the length of saying that mere one word of a Guru, if properly resorted to, can lead to liberation. The pupil therefore decides to offer himself at the lotus feet of the Guru.

આ દેહાદિ આજથી, વર્તો પ્રભુ આધીન;
દાસ, દાસ હું દાસ છું, તેહ પ્રભુનો દીન.

॥૧૨૬॥

Ä Dehädi Äjathi, Varto Prabhu Ädhin;
Däs, Däs Hun Däs Chhun, Teh Prabhuno Deen.

From now onward, let this body, etc.
behave as commanded by the Lord;
and let me be a servant, very humble,
the most humble servant of the Lord.
- 126 -

Explanation & Discussion:

Thinking that he had nothing to offer to the Guru, the pupil was overtaken by that inability. He almost despised himself for not being able to do anything commensurate to the teaching of the Guru. In view of the significance of carrying out the command, he at last decides to act in accordance with the commands of the Guru and to behave as his most humble servant. This shows his utmost modesty and his sense of subservience.

Such subservience may appear rather unbecoming to Westerners. But Indian culture is rapt with it. There are several cases when kings have offered even their kingdoms to their Gurus. King Kumärpäl had offered the kingdom of Gujarät to his Guru Hemchandrächärya, and Shiväji had presented his kingdom to Guru Samarth Swämi Rämdäs. In both of these cases the kings had taken their offerings back with the stipulation that they would reign in the interest of religion. The pupil surrenders everything at the holy feet of the Guru, and resolves that his body, senses, mind, intellect, and everything else should prevail in accordance with the instructions (and command) of the Guru. Since he does not want to waste any time for that purpose, he decides to put it into practice right away. In utmost sincerity and humbleness, he thinks of and addresses the Guru as Prabhu i.e., Lord.

षट् स्थानक સમજાવીને, ભિન્ન બતાવ્યો આપ;
મ્યાન થકી તરવારવત્, એ ઉપકાર અમાપ.

॥૧૨૭॥

Shat Sthänak Samajävine, Bhinna Batävyo Äp;
Myän Thaki Tarvarvat, E Upakär Amäp.

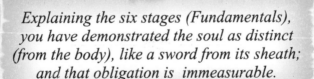

Explaining the six stages (Fundamentals),
you have demonstrated the soul as distinct
(from the body), like a sword from its sheath;
and that obligation is immeasurable.

- 127 -

Explanation & Discussion:

The Guru has removed all of the pupil's doubts pertaining to the soul, and has clearly shown the soul as distinct from the body. This is comparable to a sword and a sheath. When a sword is within its sheath, its separate existence from the sheath is not visible. However, every one, even an illiterate person knows that the sword is separate from the sheath. Moreover, whether the sheath is studded with gold or diamonds does not make any difference to the sword. It is always made of sharp steel. Similarly, the soul abiding within a body is not apparent to the sight, but its existence, separate from the body, can be understood by spiritual insight. Whether the body is strong or weak, old or young, beautiful or ugly, male or female, makes no difference to the soul. It remains the same forever.

These six Fundamentals pertain to the soul, and are laid down for the purpose of self-realization. The realization is not away from the Self, but the worldly soul has been staying away from that on account of the longings and desires arising from its identification with the body. The body is ephemeral, mortal, and subject to decomposition; while the soul is a substance on its own and stays forever. Such incompatible substances can never be the same. It is only due to delusion that they are perceived as one. That long standing delusion has been removed by the Guru. As such his obligation in the matter could hardly be exaggerated. The pupil therefore concludes his statement by acknowledging that his debt to the Guru is immeasurable.

Chapter 18: Conclusion

Now we come to the concluding part. The six Fundamentals have been explained to the full satisfaction of the pupil, but there are some vital aspects that might have escaped his attention. They are therefore brought out in the form of conclusion in the following stanzas. It should be noticed that most of the stanzas state something unique, worth remembering by heart. Some of them are worth displaying on walls as constant reminders.

દર્શન ષટે સમાય છે, આ ષટ્ સ્થાનક માંહી;
વિચારતાં વિસ્તારથી, સંશય રહે ન કાંઈ.

॥૧૨૮॥

Darshan Shate Samäy Chhe, Ä Shat Sthänak Mänhi;
Vichärtän Vistärthi, Sanshay Rahe Na Känyi.

All six schools of thought are covered in these six stages (Fundamentals);no doubt will linger on that, if pondered at length.

- 128 -

Explanation & Discussion:

As it was pointed out in stanza 44, there are mainly six schools of thought and their gist is covered in these six Fundamentals. This may perhaps seem to be a tall claim, because scholars belonging to those schools have produced voluminous literature that cannot be comprehended even during the whole life time. It is, however, clear that the viewpoints of all of them revolve around the existence or non-existence of soul and an almighty Creator. These six Fundamentals cover those aspects and conclusively show the existence of soul and non-existence of the almighty. If one contemplates over that at length, he would realize that nothing substantially remains to be stated.

The information about the six schools was briefly given while explaining the above mentioned stanza. The voluminous literature of those different schools is full of arguments in favor of the authors' viewpoints and against those who differ from them. That is hardly necessary and what is said in this Ätmasiddhi Shästra is enough for comprehending the truth. But there is scope for elaborating what is laid down therein.

આત્મભ્રાંતિ સમ રોગ નહિ, સદ્ગુરુ વૈધ સુજાણ;
ગુરુ આજ્ઞા સમ પથ્ય નહિ, ઔષધ વિચાર ધ્યાન.

॥૧૨૯॥

Ätmabhränti Sam Rog Nahi, Sadguru Vaidya Sujän;
Guruäjnä Sam Pathya Nahi, Aushadh Vichär Dhyän.

There is no disease like self-delusion;
a true Guru is an expert spiritual
doctor; there is no diet like the precepts
of the Guru; contemplation and
meditation comprise the medication.
- 129 -

Explanation & Discussion:

This is a very important stanza, which can be considered a highly precious spiritual jewel. It contains the substance of the entire spiritual realm. The four parts of the stanza lay down four highly valuable statements that need to be kept in mind by every one at all times.

The first part refers to Ätmabhränti, which means illusion about the Self. Due to the ignorance of the true Self, the worldly beings maintain illusion about their own nature. Forsaking the soul, they identify themselves with the body and its surroundings. As such, they indulge in attachment for some aspects and resentment towards others. This illusion is the main disease. The physical diseases can be cured by right treatment. Even if a disease is found incurable, it ends with death. However, illusion about the Self has been prevailing since time immemorial, and has continued birth after birth. Moreover, the worldly soul is not even aware of that disease, and therefore does not resort to any means for curing the same. Hence it is the most chronic disease.

If a person knows his disease, he goes to a doctor. Or if he is not aware of the disease, and happens to see a doctor, the latter can diagnose the disease and provide necessary treatment. If that doctor is an expert physician, the disease may be cured, or would at least come under control by his treatment. But how can one find a physician for the disease of illusion? The reply, provided in the second part of the stanza, states that a true Guru is the expert spiritual physician. The true Guru has not obtained that expertise (self-realization) by reading or other external resources. That expertise is within. He has therefore dived deep and has attained it. As such, he is the most reliable doctor for this disease.

When a doctor starts the treatment, he may insist upon some dietary restrictions, which can help in bringing the disease under control. That is called Pathya. This aspect is emphasized considerably in the Indian system of medicine. For instance, a diabetic patient is advised to reduce or avoid sweets and fats. The third part of the stanza therefore states that the instructions of a Guru constitute the dietary directives for controlling the disease. The last part deals with medication. It prescribes that contemplating about the nature of the soul and meditating over it constitute the medication to overcome the disease.

It is stated that a spiritual aspirant should stay in meditation as long as possible and when he cannot do that, he should resort to contemplation. These are two primary aspects that the worldly soul needs to concentrate on. It is obvious that no one wants to get unhappiness or encounter death. It can therefore be surmised that every living being looks for lasting happiness and immortality. Since these attributes are inherent within the soul, it would be helpful to ponder over the same during contemplation and meditation.

But this is subject to the instructions (commands) of the Guru. It is noticed that many people resort to contemplation and meditation, but their illusion of the Self does not disappear. This is due to the fact that they ignore the third stipulation (to follow the Guru's instructions). Therefore, if one follows the instructions of the Guru and resorts to the prescription of contemplation and meditation, his longstanding disease of illusion would, no doubt, be cured. If one thinks deeply over this, he will understand that there is no other way to cure illusion.

જો ઇચ્છો પરમાર્થ તો, કરો સત્ય પુરુષાર્થ;
ભવસ્થિતિ આદિ નામ લઈ, છેદો નહિ આત્માર્થ.

॥૧૩૦॥

Jo Ichchho Paramärtha To, Karo Satya Purushärtha;
Bhavsthiti Ädi Näm Lai, Chhedo Nahi Ätmärtha.

Strive real hard if you want to
attain absolute truth; do not
forsake the quest for truth
in the name of destiny, fate, etc.

- 130 -

Explanation & Discussion:

There are people who wish to attain the blissful state and like to endeavor for it. There are also those, who think that every thing happens at the destined time and our endeavoring is of no avail. The theory of Krambaddha Paryäy, for instance, states that there is a strict chronological order according to which every thing happens, and it is not possible to change or modify that order. Accordingly, what one needs to do is understand the true nature of the soul as well as its ultimate state of liberation, and then wait for the time when that state is destined to materialize. From their point of view, right understanding and the willingness to wait constitute the right endeavor.

This theory gives too much importance to the time factor. Jainism states nature (Swabhäv), right endeavor (Purushärtha), instrumental factors (Nimitta), time (Käl), and destiny (Bhavitavyatä) as the five factors that are necessary for any change to occur. Swabhäv indicates the potential of the subject to undergo a certain change. Purushärtha indicates the effort for effecting the change. Nimitta indicates the auxiliaries to be associated for bringing out the change. Käl shows the right time for the purpose, and Bhavitavyatä shows that the change is going to take place. The last one is also termed as Bhavsthiti.

All these five factors are necessary. Swabhäv is, of course, the predominant factor, because nothing can happen without potential. For instance, sand does not have the potential to yield oil; hence however much one may try, oil cannot be extracted out of sand. But this aspect has only a theoretical significance, because no one would try to do anything unless there is potential for the same.

Endeavor is therefore the first vital factor. In a way, it covers the other factors. For instance, bringing together the auxiliaries can be considered a part of the endeavor. The selection of the right time is inherent in the right endeavor, because no sensible person would make the endeavor at the wrong time. Destiny is a double edged sword. Sometimes it yields to the right endeavor and sometimes it does not. That depends upon the Karma.

Bhavsthiti is sometimes taken as a state that leads to the end of the life cycle (liberation). But such a state cannot come forth in the absence of right perception, and that perception cannot arise without endeavoring for the purpose. Thus endeavor (Purushärtha) is the most vital factor. Of the five factors, that is the only one which is under our control in the present. The seers have therefore advised to undertake Purushärtha or right endeavor by assuming that destiny will be helpful. Therefore, this stanza exhorts the aspirants to resort to the right endeavor for realizing the true nature. The right endeavor consists of giving up the tendency of indulging in craving or aversion for worldly objects. Hence one should earnestly strive to overcome the sense of craving and aversion, and not indulge in indolence in the name of destined fate.

નિશ્ચયવાણી સાંભળી, સાધન તજવાં નો'ય;
નિશ્ચય રાખી લક્ષમાં, સાધન કરવાં સોય.

॥૧૩૧॥

Nishchay Väni Sämbhali, Sädhan Tajvän N'oy;
Nishchay Räkhi Lakshamän, Sädhan Karvän Soy.

Do not give up the means after hearing
about the absolute viewpoint; make
proper use of the means by keeping
the absolute viewpoint in mind.

- 131 -

Explanation & Discussion:

This stanza provides a useful hint to the people unduly resorting to the absolute viewpoint, which was explained in Chapter 2. That view emphasizes the basic nature of the pure soul as uninteracting, unbound, unaffected, and every soul as good as the liberated one. Its purpose is to indicate the ultimate potential of the soul so that one may endeavor to manifest the potential. One must remember that though soul is inherently pure, currently it is under the impact of Karma. Although the existing Karma is eventually stripped off by bearing the consequences, the worldly soul acquires new Karma while bearing the fruits of the old Karma, due to its craving and aversion. Therefore one has to avoid such indulgence and for that purpose, he needs to resort to the appropriate means.

The people resorting to the absolute point of view conceive of the pure state of the soul as existing forever. They believe that the soul cannot be stained or defiled, and the soul's apparent impurity is illusory. They conclude, incorrectly, that nothing needs to be done to achieve the soul's purity. They remain contented with the mere knowledge of the original pure state, and stand against making any specific effort to manifest it.

Such people are called bare knowledgeable.

This stanza states that only resorting to the absolute viewpoint is not helpful. One should keep that absolute state as the objective, and try to manifest it by resorting to worship, devotion, right conduct, Self-study, etc. The true state cannot arise without cultivating detachment and renouncement, and for that purpose one needs to practice restraints, austerities, etc. Liberation can be attained by the right combination of knowledge and practice. Any one of them to the exclusion of the other would not serve the purpose.

નય નિશ્ચય એકાંતથી, આમાં નથી કહેલ;
એકાંતે વ્યવહાર નહિ, બન્ને સાથ રહેલ.

॥૧૩૨॥

Nay Nishchay Ekäntathi, Ämän Nathi Kahel;
Ekänte Vyavahär Nahi, Banne Säth Rahel.

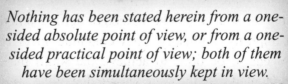

Nothing has been stated herein from a one-sided absolute point of view, or from a one-sided practical point of view; both of them have been simultaneously kept in view.

- 132 -

Explanation & Discussion:

What was implicitly said in the previous stanza is explicitly presented in this stanza. There are mainly two ways of looking at anything. One is the absolute (real) viewpoint, which is known as Nishchay Nay. The other is the practical (worldly) one, which is known as Vyavahär Nay. Both of them are equally important. The absolute viewpoint, without the practical one, would lead to illusion. It can generate fantasy and keep one self-complacent. There is thus a danger of spiritually falling downward by relying upon it exclusively.

Similarly, resorting exclusively to the practical viewpoint is also fraught with danger. That can lead to a wild thicket of rituality. One is tempted to think that lifeless worship, observance of restraints and austerities, etc. would result in the eradication of Karma. Thereby, he expects to achieve the favorable situation. He is led to believe that the increasing level of such observances would lead to an ever-increasing eradication of Karma, and thereby can attain the Karmaless state.

Such one-sided views are not helpful in spiritual pursuit. One should remember that nothing can be achieved by mere knowledge or by mere bodily activities. No activity, in the absence of soul-orientation, can do any lasting good; nor does pure concept accomplish anything in the absence of right practice. While it is necessary to know about the absolute state, it is also necessary to resort to the means for manifesting that state. One therefore needs to resort to both the viewpoints together. That is Syädväd. Resorting to any one of them, exclusive of the other, amounts to Ekänt, which should be avoided. This Ätmasiddhi Shästra has been composed while simultaneously keeping in mind both these views.

> ગચ્છમતની જે કલ્પના, તે નહિ સદ્વ્યવહાર;
> ભાન નહીં નિજરૂપનું, તે નિશ્ચય નહિ સાર.
>
> ॥૧૩૩॥

Gachchhamatni Je Kalpanä, Te Nahi Sadvyavahär;
Bhän Nahi Nij Roopanun, Te Nishchay Nahi Sär.

The concepts based on sect or creed
do not constitute right practice; the
view unrelated to the nature of Self
does not lead to absolute truth.

- 133 -

Explanation & Discussion:

There are different religions, and various sects & sub-sects in the same religion. People belonging to such sects and sub-sects insist that what they believe is right. That amounts to believing that truth would differ from religion to religion and creed to creed. Truth is one and indivisible. Therefore it is said that all the enlightened persons have the same belief and they hold the same opinion. As such, only what an enlightened person says should be accepted as truth, or that which accords with the nature of Self and leads to the path of liberation should be adopted as truth.

This may be acceptable in principle. But differences arise when it comes to the question of practice. Many sects and sub-sects arose by way of revolt against the established order. The people at the helm of affairs turned towards misusing their authority. The saintly people, who resented such misuse, therefore raised the flag of revolt and set up new standards of conduct. Unfortunately, the spirit behind those standards was lost with the passage of time. The lay followers, however, continued to stick to those standards without making out the implications thereof. That gave rise to the lifeless rituals prevalent within different sects and sub-sects. They are mechanically resorted to in the name of Vyavahär. The essence of spiritual pursuit lies in gaining equanimity, and that can be done by cultivating detachment and by pacifying the passions. Only that Vyavahär should therefore be undertaken, which leads to detachment and to the calming down of the passions.

Similarly, the absolute concept is useful only to those who have experienced the purity of the soul. The illusory identification with the body is the root cause of the worldly life and that identification cannot cease simply by talking about the absolute nature of the soul. Aside from realizing the nature of the soul, the absolute viewpoint should be helpful in leading to right practice (Sadvyavahär). Otherwise, it would simply be meaningless.

As it stands at present, often there is a lack of purpose in the so-called Vyavahär. Similarly, there seems to be little noticeable spiritual development among the holders of the absolute point of view. The situation is thus less than satisfactory, and there is scope for improvement on both sides.

આગળ જ્ઞાની થઈ ગયા, વર્તમાનમાં હોય;
થાશે કાળ ભવિષ્યમાં, માર્ગભેદ નહિ કોય.

||૧૩૪||

Ägal Jnäni Thai Gayä, Vartamänmän Hoy;
Thäshe Käl Bhavishyamän, Märgabhed Nahi Koy.

> *There had been enlightened persons*
> *in the past, they are at present,*
> *they will be in the future; but their*
> *paths are not different in any way.*
>
> *- 134 -*

Explanation & Discussion:

While discussing the last stanza, it was pointed out that in view of the different beliefs of sects and sub-sects, one should accept what the enlightened person says. In that connection, it is here said that enlightened beings arise in every epoch. We know from history that there were such entities in past, and there are such entities at present also, though we may not be aware of them. For instance, when Shrimad was alive in the 19th century, very few people knew that he was enlightened. Thus, our unawareness does not mean that there cannot be such entities now. Similarly, they are bound to arise in the future. All of them describe the same path. There is no difference in their outlook. There is only one path of liberation. The objective is to be free from the continuing cycle of birth and death, and the path for that purpose is right insight and the endeavor to stay away from attachment and resentment.

સર્વ જીવ છે સિદ્ધ સમ, જે સમજે તે થાય;
સદ્ગુરુઆજ્ઞા જિનદશા, નિમિત્ત કારણ માંય.

॥૧૩૫॥

Sarva Jiv Chhe Siddha Sam, Je Samaje Te Thäy;
Sadguruäjnä Jinadashä, Nimitta Käran Mäny.

All souls are like liberated ones; one
who understands gets liberated. Precepts
of the true Guru and the state of omniscience
are among the instrumental causes.

- 135 -

Explanation & Discussion:

This is a very significant stanza, which lays down the entire canon from the absolute as well as the practical view points. All souls have the same properties of perception, knowledge, and bliss. Therefore, from the absolute viewpoint there is no difference between the liberated souls and the worldly ones. In reality, however, there is a difference. The liberated souls have manifested those properties, while the worldly ones have not. If one ignores or overlooks that reality, he will never be liberated. He, who knows the inherent attributes of the soul and accepts the present reality, would definitely strive to manifest the inherent capabilities and attain liberation. The first line of the stanza therefore states that one who understands the reality can get liberated.

Every objective needs some means that become instrumental in achieving that objective. Such means are termed as Nimitta. The means can be live or lifeless. For instance, a pot is made out of earth, while the potter, wheel, etc. are instrumental in making it. The second line of this stanza lays down that the commandments of the Guru and the state of the omniscient Lords are instrumental in attaining liberation. If therefore one wants to get liberated, he needs to carry out the commandments of the Guru while keeping the state of the Lord as his objective.

The main commandments of the Guru are to calm down the defiling instincts. For that purpose one should remain meticulously vigilant while undertaking any activity. He should stay vigilant while moving, speaking, receiving what is needed, displacing anything, and disposing of useless material. These are termed as the five Samities. The state of the Lord symbolizes the steadiness of mind, speech, and body. These are known as the three Gupties. The five Samities and three Gupties constitute the essence of Jain canons. They are collectively called Ashtapravachanmätä, meaning the eightfold message of the omniscient's sermon, which is considered as good as motherly affection.

ઉપાદાનનું નામ લઈ, એ જે તજે નિમિત્ત;
પામે નહિ સિદ્ધત્વને, રહે ભ્રાંતિમાં સ્થિત.

॥૧૩૬॥

Upädänanun Näm Lai, E Je Taje Nimitta;
Päme Nahi Siddhatvane, Rahe Bhräntimän Sthit.

> *One, who forsakes the instrumental*
> *factors in the name of absolute*
> *causation, would stay deluded and*
> *cannot attain the liberated state.*
>
> *- 136 -*

Explanation & Discussion:

This stanza is also very significant as it lays down the theory of causation in the right perspective. Every thing occurs by virtue of several factors, which are termed as causes. All such factors can be classified into two categories of Upädän and Nimitta. Upädän is the absolute cause. It relates to the matter or the substance, which undergoes change and is therefore the cause of its own changing states. For instance, for making an earthen pot, earth is the basic requirement, without which the pot cannot be made. If one tries to make it from sand or water, he cannot do it. This is because earth has the potential to be turned into a pot, while sand or water does not. Earth is therefore termed as the Upädän or absolute cause of the pot. The instrumental cause is termed as Nimitta, which has been explained above.

The potential of something to turn into some other form or state is called its Upädän. The soul, because of its potential to attain the liberated state, is the Upädän for the state of liberation. Lifeless objects do not have that potential of liberation, and do not therefore become Upädän for that purpose. Thus the potential to do something or to turn into some form is the essential aspect of Upädän. This should be kept in mind, because often there is misunderstanding about this.

Some people have the tendency to underrate the importance of Nimitta. They contend that Upädän is the only real cause, and when something is going to happen, Nimitta is bound to be there. Actually both of them are equally essential. For instance, the earth may be lying somewhere for millions of years, but it does not turn into a pot, until some one picks it up, cultivates it by mixing it with water, and puts it on a turning wheel. Similarly, in spite of the potential to attain liberation, the worldly souls have been wandering since long in absence of the right guidance and active vigor.

This stanza states that if one insists upon Upädän and forsakes Nimitta, he cannot attain liberation. By virtue of the knowledge about the soul, one may think of the state of liberation to emerge out of the soul's nature and might even call for that state to emerge from within. But without heeding and carrying out the commandments of the Guru and without keeping the state of omniscience as his objective, he cannot attain liberation. If someone therefore exclusively insists on Upädän, he would merely stay bare knowledgeable. He is destined to remain under delusion, and would never attain liberation.

મુખથી જ્ઞાન કથે અને, અંતર્ છૂટ્યો ન મોહ;
તે પામર પ્રાણી કરે, માત્ર જ્ઞાનીનો દ્રોહ.

॥૧૩૭॥

Mukhathi Jnän Kathe Ane, Antar Chhutyo Na Moh;
Te Pämar Präni Kare, Mätra Jnänino Droh.

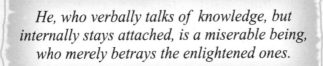

He, who verbally talks of knowledge, but
internally stays attached, is a miserable being,
who merely betrays the enlightened ones.

- 137 -

Explanation & Discussion:

The above stated position of the bare knowledgeable person is described here in a different perspective. Such a person has simply learnt about the blissful potential of the soul but has not done anything to realize it. Had he realized this, his ego and attachment for worldly objects would have melted down. Instead of overcoming ego and attachment, the bare knowledgeable person would contend that attachment to worldly objects relates to the body and mind; soul has nothing to do with it. This displays his infatuation. He overlooks the fact that the lifeless body does not have any longing or desire, it is only by virtue of the soul's inspiration that the body acts in a particular way. By thinking and talking about enlightenment without overcoming attachment and infatuation, one actually works against the concept of enlightenment.

Since such a person is likely to continue indulging in the wrong mode, it would create an adverse impression in the minds of others. They may also be led to think that his Guru might be like him. Thus his behavior becomes instrumental in casting aspersion on the enlightenment of the Guru. By being bare knowledgeable, such a person thus betrays the image of the enlightened entity.

દયા, શાંતિ, સમતા, ક્ષમા, સત્ય, ત્યાગ, વૈરાગ્ય;
હોય મુમુક્ષુ ઘટ વિષે, એહ સદાય સુજાગ્ય.

॥૧૩૮॥

Dayä, Shänti, Samatä, Kshamä, Satya, Tyäg, Vairägya;
Hoy Mumukshu Ghat Vishe, Eh Sadäy Sujägya.

Compassion, tranquility, equanimity,
forgiveness, truth, renouncement,
and detachment are ever-present in
the heart of a liberation seeker.

- 138 -

Explanation & Discussion:

The term Mumukshu literally means one who is desirous of liberation. Shrimad has defined the term (Vachanämrut # 254) as one who, being tired of all the sense of attachment and infatuation, endeavors only for liberation. We call him a liberation seeker or truth seeker. This stanza describes the following seven attributes as essential for a real liberation seeker.

Dayä: This means compassion. It is emphasized as the basis of religion, and denotes the softening of the heart on seeing the pitiable condition of others. The liberation seeker has compassion for himself as well as for others. Such a person knows that indulgence in craving and aversion has caused the unending series of birth and death, and as such has subjected himself to untold misery and pain. He would therefore try to avoid such indulgence so as to avert that misery and pain. This is termed as self-compassion. Disaffection for worldly wandering also amounts to self-compassion.

One, who has self-compassion, is invariably compassionate to others. Realization of sufferings borne by him keeps him aware that if he causes pain to others, he will acquire unwholesome Karma that would again extend suffering to him. As such, not only does he refrain from causing any suffering, but he would also try to restrain others from causing the same. Out of compassion, he would lead other beings towards the right path so that they can be free from suffering.

Shānti: This means peace. But the concept of peace is not restricted to outward calmness. The emphasis is on internal peace, which arises when one feels tired of all worldly activities and stays merely as an unimpassioned spectator of whatever happens. Worry, diseases, and concern (known as Ādhi, Vyādhi, and Upādhi) are the three types of distress in the worldly life. By being free from all such distress and affliction, one can experience the peace and tranquility within.

Samatā: This means equanimity. It denotes staying indifferent to favorable as well as unfavorable situations. The equanimous person is free from the sense of likes or dislikes, pleasure or pain, etc. He stays above the sense of respect and disrespect or friends and foes, and maintains his equanimity in all circumstances.

Kshamā: This means forgiveness. If we perceive someone as not behaving to our expectations, we are prone to become angry. The attribute of Kshamā prescribes to forgive those who seem to be at fault. Lord Mahavir forgave all those who caused him pain and even terrible distress. Forgiving is a great virtue. It is vitally and closely related to the concept of Ahinsā (non-violence). All possible emphasis is therefore put on forgiveness.

Satya: This means truth, but it does not merely mean not to lie. Truth has a far wider connotation. It indicates everlastingness. Whatever lasts forever is truth. Since the soul is everlasting, conviction of the soul is real truth. In routine life too, unless one has such a conviction, he would tend to resort to lies for the sake of worldly benefits. But the person, who is convinced of the soul, would remain scared of such indulgence. The understanding of the soul is therefore considered the supreme truth.

Tyäg: Literally this means giving up. It can be external as well as internal. Renouncing the worldly objects is external Tyäg. Internally, it means giving up of craving, aversion, and all other instincts, which are extraneous to the soul. Once a person has grasped the truth, giving up the extraneous aspects automatically comes forth.

Vairägya: This means detachment. It denotes absence of attachment and resentment. Renouncement and detachment are mostly used together and they seem to be alike. The difference between the two is that detachment is a state of mind, while renouncement indicates physically giving up.

These seven attributes are interrelated, and can be developed one after another starting with compassion. One, who has the compassion at heart, tries to maintain peace of mind. Peace can lead to equanimity, and that can give rise to forgiveness. When all of these attributes are in place, one can think of resorting to truth. In other words, he tries to remain tuned to the soul. For staying that way, one has to give up all those aspects that go against the well being of the soul. If he cannot give up some of them, he at least develops detachment for them. All these attributes help in maintaining Self-awareness, and are indicative of one as a liberation seeker. If one does not hold them, he is evidentally not a liberation seeker. It is therefore said here that they are always present in the heart of a truth seeker.

મોહભાવ ક્ષય હોય જ્યાં, અથવા હોય પ્રશાંત;
તે કહીએ જ્ઞાનીદશા, બાકી કહીએ ભ્રાંત.

||૧૩૯||

Mohbhäv Kshay Hoy Jyän, Athavä Hoy Prashänt;
Te Kahie Jnäni Dashä, Bäki Kahie Bhränt.

The state, where the sense of
attachment is either eradicated or
is calmed down, is called the
enlightened one; all else is delusion.

- 139 -

Explanation & Discussion:

Throughout the present discussion, we had the occasions to talk about an enlightened entity and the enlightenment gained by his grace. The characteristics of the true Guru given in stanza 10 would be helpful in identifying an enlightened entity, but how does one make out whether he has gained enlightenment? This stanza gives a yardstick for that purpose. It states that enlightenment arises only when delusion is overcome. As discussed earlier, enlightenment is inherent in the soul, but it has been overshadowed by the impact of delusion. If that delusion is removed, enlightenment becomes manifested.

Whether it is perception-related or character-related, delusion can be overcome by the process of destruction or by pacification. In either of these cases, the deluding Karma ceases to be operative. As such, enlightenment shines out.

Enlightenment changes one's entire outlook. In that light, he clearly makes out the utter transitory nature of the worldly life. The worldly objects therefore no longer seem attractive to him. That absence of attachment towards the worldly life is itself the sign of overcoming   delusion. Those, who think of enlightenment while remaining attached to worldly aspects, merely delude themselves. Pitiable is the state of such deluded beings!

સકળ જગત તે એંઠવત્, અથવા સ્વપ્ન સમાન;
તે કહીએ જ્ઞાનીદશા, બાકી વાચાજ્ઞાન.

||૧૪૦||

Sakal Jagat Te Enthvat, Athavä Swapna Samän;
Te Kahie Jnäni Dashä, Bäki Vächäjnän.

When the entire universe looks like
used (rejected) food or a dream,
it is called the enlightened state;
otherwise it is mere verbal knowledge.

- 140 -

Explanation & Discussion:

This stanza gives other significant signs of enlightenment. To an enlightened person, the entire universe seems like left over or rejected food. This concept can be better understood by analyzing the worldly phenomenon. It is now a scientific truth that the world consists of infinite atomic particles pervading everywhere. The physical bodies as well as everything else in the world are composed of such particles. The worldly souls adopt the particles at the time of formation of the bodies, and leave them at the time of death. In addition to this, they also adopt such particles in the form of Karma. The process of adopting and leaving has thus been going on continuously in each lifetime. During the infinite time that has elapsed, every particle in the world must have been adopted by each soul several times. As such, the entire world consists of the particles that have been adopted and released. Is that situation not comparable to used or left over food?

To the enlightened, the entire universe therefore seems like used rejected food and is considered worthless. It is similar to the things that need to be disposed of like vomited food. To take an illustration from routine life, if left over or vomited food is strewn over the dining table, no one would like to occupy that place. To the enlightened beings, every thing in the universe is comparable to that situation. On this very account, when Rathnemi, the brother of Lord Neminäth, displayed his attachment for Räjul, she brought him back to detachment by comparing his attachment to vomited food.

As an alternative, the stanza states that an enlightened person looks at everything in the world as a dream. Quite a few fascinating objects or situations may appear in a dream and the dreamer may even enjoy the same. But dreams are not true, as they disappear at the instant of awaking. As the dreaming person wakes up, he realizes that he was simply availing of the dream, and the fanciful situations presented had no reality. Similarly, all the worldly situations look ephemeral and unrealistic to enlightened beings.

The identification and attachment that the worldly soul feels with the body and other environments is thus illusory, and arises out of its ignorance and unawareness of the self. The enlightened being considers all worldly situations dreamlike, and therefore does not attach importance to any of them. Since it is not possible to get the truth without overcoming illusion, only he who has set aside the illusion of the dreaming state, can be considered enlightened. Those so-called enlightened persons who do not satisfy this criterion, are merely verbally knowledgeable.

સ્થાનક પાંચ વિચારીને, છઠ્ઠે વર્તે જેહ;
પામે સ્થાનક પાંચમું, એમાં નહિ સંદેહ.

॥૧૪૧॥

Sthänak Pänch Vichärine, Chhatthe Varte Jeh;
Päme Sthänak Pänchmun, Emän Nahi Sandeh.

Pondering over the (first) five
stages (Fundamentals), if one acts as
stated in the sixth, he would undoubtedly
attain the fifth (liberation) stage.

- 141 -

Explanation & Discussion:

The Letter of Six Fundamentals (Appendix-II) states that the enlightened entities have described the teaching of these Fundamentals for the sake of removing the sense of ego and attachment of the worldly soul. That sense arises from one's dreaming state, which has been prevailing since the time without beginning. If the soul realizes that its true nature is beyond that state, it would easily come out of it and gain right perception. By acquiring right perception, it would attain liberation in the sense of realizing its true Self. Contemplation of these Fundamentals can thus lead it to experiencing its own natural purity, perfection, imperishability, and infinite bliss.

Of the six Fundamentals, the first five need to be properly understood, and the last is meant for practicing. This stanza therefore lays down that if one digests the first five Fundamentals by contemplating over them, and then if he puts into practice what is stated in the sixth, he would surely attain liberation. In other words, if one is convinced of the soul and its wandering, and proceeds on the path of liberation as stated in the sixth, he would reach the destination (liberation). Since liberation (Moksha) is dealt with in the fifth Fundamental, it is said that he would attain the fifth stage. It should be noted that this stanza does not promise that reward to those who merely read or listen to this scripture (Ätmasiddhi Shästra), as is often said or believed. It stipulates the strict conditions of understanding and contemplating the first five Fundamentals, and then earnestly practicing the sixth for attaining the said reward.

દેહ છતાં જેની દશા, વર્તે દેહાતીત;
તે જ્ઞાનીના ચરણમાં, હો વંદન અગણિત.

॥૧૪૨॥

Deh Chhatän Jeni Dashä, Varte Dehätit;
Te Jnäninä Charanmän, Ho Vandan Aganit.

> *My innumerable obeisance be*
> *at the feet of the enlightened,*
> *who behaves transcendentally*
> *even though being embodied.*
>
> *- 142 -*

Explanation & Discussion:

While commencing this composition, the obeisance was offered to the enlightened Guru. That was done for securing his blessing for the work. Since that work is now over, the obeisance is offered to the enlightened entities, staying beyond the physical mode while being embodied. Such entities are mainly the omniscient Lords, who are in the transcendental state. Of course, it is hard to explain that state verbally. However, one can try to comprehend the same in terms of the ladder of spiritual elevation.

There are 14 stages of elevation, which are analogous to the rungs of a ladder. The ascendance on the ladder is mainly in the form of overcoming delusion. Most of the worldly souls are under delusion since time immemorial. They are ignorant of their true Self, and as such their perception remains deluded. They are used to reacting to different situations with craving or aversion. This leads to the acquisition of Karma, and for bearing the consequences thereof, they continue to take birth after birth. The life cycle has thus been going on since That cannot stop, unless the soul learns about its true Self. This is the baseline of the ladder or the 1st stage, known as Mithyätva.

The perception-related delusion is overcome in the 4th stage, at the time of gaining right perception. As the aspirant goes ahead, the perception gets clearer, and thereby the character-related delusion also continues to decrease. This is concomitant to climbing on the succeeding rungs of the ladder. If the progress stays uninterrupted, one eventually reaches the 8th stage, which is termed as "unprecedented". Thereafter, the progress in overcoming delusion is swift. It culminates in the 12th stage, when the character-related delusion is totally overcome. The rest of the defiling Karmas are instantly destroyed thereafter and the person attains omniscience. This is the 13th stage.

But that does not mean the end of embodiment, because one has to remain embodied till the end of that life. As such, the activities related to embodiment continue to take place. The omniscient Lord, however, remains indifferent to physical aspects and stays transcendental. In this stanza, the obeisance is offered to such transcendental entities. When the omniscient Lord ends the current life, it gives up the body (14th stage) and becomes a liberated soul.

Here the question may arise, 'The omniscient Lords have other significant attributes like infinite perception, infinite knowledge, infinite bliss, etc. Why are those attributes not called for while offering obeisance?' The reason is clear. This work has been composed mainly for those aspirants who still have a sense of identification with the body. The purpose of this composition is to get them out of that sense. It is therefore necessary to bring to their notice the state of dissociation from bodily instincts. Obeisance to the transcendental nature of the Lords can be helpful in contemplating about that state.

Moreover, there can also be other entities (mainly belonging to stages 4 to 7), who stay indifferent to physical modes. Whether the body gets food or rest, whether it gets hurt or afflicted by any disease, is immaterial to them. They are self-realized souls, and stay tuned to the true nature of the soul. Since the sense of indifference prevails in their minds towards all bodily aspects, such entities can also be termed as living transcendentally.   Shrimad, of course, belonged to that category. This stanza is meant to offer obeisance to such entities as well.

It should be noted that obeisance to the omniscient Lord is not to be offered once, twice, fifty times, or a hundred times. The word used for the purpose is Aganit, which means uncountable number of times. As such, obeisance is to be offered to the omniscient entities for all time so as to remain aware of their transcendental state.

સાધન સિદ્ધ દશા અહીં, કહી સર્વ સંક્ષેપ;
ષટ્દર્શન સંક્ષેપમાં, ભાખ્યાં નિર્વિક્ષેપ.

Sädhan Siddha Dashä Ahin, Kahi Sarva Sankshep;
Shatdarshan Sankshepamän, Bhäkhyän Nirvikshep.

Herein has been succinctly described
the state of liberation and its means;
the six schools of thought also have
been explicitly stated in brief.

APPENDIX - I

SELF-REALISATION
(By: Revered Brahmachäriji)

1. *As real self I never knew,*
    So suffered I eternal pain;
    I bow to Him my master true,
    Who preached and broke eternal chain.

2. *In this degrading Age,*
    Who knows - Salvation-way mostly unknown?
    For seekers true, this Gospel shows,
    Unhidden as their fingers own.

3. *Some follow rites forgetting self,*
    Some learned fools believe freedom;
    Misled are both, none knows the self,
    Merciful state, I feel for them.

4. *The first are stuck in outward deeds,*
    With heart unturned, they save and serve;
    But prohibit they knowledge-seeds,
    Believing old as gold preserve.

5. *No bondage, freedom new or old,*
    The others preach, in words, the soul;
    Attachment all in acts behold,
    So word-wise, they get not the goal.

6. *Unattachment and all fruitful,*
    If you have knowledge of the soul;
    Of self-knowledge they are the tool,
    The real knowledge is the goal.

7. *And if the heart contains no merits,*
    The real knowledge cannot shine;
    If only satisfied with merits,
    They prove the block to knowledge fine.

8. *Whatever, wherever is fit,*
    The seeker understands and acts;
    Without this virtue, count unfit,
    For seekership of real facts.

9. *Who serves true master's feet, obeys,*
        Leaving aside his whims and views;
    He knows the truth what master says,
        Ascertains his own self abstruse.

10. *Self-knowledge, equal eye to lot,*
        Behaves as destined, speech unique;
    Authentic in all schools of thought,
        True Teacher's qualities mystic.

11. *Indirect Jin (Lord) cannot oblige,*
        As does the direct Teacher true;
    Without this key, would not arise,
        The thought of self or searching through.

12. *Without true Teacher's exposition,*
        None can know the Lord as Lord;
    In ignorance no obligation,
        Such understanding makes him God.

13. *True scriptures soul and all expound,*
        To seekers fit, unerring guide;
    Where direct Teacher is not found,
        'Tis next best for one's safer side.

14. *Or whatever true Teacher said,*
        For thinking deep, daily practise;
    Forgetting sects, popular head,
        Opposition of families.

15. *If one controls his self-conceit,*
        Gets surely as infinite souls;
    The final state that is most fit,
        So says innocent Jin in scrolls.

16. *One's self-conceit is checked at once,*
        In direct Teacher's nearness;
    To root it out use other means,
        It grows two-fold in general sense.

17. *If one has true Teacher's guidance,*
        Putting aside one's whims and views;
    Sectarian ways, obstinateness,
        'Tis termed true Faith, for direct cause.

18.   One cannot kill by self-conceit,
            Foes, pride and all, but seek refuge;
      True Teacher's, easily defeat,
            All mighty foes' extinction huge.

19.   Who knew full soul, attained Godhood,
            By means of sermons such sublime;
      Reveres his Teacher of true mood,
            Not yet perfect for former crime.

20.   Such system of Reverence so deep,
            The Lord proclaimed in holy Books;
      Profit thereof they only reap,
            Few fortunates, who know the nooks.

21.   If any untrue teacher takes,
            Advantage of such reverence;
      Goes down into the deep birth-lakes,
            Delusion great is dangerous.

22.   This fact the seekers understand,

23.   The bigots draw the sense perverse;
      Impartial description, attend,
            Of bigots' badges, soul-aimless.

24.   Some bigots follow false teachers,
            Who outwardly renounced the world;
      Or their hereditary preachers,
            But soul-aimless, believe their word.

25.   Some confine their own talent,
            In pompous Godly congregation;
      Jin's pictorial form and height,
            Or superhuman revelation.

26.   Even in presence of true Teachers,
            The bigot takes the perverse side;
      Confirms his former false preachers,
            To mostly gratify his pride.

27.   Celestial abodes, universal lores,
            He takes for inherent knowledge;
      Sectarian forms and creed adores,
            Believing cause of final stage.

28.   Is proud of vows, ignorant all,
                Of mental yearnings for world-fame;
            He does not heed to inner call,
                Thus loses chance, remains the same.

29.   Or talks of original state,
                Of souls, refutes practical ways;
            Lip-wisdom is not heaven's gate,
                Without true means he wastes his days.

30.   He who follows one unduly,
                Not expert in true soul-notion;
            Neither practising it truly,
                Is drowned in this vast world-ocean.

31.   For one's prestige and selfishness,
                If one lets his ideals go;
            Consider that too foolishness,
                The bigot he unfit also.

32.   Controls no passions and the heart,
                Contains no unattachment true;
            No frankness and no open heart,
                Unfortunate that bigot too.

33.   The bigot's badges thus described,
                To give up bigotry for good;
            Soul-seekers' virtues now prescribed,
                Are for attaining supreme good.

34.   Sainthood is there where's true self-knowledge,
                Soul-seekers follow such true Teachers;
            Not family-priests or one who plays,
                On worldly stage the part of preachers.

35.   The company of the Teacher true,
                Directly does the greatest good;
            Soul-seekers all accept this view,
                Complete obedience understood.

36.   The path of perfection is the same,
                In all times past, present, future;
            It's path practical worth the name,
                Acceptable if helps soul-nature.

37. Determines thus and tries to find,
       The proximity of true Teachers;
    No ideal else that eats the mind,
       The soul alone for all soul-seekers.

38. See seekership in soul-compassion,
       Suppression of all passions four;
    The hope of only liberation,
       Dejection of such rebirth-tour .

39. Unless one reaches such a state,
       No company of teachers good;
    Nor soul-suffering gets a gate,
       Cannot attain the freedom-road.

40. While one comes up to such a state,
       The sermon of the saint awakes;
    The inner-thought that is good fate,
       Soul-seeker's sleep so deep it breaks.

41. With inner-thought, self-knowledge shines,
       That knowledge delusion roots out;
    The topmost state the seeker climbs,
       Thus gets the salvation, no doubt.

42. Six facts I say in this Gospel,
       A dialogue between the two;
    To stir the inner thought so well,
       For bringing home the path so true.

43. The soul exists, see it eternal,
       Accepts bondage, receives the fruit;
    It can be free, take means devotional,
       Ignorance is the bondage-root.

44. Six subjects or six schools of thought,
       Are here described as seers great;
    In abstract scriptures strictly taught,
       For understanding soul concrete.

45. The pupil doubts the soul's existence,
       Is out of sight, its form unknown;
    In any way no experience,
       No-where is soul, cannot be shown.

46. The body, senses or the breath,
      Can be the soul, all else is false;
How one can know the soul ere death?
      No clear signs as I see the walls.

47. If there's the soul, why it's not known?
      As pots and clothes, it should be seen;
If there is soul's existence own,
      Arguments mine are true, I mean.

48. Thus there's no soul, futile all means-
      For freedom of the soul-of saints;
Destroy my doubts by any means,
      To make my heart free from all taints.

49. The Teacher true does so explain,
      The body and the soul seem one;
Distinct are both, the signs are plain,
      Remove body-infatuation.

50. The body and the soul seem one,
      Distinct are both, but this deceives;
Alone the body-infatuation,
      Distinct are both as swords and sheaths.

51. Ah! one that sees the sight and knows,
      Experiences one unconcealed;
Indisputable sign that shows,
      The soul itself to all revealed.

52. Each sense has its own subject-knowledge,
      The knowledge of all sense-subjects;
The soul possesses, it's not strange,
      The ear hears, the soul rejects.

53. The body cannot know the soul,
      Nor senses, neither knows the breath;
All do their deeds, if there's the soul,
      If it goes off, it is called death.

54. In all the states the soul separate,
      Is seen always as consciousness;
Distinctive mark is accurate,
      To ascertain the soul's presence.

55.   *You know the pots and clothes and all,*
        Thus them believe but not the knower;
    If pots and clothes exist big, small,
        Why not the soul with knowledge-power?

56.   *Supreme in thought, though bodies thin,*
        In fat, strong bodies no cleverness;
    This proves that the body is the inn,
        And not the soul, there is no oneness.

57.   *The nature of the soul and matter,*
        Is clearly quite different;
    Can never be of one character,
        See ages all: past, future, present.

58.   *Of one that doubts the soul's existence,*
        He himself the soul must be;
    Without the doubter's obvious presence,
        Can there be doubt? Surprises me.

59.   *By thinking deep upon your points,*
        Of soul's existence, I allege;
    That there must be the soul who joints,
        The conversation of this knowledge.

60.   *The second doubt now I put forth,*
        The soul cannot be eternal;
    The contact of the body's birth,
        Destruction of union visual.

61.   *Or things are transient, constant change,*
        Is seen in every living being;
    And substances without knowledge,
        I see, thus, there' no eternal thing.

62.   *The body is only adherence,*
        The object seen, lifeless with forms;
    Who knows the soul's genesis, hence,
        Or death thereof? Think of the norms.

63.   *The seer of the rise and fall,*
        Must be quite different from the scene;
    Can hear the dead their death-roll-call?
        Or ere one's birth what can be seen?

64. Compounds of elements can be seen,
        But not the soul that's original;
    The soul is the seer and not the seen,
        Nothing can create the soul eternal.

65. From matter consciousness may rise,
        Or consciousness might it create;
    Is not the experience of the wise,
        It never happens, say the great.

66. If out of any element,
        One is not created at all;
    It cannot be put to an end,
        The soul is seen thus eternal.

67. In beings like snakes anger's untaught,
        It shows the former birth's habit;
    Therefore the wise have deeply thought,
        The soul has lost last body, not it.

68. One sees in childhood, youth and age,
        There's knowledge of being the same;
    So see the soul's all states but change,
        Remaining ever the substance same.

69. One who describes absolute change,
        Of everything at every moment;
    Must be the same who knows and says,
        This falsifies his own statement.

70. Nothing is lost absolutely,
        See water changes as the steam;
    If consciousness is off totally,
        Find out the ocean of soul-stream.

71. The third doubt as the pupil's plea,
        The soul himself does no bondage;
    Or bondage acts itself ugly,
        Affixed by nature, or as knowledge.

72. The soul is unalloyed for ever,
        'Tis bondage that is really bound;
    Or God is goading, what's soul power?
        Therefore the soul remains unbound.

73.   It's of no use to try for freedom,
        The soul binds not, else binds for ever;
    Thus I see carelessness is wisdom,
        Unchanged is nature whatsoever.

74.   In bondage if the soul not acts,
        Who can accept the bondage worse?
    Examine minutely the facts,
        No conscious acts in lifelessness.

75.   In any way if soul is still,
        No bondage it acquires ever;
    It's thus no nature's work so ill,
        Nor character of soul's own power.

76.   If soul is so bondageless quite,
        To you it appears not why?
    Unalloyed is soul, that's right,
        To one who knows his self, else dry.

77.   God does not bind, nor helps creation,
        Perfection (purity) of the soul is God;
    If He instigates, where is perfection?
        Nothing He does, such is the Lord.

78.   If one himself really knows,
        The soul behaves in only knowledge;
    But binds himself in ignorance,
        As childish plays in younger age.

79.   The soul may bind, but not receives,
        The fruits thereof, who likes the worse?
    No knowledge lifeless bondage has,
        How can it allot the fruit as worth?

80.   Believe fruit-giver God impartial,
        Defective Godhood sounds unwell;
    In any other ways the soul,
        Receiver of the fruits, don't tell.

81.   Without good God chaos must shine,
        No proper place for good, bad deeds;
    To distribute ill fruits or fine,
        Impartial person must be needs.

82.   *The soul-activity is animate all,*
      Impure thoughts are self-bondage;
  Soul-strength vibrates, infinite small,
      Gas-forms of bondage form the cage.

83.   *Understands not nectar or poison,*
      That it should cure or kill the eater;
  The soul gets fruits of what is eaten,
      Thus bondage bears fruits bad or sweeter.

84.   *See one errant and one empress,*
      Without some cause, no results strange;
  Both human beings, unevenness,
      Is due to bad or good bondage.

85.   *Fruit-giver God is not required,*
      By nature bondage fructifies;
  No more the soul juice enjoyed,
      The bondage falls, without surprise.

86.   *The place and things of various kinds,*
      There are eternal heaven and hell;
  The truth is deep beyond your finds,
      It's here exposed in a nut-shell.

87.   *The soul may bind and get the fruit,*
      But never can it get the freedom;
  Infinite time has passed, the root-
      Of birth and death is not undone.

88.   *Good deeds give heaven and bad, hell,*
      The soul is errant and world, wheel;
  What state is bondageless, please tell,
      Try any way, result is nil.

89.   *As good or bad deeds give the fruit,*
      Non-action too is fruitful, due;
  O wise ! with talent see acute-
      There's freedom from the bondage true.

90.   *Infinite time has passed till now,*
      For good or bad ideas maintain-
  The chain of bondage anyhow,
      At hand is freedom, break the chain.

91.   *Absolute loss of bodies and all,*
       Puts forth the freedom-state-renown;
   Eternal status of the soul,
       With happiness infinite own.

92.   *May there be freedom of the soul,*
       There's no unrefutable means;
   By which, of time infinite all-
       The bondages may loose bobbins?

93.   *Or many a creed and schools of thoughts,*
       Show steps to freedom differently;
   What step is true, I can't make out,
       What must I choose, (I) ask reverently.

94.   *What caste or garb leads one to freedom,*
       Is not determined, all differ;
   The true religion must be one,
       So many baffle, when they whisper.

95.   *Thus I conclude the means of freedom,*
       Does not exist in any way;
   What is the use of such a wisdom,
       Of soul's existence, ever-stay?

96.   *Your five replies satisfied me,*
       About that I am doubtless now;
   If I now know the means ah! me!
       Full fortunate I feel freed how!

97.   *Convinced you are of five replies,*
       The same way means you shall know soon;
   An answer comes, the doubt soon flies,
       The way to freedom is a boon.

98.   *The bondage-cause is self-ignorance,*
       Self-steadiness is freedom-cause;
   Ignorance is like darkness, trance,
       The knowledge-torch brings it to pause.

99.   *The bondage-causes, whatsoever,*
       Follow path of bondage;
   Destroy those causes, being clever,
       That's path of freedom for all ages.

100. *Attachment, hatred, ignorance,*
    Are three chief knots of bondages;
The path of freedom, find at once,
    If they fall off, leave no traces.

101. *The soul that's living, conscious, beauty,*
    Quite free from all deluding views;
That leads to perfect purity,
    Serves for the means of freedom huge.

102. *The bondage has infinite forms,*
    The chief are eight, with one foremost;
`Deluding Karma' the name adorns,
    To cut it off, take pains utmost.

103. *It pollutes Faith and Conduct both,*
    Unfailing means accordingly;
Enlightenment by Teacher's truth,
    Unattachment true distinctly.

104. *All experience that passions bind,*
    Their antidotes as forgiveness;
Make one free from that bondage-kind,
    No doubt there is, it's common sense.

105. *If one gives up self-guiding-whim,*
    And blind religious pursuit, creed;
By following this Gospel-cream,
    he has few births, no doubt indeed!

106. *Six questions of six doctrines asked,*
    Foundation of True Faith They lay;
If mind in these is doubtless fixed,
    The path of freedom that's saints say.

107. *Look not to caste-or garb-distinction,*
    The path aforesaid is essential;
Whoever takes it gets liberation,
    No distinction in status final.

108. *Mark knowledge-thirst, inner compassion,*
    Suppression of all passions four;
The hope of only Liberation,
    Dejection of such rebirth-tour.

109. To such aspirants true Teacher's preaching,
   Inculcates faith, awakens vision;
   They are inspired by such true teaching,
   They deeply think for purification.

110. They give up bias for blind faith,
   Self-guiding views, follow precept;
   Of true Teachers, earn right pure faith,
   Where's no discord or party-spirit.

111. Either they have soul-experience,
   Attention to it continuous;
   Or self-existence-conviction,
   Internal vision's Faith so glorious.

112. As Faith grows deep, false faith falls down,
   Rises right Conduct gradually;
   Full non-attachment is the crown,
   Of Conduct right perpetually.

113. Continuous flow of knowledge pure,
   Of one's self-nature unalloyed;
   Is termed the perfect knowledge sure,
   Liberated he is though embodied.

114. A dream of million years ends soon,
   When one awakes, so self-knowledge;
   When shines, goes off one's self-delusion,
   Of time eternal, 'tis not strange.

115. Let go the body-infatuation,
   And you will not have bondage new;
   You will not have deed-fruition,
   This is Religion's secret true.

116. This true Religion leads to Freedom,
   You are image of Liberation;
   You are undisturbable wisdom,
   You are infinite knowledge, vision.

117. Enlightened, pure, full consciousness,
   Self-brilliant, home of happiness;
   What more to say? Have eagerness,
   Think deep and you shall realize this.

118. This sums up all absolute view,
    Of all wise men, who knew the soul;
  The dialogue ends, The Teacher true,
    Absorbs himself in nature cool.

119. The pupil praises his true Teacher,
    "I know what I had never known;
  By teaching of my own true Teacher,
    Ignorance passed and knowledge shone.

120. I knew my self pure consciousness,
    Immortal, ever-lasting, strong;
  Above all body-states lifeless,
    Perpetual existence, no wrong.

121. In delusion one does the deeds,
    Receives the fruits, but non-doer;
  He is, when sows the knowledge-seeds,
    And constantly remains the knower.

122. Or as pure consciousness it acts,
    The fruit as consciousness it reaps;
  Without volition see these facts,
    Thus call the soul as does, receives.

123. The perfect pure state of one's self,
    Is taught to be true Liberation;
  The way to it is right one's self,
    This true Saint's path is intuition.

124. Thanks! the Holy True Teacher,
    Unfathomable ocean of compassion;
  I'm highly obliged, Oh! good Teacher,
    The pupil poor has no expression.

125. What should I offer to you, Lord?
    In soul-comparison all is trifle;
  The soul is gifted by the Lord,
    I wish to act to your oracle.

126. Henceforward this my body and all,
    Are at Your feet, I wish to serve;
  Your humble servant, poor soul,
    Even servant's state I don't deserve.

127. *Explanations of doctrines six!*
          As swords from sheaths so clearly:
     The self is shown by you distinct,
          You obliged me immeasurably."

128. *Six schools of thought lie in six doctrines,*
          If one thinks deeply in details;
     The vital truth he ascertains,
          Undoubtedly, he never fails.

129. *There's no disease as self-delusion,*
          The well-versed doctor's Teacher true;
     The Teacher's precept's prescription,
          Thought-concentration's medicine due.

130. *If you hope for Soul-Reality,*
          True self-effort you must begin;
     Depending on fate, destiny,
          Destroy not self-searching, I mean.

131. *By hearing words of view absolute,*
          Let not one give up formal means;
     Attending to the view absolute,
          One should perform all freedom-means.

132. *Neither absolute view one-sided,*
          Nor stand-point practical alone;
     In this Gospel is emphasized,
          But both together are due shown.

133. *Sectarian views, self-guiding whims,*
          Are not right stand-point practical;
     Nor right absolute view, it seems,
          Without self experience, it's oral.

134. *There were the seers long ago,*
          There are in present time alive:
     In times to come they shall be so,
          The path's the same that they revive.

135. *All souls are like the perfect ones,*
          Self-knowledge leads to perfection;
     Auxiliary cause is obedience-
          To Teacher's word, Jin-condition.

136. Who put forward the subject-cause,
   And leave the auxiliary one;
  In delusion they firmly pause,
   And can't attain the perfection.

137. Lip-wise are some, pretending heart,
   They have no love lost for the seer;
  They aid senseless, play pitiable part,
   Have seer's show, delusion-dear.

138. Awakened seeker's heart contains,
   Compassion, peace, forgiveness, truth;
  An equal-eye in loss or gains,
   Unattachment, donation, ruth.

139. You find extinction or suppression,
   Of infatuation as a rule;
  In seer's heart, there's no delusion,
   Else-where you find delusion full.

140. The seer's state is thus described,
   The world to him is like a dream;
  Or left-off food when satisfied,
   The rest are lipwise, not supreme.

141. Who thinks of first five doctrines well,
   According to the sixth who acts;
  Attains the fifth, great seers tell,
   No doubts maintain in these true facts.

142. I often bow to him who lives,
   Though in body, above it;
  The seer's word always survives,
   The North-pole-star resembles it.

APPENDIX - II

LETTER OF SIX FUNDAMENTALS
(Chha Padno Patra)

Obeisance with intense devotion to the true Guru, the conferor of the unique shelter.

The enlightened entities (persons), who have realized the true nature of Self, have laid down the following six Fundamentals as the supreme abode of right perception.

First Fundamental: -

"There is existence of the soul." Just as there are physical objects like pot, cloth, etc. so is there the soul. As the properties of pot, cloth, etc. provide the evidence of their existence, so the obvious property of consciousness to manifest itself as well as to know others, is the evidence of existence of the soul.

Second Fundamental: -

"The soul is eternal(everlasting)". Pot, cloth, etc. last only for a certain time; but the soul stays forever. Pot, cloth, etc. are composed of some materials, but the soul is a substance on its own, because no composition can be visualized for producing the soul. Consciousness cannot arise out of any composition, so it is not a product. Being non-composible, it is imperishable; because what cannot be produced by any composition, cannot merge into anything else.

Third Fundamental: -

"The soul is Kartä (doer or actuator)". All objects are associated with some activity. All of them are seen with some or other change in their states. The soul also is imbibed with activity. Being imbibed with activity, it is the Kartä of that activity. The omniscient Lords have stated three types of activities. In absolute pure state, when the soul stays tuned to its nature, it is the Kartä of its own nature; in usual practice (which can be experienced; which comes in close contact), it is the Kartä of material Karma, and nominally it is the Kartä of buildings, towns, etc.

Fourth Fundamental: -

"The soul bears the consequences."All the activities are fruitful, they are not futile. It is the obvious experience that whatever is done, the consequences have to be borne. Consumption of poison or sugar, and contact with fire or snow do not fail to produce their consequences. Similarly, if the soul indulges in defiled (impure) or undefiled (pure) state, that state too is bound to be fruitful and produces its consequences. The soul being the Kartä of that Karma, it bears the consequences.

Fifth Fundamental: -

"There is liberation." The soul has been described above as being Kartä of material Karma and hence subject to its consequences. That Karma can be terminated as well; because even if the prevailing defilement, etc. are very acute, they can be reduced, by discontinuance of practice, by avoiding contact, and by calming them down. They are reducible and can be destroyed. The state of bondage thus being destructible; the pure nature of soul, devoid of bondage, is the state of liberation.

Sixth Fundamental: -

"There are means to achieve liberation." If bondage of Karma simply continues to occur, its cessation can never be possible. But there are means like knowledge, faith, staying tuned to Self, detachment, devotion, etc. which are manifestly opposite of bondage of Karma. By the intensity of those means, bondage is loosened, it subsides, and can be destroyed. Hence, those factors of knowledge, faith, restraint, etc. are the means for attaining liberation.

These six Fundamentals, called by the blessed entities as the primary abode of right perception, are stated here in brief.

The soul, which is close to liberation, would easily find them appropriate and entirely convincing. Consideration of these Fundamentals in all perspectives would lead to the rise of discernment within. The supreme entities have pronounced these six Fundamentals as beyond all doubts. Discernment resulting from these six Fundamentals can make the soul to comprehend its true nature.

The enlightened entities have laid down the teaching of these six Fundamentals to remove the sense of ego and attachment of the soul arising from its dreaming state (ignorance), which has been prevailing since the time without beginning. If a soul realizes that its true nature is beyond that dreaming state, it would easily awake and gain right perception. By right perception, it would attain liberation in the sense of realizing its true Self. Sense of exultation, grief, or other interaction would not occur to the soul from any transient, impure, or other mode. That contemplation would lead it to experience, from close proximity, its own natural purity, perfection, imperishability, and boundless bliss.

The soul has been accustomed to identify itself with the states arising from time to time. It would now gain clear, visible, vivid, and manifest experience of being completely distinct from those states. The interaction with the transient and other objects would not be perceived by it as desirable or undesirable. It would feel gratified by knowing and experiencing its own true Self as the abode of perfect purity, free from affliction of birth, old age, death, disease, etc. All those, who are convinced of the soul by the words of supreme entities in the form of these six Fundamentals, have realized their true state. In the past they have been freed from worries, disease, affliction, and all other interactions; presently they do so and in future the same will happen.

Let our highly devoted obeisance be to the enlightened entities, who instructed us to abide at ease within our true Self, that can end the affliction of birth, old age, and death forever. The true nature of the soul can be manifested by continuous daily adoration of their innate compassion. The lotus feet of all such entities may always be in our hearts.

It is not possible to define the attributes of the enlightened persons. Adoption of their instructions leads to manifestation of the true Self as evidenced by these six Fundamentals. By manifestation of true Self the soul attains everlasting bliss and becomes fearless. The enlightened entities have conferred unrewardable supreme disposition without desiring anything whatsoever by virtue of their innate compassion. Yet they have never even imagined that some one is my pupil or he is mine because he is my devotee. Repeated obeisance with intense devotion be to such enlightened entities.

Such entities have laid down devotion for true Guru solely for benefit of the pupil. They have laid down devotion so the tendency of the pupil would stay towards the state of Guru's soul. Self-indulgence would end by witnessing the Guru's unprecedented attributes and self-realization would follow effortlessly. The repeated and all time obeisance be to that devotion and to those enlightened entities.

Omniscience has not been presently manifested. However, it has been clearly known as a potentiality by virtue of the words of the enlightened entities. Omniscience exists as, a matter of faith, a state to be contemplated, and a state to be aspired. From the absolute point of view it has been existing. The repeated obeisance with supreme devotion be to the benevolence of the enlightened entity by whose grace this soul easily became worthy of attaining omniscience, the manifestor of unobstructed bliss.